TO
SETTLE
YOUR
CONSCIENCE

TO SETTLE YOUR CONSCIENCE

Rev. Cass Kucharek

Our Sunday Visitor, Inc. / Noll Plaza / Huntington, IN 46750

The Nihil Obstat and Imprimatur are official declarations that a book or pamphlet is free of doctrinal or moral error. No implication is contained therein that those who have granted the Nihil Obstat or Imprimatur agree with the contents, opinions or statements expressed.

Nihil Obstat:
Rev. Lawrence Gollner
Censor Librorum

Imprimatur:
✝Leo A. Pursley, D.D.
Bishop of Fort Wayne-South Bend

ISBN: 0-87973-877-4
Library of Congress Catalog Card Number: 73-91902

Cover Design by James E. McIlrath

Published, printed and bound in the U.S.A. by
Our Sunday Visitor, Inc.
Noll Plaza
Huntington, Indiana 46750

877

Dedicated to the poor people of this earth,
sinners,
the troubled, sorely distressed,
the worried;
they cry, the sick of soul and heart,
fallen, bleeding,
and still reach out
to touch the hem of His garment,
through tear-stained eyes,
they try to grasp His hand
and walk with Him,
the gentle Master loves them all,
and died for them,
to give them peace,
compassion,
courage,
and to make them God-like,
the poor people of this earth.

PREFACE

To Settle Your Conscience, while not pretending to sound the moral depths of human conduct, does propose to help Catholics solve their ordinary ethical difficulties by means of the Christian moral principles here presented. It was written chiefly as a guide for practical Catholics who, because of deficient religious instructions and training, simply do not know how to cut through the maze of complicated problems and difficulties that this modern, complex age presents. Nor do recent converts face less bewilderment. And these difficulties have been intensified by the many conflicting theories, controversies and confusion in many areas of morality in the turbulent era following the Second Vatican Council.

We know that moral acts cannot be judged in a vacuum. They must be applied in concrete circumstances, in a *total context* that is becoming bewilderingly complex, many times impossible to unravel even by educated Christians. But there are principles which, if correctly understood, can help solve many problems of conscience. The Church may never have declared *ex cathedra* regarding morality but in its ordinary teaching it has given us and will continue to give us countless aids for helping us to form our consciences. This book contains nothing new, only these tried and true instructions and teachings. It contains little of what some may call "the major influences of contemporary theology," a theology which still has to be accepted by the official teaching authority of the Church.

Avant garde theologians certainly have their place in the Church but pastors of souls, directly involved with the People of God, cannot adopt each new theory and unreservedly apply it to their flocks. If a pastor does that, what will he do when the new theory is supplanted by a newer one? Discard the souls "that didn't work out" under his care into the unwanted file too? Theologians can afford to speculate; pastors and parents cannot. As one mother of six put it, "If the new morality does not work on my kids, Father, they will be moral cripples for time and eternity. I can't just throw them out then on the garbage heap with the theologians' outmoded theories."

Exaggeration? Perhaps, but parents experienced with the wanting pedagogic and psychological theories of yesteryear are rightly concerned. At least some of the bygone pedagogic and social theories had been bolstered originally with pilot projects, progress reports, data and rates of achievement. Can the same be said for the proposals of the new morality?

We are well aware that the "new trends" in morality would have everyone make up his own mind about the goodness or badness of the course of action he must take. There is some merit in this but when a confused soul approaches a priest with a problem of conscience, it is quite evident that this soul could not unravel the difficulty by itself. It does little good to tell such a soul that moral judgments must be based on the evolving concept of man's nature and the concrete situation he is in.

Yet that is exactly what the proponents of the new morality would have us do. Too often we hear at retreats and parish missions, "I can't even get a straight answer from our priests, Father. If I knew the answer, I wouldn't have asked them. When I go to a doctor and tell him I have this sharp pain deep inside, that maybe it's appendicitis, he doesn't tell me to go home and then when I have made up my mind, come back and tell him to operate." Again, exaggeration? Perhaps, but very often writers, priests included, forget that most people, the ordinary folk of America, are neither experts nor educated in theology. The silent, uncomplaining majority, have neither the time nor the opportunity to learn theological subtleties and niceties. Now since Vatican II, more than ever, they are bewildered, crying out for some straight answers to their troubled souls. And many have thrown up their hands in despair.

As People of God, they have every right to ask help in solving their consciences. They are uncertain, troubled and confused. They ask for bread. Are we to give them the stone of uncertainty? If this is the "in" thing to do, then this book is "out," way out, because it gives straight answers to the perplexed, to the troubled. It calls mortal sin a mortal sin and it is unashamedly chock-full of what is seriously wrong and what is venially sinful in regard to particular actions.

To the cry of "legalism," we answer that Christ's system of morality did not sow doubt, uncertainty and anxiety but that it brought peace to the souls and minds of the troubled and distressed. That is what this book is about: to help *settle consciences,* not to confuse them; to bring peace of soul, not disquieting anxiety and doubt.

Neither can true pastors of souls forget those under their care who tend toward scrupulosity. They are good souls, disturbed and distressed beyond measure by troubles and problems which beset them daily but which would fade into nothingness if correctly and clearly understood. This is another reason why this book is not afraid to set down and explain in abundant detail not only the obligations of every Christian but also the exact sinfulness or degree of guilt involved in various violations. It is also meant for those who could avoid many great falls, if they knew just what is seriously wrong and what is venially sinful in regard to particular actions. No less is it intended for those who, not knowing how to judge prudently whether or not they have consented fully to a temptation, give in all the way simply to avoid the ceaseless, torturing doubts which would follow the conflict. These too must be helped.

In all of these purposes, there is one common denominator for which this work was undertaken: to help all these souls *to settle their consciences,* to help them understand the burden that is in reality light and the yoke that is sweet instead of the seemingly impossible weight that crushes them in their present state.

The language used is intended to be such as to be fully understood by all. When technical terms are used they are duly defined and explained in words which can easily be grasped and understood. The many examples and cases following the explanations further illustrate the matter in question.

May this little volume serve as a handy reference for the speedy solution of the common moral difficulties encountered by Catholics in everyday life. In helping those who chance to read or consult it, may it spur them on to the more positive heights of true heroism — sanctity — by dispelling the mists of doubts and scruples which obstruct the way to this mountain of holiness!

Cass Kucharek

CONTENTS

Chapter I

GENERAL PRINCIPLES OF MORALITY

A newborn baby is little more than a bundle of feelings. Totally lacking the use of reason, he relies completely on his feelings to satisfy his needs. When uncomfortable, hungry or cold, he will cry — the only way he can make his needs felt. No one blames him for anything even if, by his excessive crying, he angers his parents precisely because he cannot judge, cannot reason.

As the child grows, he slowly learns that there are others in his world besides himself, that there are things he must do, things he must avoid — rules to which he must conform — if he wants to meet with approval, satisfaction and rewards. He becomes aware of affection, of being loved and wanted. If he does not conform, he notices that he meets with disapproval, that he receives less affection and love. He may even be punished outright if he persists in doing certain forbidden things. So he learns to compromise, to defer some of his passing wants for something more gratifying: approval, love and affection. Gradually, almost unnoticeably, his reason begins to stir.

What happens, first of all, is that the child becomes aware of what adults term a relationship between him and others in his world. This relationship is affected by his own conduct and acts as well as by those of others around him. What may have been conditioned merely by reflex action, emotions, etc., gradually becomes conditioned by the use of reason as the child grows older. The more he gains the use of reason, the more he begins to understand why he is expected to act in a certain way, why he must weigh the consequences of his actions, and why his relationship with other people is affected. In the process he also becomes aware of the reasons why he is considered more blameworthy than when he was smaller, when he "didn't know any better," or if we may put it another way, when he could not use his reasoning powers as well.

In the child's world the norms (the rules to which his actions were expected to conform) were probably for the most part arbitrary, man-made, imposed by parents, by brothers and sisters, or by teachers. It was *their will* that he had to obey. There were rules to be obeyed at home, on the street, at gatherings, in polite society. His relationship with others was affected adversely or favorably by his actions of disobedience or obedience.

In the adult world the laws or "rules" are usually far from being arbitrary.

Though many are man-made by governments and the Church for good order (and may change with the circumstances of the times), others are made by God Himself (and are unchangeable, no matter what the circumstances). God has indeed set down His laws: the natural law and the divinely revealed precepts as interpreted by the teachings of His Church. God's law is *His will* for us, what He wants of us. Only insofar as our actions (our conduct) conform or do not conform to these divine laws that they are good or bad.

Our relationship or friendship with God is also thereby affected. If we disobey, our friendship (sanctifying grace) with God is lessened or may even be ended (through serious, deliberate disobedience); but if we obey, it is strengthened. If we are His friends when we die, we will be happy with Him forever in paradise; if not, we will be damned, unhappy for all eternity.

God's laws were not given us for our harm or displeasure; on the contrary, they are for our good and for our happiness (just as a parent's "rule" for the child that he never play with matches or a sharp knife). They are the guides which tell us clearly what we must do and what we must avoid if we are not to hurt ourselves and stay God's friends. Our moral judgment or conscience, to be right, must be formed according to these laws; otherwise, it may be erroneous, false. That is why getting to know these laws, these guides, is so important for us . . . and that is what this book is all about!

LAW AND CONSCIENCE, THE NORMS OF MORALITY

A deliberate act is good or bad depending on whether it does or does not conform to the norms of morality (essentially the will of God for us) as expressed by *law* and *conscience*. The external, objective guide of conduct is law; the internal, subjective guide is conscience. Of the two, conscience is more important for the individual person, since it is only through conscience that he can apply the objective law to his each and every action. On the other hand, the true formation of conscience is based on law. Both interact; both complement one another.

Law, in a broad sense, is that which regulates the actions of a thing. Thus, we speak of the laws of nature: the various laws of physics, chemistry, science, etc. The astronauts who went to the moon, for example, had to obey such laws of nature to carry out their mission successfully; if they had disregarded any one of many such laws they would have been dead within seconds. Conformance to the laws of nature was a matter literally of life and death for them.

In its strict and proper sense, however, law is a reasonable regulation issued and promulgated (made known) by one in authority over a group for whose common welfare the law is intended. If we take this definition apart we find that a proposed law or regulation must have certain, necessary elements in order that it have any binding force; if not, it does not oblige us.

To put it another way, to be binding a law must be: (1) *reasonable* — e.g., a law forbidding the wearing of hats would not be reasonable; (2) *aimed at the common welfare* — this requires that the law be just, morally good, and necessary for, or at least conducive to, the common good; e.g., a law which states that employees of the government are no longer bound by traffic laws would not be conducive to the common welfare; (3) *issued and promulgated by those having authority over the group* — e.g., a hunting law for the state of Michigan cannot be made by the governor of Ohio, because he has no authority over the people of Michigan. Until a law is promulgated (made public and declared binding) it is not a law and, therefore, does not bind its subjects.

God's laws always have these necessary elements but human, man-made laws sometimes may lack one of them and so do not oblige us in conscience.

KINDS OF LAW

I. *Eternal law* is God's divine plan, the plan He used when He created the world, established the order of nature, keeps it in existence, and forbids its disturbance. God in His limitless wisdom, from all eternity, saw all the possible things with their possible, varied arrangements and decreed the creation of an ordered world in which all things are ordained toward their proper, determined end.

II. *Natural law* is the eternal law as it applies to man and as it is recognized by mankind through the light of reason. It gives man the fundamental notions from which he derives the rules governing his relations with God and with his fellowmen. The natural law obliges all men and is "written in their hearts," as we know from St. Paul (Rom. 2:14-15). It can be expressed in one general norm: "Do good and avoid evil." In this we are given the general principles from which we can derive more particular conclusions. To this general norm each of the individual precepts can be reduced; e.g., do not kill, do not steal, worship God, preserve your health, and so on. Natural law is basically the reason why people will say, "It's *natural* to preserve one's life," though it is possible for man to become so depraved that his mind will be blinded even to these fundamental truths (cf. Rom. 1:19-32).

III. *Divine positive law* is the law given to us by God through divine revelation. This law declares and defines the natural law more specifically by applying it to particular situations and cases; thus, the Ten Commandments revealed to the human race on Mount Sinai are an example of divine positive law and are really an explicit codification of the natural law. The precepts contained in the Sermon on the Mount, the precepts concerning the sacraments, etc., are other examples of divine positive law.

Divine laws are absolute and cannot be changed by man, no matter what the situation. They are not a survival of an archaic Greek mentality as some would have us believe. Divine laws, like the laws of nature (indeed laws of nature are part of God's laws), remain true no matter what the circumstances or consequences. If I step off a plane in midair, for example, the law of gravity will hold and I will fall to my death. No amount of wishful thinking will change that fact. Truth is truth no matter how many people will deny it or refuse to recognize it.

Though disobedience to God's moral laws may not have the immediate, drastic consequences as would the disregard for the laws of nature, nonetheless God's moral laws are just as true and absolute. Modern man, used to evolution and dramatic changes on every side, sometimes attempts to deny the absolute standards which God has set for man; thus, anyone voicing maxims such as "marital fidelity is old-fashioned" is really denying the absolute values of God's moral laws.

More dangerous to truth and morals are the various forms of situation ethics so prevalent in our day. There was the older form of situation ethics: this consisted in a slavish application of human laws, a rigid obedience to a "legal situation" which was said to justify transgressing God's law. In other words, according to the older form of situation ethics, a man could disregard fundamental divine commandments and even the demands of natural law in order to obey human precepts and human traditions.

If this were true, no one could have been condemned at the Nuremberg trials: how many Nazis tried to excuse their crimes with a plea that they were acting under orders! In Matthew's Gospel, Christ condemned this mechanical application of human laws in the Pharisees: "Pharisees and scribes from Jerusalem then came to Jesus and said, 'Why do your disciples break away from the tradition of the elders?' Jesus answered: 'And why do you break away from the commandments of God for the sake of your tradition?' "

The newer, more modern form of situation ethics (sometimes called "the new morality") is even more insidious. This system, if we may call it such, does admit the existence of moral laws; Christians, in fact, are urged to consider these norms carefully before acting. So far so good. According to proponents of this "new morality," however, no moral law has any absolute value and so a Christian for the sake of love may seek his self-fulfillment and true expression of love for neighbor in a way opposed to the general moral principles. Anything may be done, it would seem, provided a man is careful that he does it out of true and unselfish love (sometimes called "agapeic" [from the Greek *agapē* — "love"]) . . . which generally is reducible to a form of utilitarianism or pragmatism. Accordingly, proponents of this system would have us believe that a person, in certain situations or circumstances, may even commit adultery or rape, have premarital sex, or publicly disown God provided he has the right intention. This "law of love" can even justify murder. For example, I can put to death a person in intense pain if I do it out of love, much as I would shoot a horse because I cannot stand to see it suffer!

Frankly, such "new morality" is nonsense and could be dismissed as wistful thinking were it not for one fact: it is seriously being taught in our schools, even in some Catholic ones. "Premarital sex is neither to be encouraged nor discouraged. If it helps one to mature, to grow in love and thoughtfulness, it's all right." Does it sound familiar? Something the children brought back from school? It may be, for it is almost straight out of a textbook of "new morality." Simply and truly, love in this pragmatic or utilitarian sense is not and was not ever the basic principle of Christ's ethics. Christ's fundamental principle of ethics was and is "to do in love what *truth* demands."

IV. *Ecclesiastical or Church law* is that law which the Church makes in virtue of the authority given her by God. In no way can the Church ever contradict the divine law, whether natural or divine positive law. In spite of countless difficulties, the Church has defended the divine law down through the ages not only in her teaching but also in her legislation.

Why is it necessary for the Church to have detailed external laws, when the law of Christ is primarily internal? Fallen human nature is far from perfect: man in his present state is born with a tendency to self and self-love and not to the self-effacing love of God and neighbor. Though particular, external laws do not fathom the total demands of our love for God, they are valuable insofar as they point out the minimum and basic demands of the law of love. Love, after all, is not merely an emotion; it always seeks to do the will of the beloved — in this case, God.

In some instances Church law merely points out to us how the law of God is to be kept as to time, place or manner; thus, we are commanded by God to worship Him, but the Church fixed particular days for divine worship and the manner in which we are to fulfill this duty as a minimum expression of our love for God. But that is all the Church's external law is: the minimum requirement. That is why good Christians are never satisfied merely to fulfill them but will make the most of any opportunity to show their love for God. The Scriptures frequently admonish us of the duty to do penance; the Church fixes the time for doing penance (e.g., Lent), to help us not to forget that duty . . . again, reminding us of the minimum requirements. Such types of laws she may change whenever she deems it best for our welfare. In no longer obliging Friday abstinence, she was not decreeing anything contrary to God's law, for she told us to do penance in other, more positive ways. The general laws of the Church regarding discipline are found in the Code of Canon Law (*Codex Juris Canonici*).

True love is far from being rigidly legalistic, static or satisfied only with minimum requirements; on the contrary, it grasps every opportunity and eagerly searches out ways to show itself. Parents, after all, who dutifully fulfill all their legal obligations towards their children, can still be empty caricatures of fatherhood and motherhood. Truly loving parents, in addition to fulfilling their strict obligations towards their chidren, will show their love for them in innumerable ways to which they are not required. Ask a mother to count the ways! The Christian's answer to the love of God is the same. If it is merely legalistic, searching out the absolute minimum required by law, it can become a caricature of true love, akin to that of the Pharisees. Those who rely primarily on external law and its coercive force can be more unchristian than unbelievers. For the truly Christian, there is no coercion; their living, their actions, are prompted by the love of God in a constant and unending giving of themselves.

V. *Civil law* is law made by civil authority. Since the temporal good of citizens is connected with their eternal salvation and hence with the practice of virtue, God gives legitimate civil leaders the authority to make just laws for the common good of their subjects. If any proposed civil law disagrees with divine law (from which it actually derives its force), it is not a law but a corruption of law which has absolutely no binding force in conscience. Strictly speaking, therefore, any civil law which disregards the natural rights of man or invades the rights reserved for the Church by God is not actually a law, and therefore, *morally* speaking, is not binding.

If civil laws fulfill all the conditions required — that they be reasonable, made for the common good, promulgated by legitimate authority which intends to bind its subjects in conscience — then, and only then, do they oblige those for whom they were made. Our federal and state laws are truly civil laws. In transgressing true civil laws we are violating not only the order established by God but also His authority which He delegated to the State. That is the reason why civil laws can oblige also in conscience. We may say, however, that many civil laws of themselves do not oblige in conscience, because they are intended by the lawmakers to be merely penal.

Merely penal laws are those which, while not binding us in conscience to do what they prescribe, do oblige us to submit to whatever penalty is inflicted upon us for their violation. Therefore, in disobeying a merely penal law, the transgressor does not commit any sin; but if the authorities detect and impose a just penalty on him, he is then bound in conscience to submit to that penalty.

How is one to know which civil laws are merely penal and which bind in conscience? If, in promulgating the law, the legitimate legislator says or intimates that a particular law obliges in conscience, then it is clear that it so obliges; but if he says that it obliges under pain of such and such a punishment for its violation, then we can reasonably conclude that this is merely a penal law. Disobedience to merely penal law, however, may easily offend against some other virtue such as truth, justice or charity.

EXAMPLES:

1. Mr. Good more than once broke the hunting and fishing laws by participating in these sports in restricted areas a few days before the season opened. In so doing he did not commit any moral fault. One fine day Mr. Good is apprehended and fined; he is bound in conscience to pay the fine.

2. Mrs. Killjoy speeds fifty miles an hour in a thirty-five mile-per-hour zone. Mrs. Killjoy does not sin in doing so, but if she is given a ticket or an overnight jail sentence, she is then obliged in conscience to pay it or spend the night in jail. When we say that she does not sin, however, we mean that she is not sinning because of disobeying the penal law. She does sin if she is endangering either her own life and limb or those of another.

CONSCIENCE, THE SUBJECTIVE GUIDE

Many people have disastrous misconceptions of conscience: many confuse it with feeling, fuss, fuddle and whatnot. Some have vague, hazy notions of what conscience really is; others have definitely bogus notions about it. Small wonder, then, that these people become muddled in preparation for confession. Each one attempts to examine something he presumes to be his conscience, which is not conscience at all but a vague feeling of guilt or an indefinite fear that is gnawing at his heart, a fear of he knows not what. The fact is that many don't know what they are examining, perhaps some woolly notions dragged up by the ears from the dark cellars of their subconscious minds.

Needless to say, misconceptions about conscience walk hand in hand with their sisters: intuition, obstinacy, scruples and fanaticism.

Even people who are cheerfully confident that they have correct ideas about conscience should read to find out whether their ideas about it are not slightly bogus. If we are one of those who think that conscience is a special faculty, a kind of inner voice whispering categorically of right and wrong, then we should definitely inquire further, for that is a bogus notion.

True, conscience is in the soul; so far so good. But philosophers and theologians teach that in the soul there are two faculties — intellect and will. Nowhere do they teach that there is a third one — conscience; it is not something existing on its own, a separate, permanent reality like the mind and will. But since conscience is found in the soul, then it must obviously be found in these two faculties. Conscience is merely the *judgment pronounced by the intellect about the moral goodness or sinfulness of an intended action,* the conclusion that the intellect comes to after applying the objective laws of morality to a specific action. More briefly, it is a practical moral judgment. Like any judgment, it is based on reason. An example will show how conscience works. While in Benny's Diner this afternoon, Johnny sees a dollar bill left on the counter. Nobody comes to claim it, and the dollar looks mighty attractive to Johnny. Something like this goes on in his mind: "Stealing is wrong; if I took this dollar it would be stealing; therefore, if I took this dollar it would be wrongful."

Perhaps most of the time we are not conscious of any such process of reasoning in making our practical moral judgments. If we are not, it is either because the conclusion is immediately obvious, or we have been well instructed previously about the matter in question, or perhaps we have thought it out beforehand. This is why many decisions are made without any hesitation — "in a flash." This, we may add, is where we get the idea of conscience as a voice. Nevertheless, whether the reasoning has taken place in the past or in the present, its conclusion (the decision) is always the result of a reasoning process.

Now, just as in sports the game of baseball has certain rules and regulations telling the players what will make them "out" and what is necessary for scoring (e.g., they must reach base, must not be tagged off base, etc.), so in the moral sphere there are various types of law which tell men what they must do and what they must not do to perform morally good acts, that is, what is the minimal will of God whom we try to love and therefore to please. These are the objective external guides for regulating the actions of baseball players in sports and of human beings in life.

In baseball, the umpire applies the objective rules and regulations to the individual actions of the players and accordingly pronounces the verdict: "safe" or "out" or "score." In life, the intellect (in conjunction with the will) applies the various types of law to the particular acts of the person and accordingly pronounces them good or bad; this is exactly what conscience is . . . the moral umpire. The umpire may be wrong in some cases. Still it is he who judges and it is his judgment which must be accepted. Conscience may also be wrong sometimes, especially in trying to unravel the complexities of living in the modern world; still, it is the individual person's final judgment of what the Lord wants, what is good and what is wrong, and so he must always be guided by it. In other words, a person may sometimes misunderstand the demands of the Lord but he must do what he thinks the Lord wants.

Everyone perceives "the voice of his conscience," that is, the practical moral judgment made by the intellect. This judgment (conscience) states that the act which we are about to perform is good (pleasing to God) or bad (displeasing to God) accordingly as it conforms or does not conform to the will of God made known to us through His law (divine, ecclesiastical or civil). If the intellect judges our action as morally good, it gives its approval; if it judges our action as morally wrong, it vehemently disapproves of that action. The word "conscience" itself means "with knowledge" or "with awareness," and implies that the person is acting with knowledge or awareness of God's will as expressed in a law's obligation regarding a particular act.

What conscience (the moral judgment formed by the intellect) forbids, we must avoid; what it commands, we must do; when it marks something as permissible, or preferable, but not obligatory, we have a choice. Strictly speaking, this is called *antecedent conscience;* whereas the judgment that is passed on an action after it is performed (and which is usually accompanied by a feeling of remorse or peace, as the case may be) is called *consequent conscience.*

Consequent conscience is usually accompanied by a feeling of remorse or peace. Note we have said "is accompanied by," not *is the feeling* of remorse or peace. Guilty feeling is an *indication* and may establish a probability that a person has acted sinfully, just as a feeling of satisfaction and peace is an indication that one has acted virtuously. It is an indication and no more, for a guilty feeling may not at all be induced by conscience, but may be due to some phobia or a vague notion arising from the subconscious mind. Feelings must never be accepted as infallible guides in moral matters. We should never pay too much attention to feelings, or we may become unstable, with warped personalities. Neurotic anxiety has no place in Christianity. If we do have feelings of guilt, we should investigate whether these feelings have any *reasonable* foundation; if we cannot find any reasonable basis for these feelings, we should dismiss them as we would the gossip of old Mrs. Thingumbob.

The judgment of conscience, as we have said, may sometimes be wrong. It is not infallible, for it is based on knowledge of the law (God's will for us as expressed in law) which the mind has at the time of the decision; and the mind, as all of us know, is not infallible either. (But if, after prayerful consideration of all values involved, we decide on a definite course of action, we need have no worry about displeasing God.)

We must, therefore, distinguish several types of conscience according to the various qualities by which each one is characterized.

TYPES OF CONSCIENCE

I. A *correct conscience* (moral judgment) is one which tells a person that a certain thing is good or bad, and this decision is in agreement with what that thing actually is according to the objective law.

EXAMPLE:

Miss Cherry Blossom's conscience rightly told her that the "little white lie" she was about to tell would be sinful, even though she cannot see how it would hurt anyone if she told it. The moral law says that a lie is always wrong and small lies are venially sinful. Miss Blossom's moral judgment is in agreement with that law; therefore it is correct.

II. A *false conscience* is one which judges an action incorrectly; that is, it judges a good action evil or an evil action good.

Especially in judging evil actions as good ones, a false conscience can have disastrous results. Adolf Eichmann, after all, claimed that he acted with a clear conscience in helping to liquidate millions of Jews. That the world did not agree with his claim is clear from the verdict of his trial. But what of lesser men and smaller values? Only God can judge the actual guilt of a person who acts with a false conscience. What may be obvious to one person may not be so clear to another.

In fundamental notions of right and wrong (those "written in the heart of man") a false conscience is probably no excuse at all. This we have on the word of God: "Ever since God created the world his everlasting power and deity — however invisible — have been there for the mind to see in the things he has made. That is why such people are without excuse: they knew God and yet refused to honor him as God or to thank him; instead, they made nonsense out of logic and their empty minds were darkened — that is why God left them to their filthy enjoyments and the practices with which they dishonor their own bodies . . ." (Rom. 1:20-25). Moral judgment, which goes with knowing about God, disappears and all kinds of monstrous behavior result. There can hardly be any doubt how God will judge such: "God's verdict is: that those who behave like this deserve to die . . . and yet they do it; and what is worse, encourage others to do the same" (Rom. 1:32).

EXAMPLES:

1. Mrs. Turningtop believes that her grocer has cheated her of five dollars. She does not try to discuss the matter with him reasonably, for her conscience tells her that she can secretly take that amount from him without sin. Her conscience is not in agreement with the moral law and so is incorrect or false.

2. Angela thinks that it is a sin for women to smoke cigarettes. Angela's conscience is false.

In judging good actions as evil, a false conscience also has sad results, for it makes a person guilty of as great a sin as his false conscience represents his act to be — for the will to sin is there. Thus:

A. In performing a sinless act or a venially sinful act, thinking that it is gravely sinful, a person is adjudged guilty of grave sin, if he does it with full deliberation and malice aforethought. In the preceding example (No. 2), if Angela thought that it would be gravely sinful for her to smoke and she smoked anyway, she would be as guilty as if she had done something actually forbidden under pain of serious sin.

B. If a person performs a sinless act, thinking that it is venially sinful, he is , guilty of venial sin. Again, if Angela thought smoking venially sinful, she would be guilty of venial sin if she smoked.

Sometimes it happens that a person fears he is committing a sin even if he has no choice but to act as he is doing. Such a person is not guilty of any sin, because his act is not free; consequently, he cannot be held responsible for it. In order that an act be sinful, it must be performed *with freedom* — with an option to choose right from wrong — and if a person fails to recognize this in a given case, it does not alter the fact of his action not being free. Despite the person's fear that he is sinning in choosing either one of the only two alternatives equally sinful open to him, the conditions for guilt are not present and so there can be no sin.

EXAMPLE:

Mrs. Goodhart's husband is very sick, and she is taking care of him. When Sunday morning comes there is no one else available to take over her duties, and it would be dangerous to leave the patient alone. Not being sufficiently well informed to know that her task of charity automatically excuses her from the obligation of attending Mass, she knows that if she leaves and goes to Mass she will be sinning seriously against charity and duty; she likewise believes that if she stays with her sick husband and misses Mass, she will be guilty of grave sin. Nevertheless, she stays with her husband. In this case, Mrs. Goodhart does not sin at all, even though she thought that she was committing grave sin; for, under the circumstances, she could not avoid an imagined sin, no matter what she did.

The perplexed person in such a case has the erroneous idea that it is sometimes necessary to do wrong; actually, there is never a point at which one must choose between two lines of action, each immoral. A perplexed person who, however, is confronted with two alternatives, both of which he believes to be sinful, should choose that which seems less wrong. No sin will then be committed, for he is not free. If one of the two alternatives seems only slightly less wrong than the other, it is not gravely sinful to choose the slightly greater evil.

It should be clear by now how important it is for us to inform ourselves of the correct principles of morality (God's precepts, laws, etc.) and their application. We are never too old to learn, never too old to change our ideas if they happen to be wrong. So much depends on our minds, on whether or not our ideas of morals are correct. The mind naturally tends to be colored and dulled by prejudice, fashion and environment. Fashions are changeable; the principles of morality are not. But how many people, good people, confuse the two! A knee-length, sleeveless dress in the Victorian era might have been a serious incitement to lust, but today it arouses no normal man to passion. How we must guard against confusing conservatism with conscience, and manners with morals! Certainly ideas are not necessarily correct because they are old-fashioned; neither are they right simply because they are modern.

Most of us tend to canonize the fashionable ideas and conventions of our own generation. Granny, for example, confident of her modesty in ruffles and crinolines, thinks the thoroughly modern Miss Millie is slithering into hell in her mini-skirt; while modern Miss Millie, equally self-opinionated, thinks Granny a stubborn old fool. Both sit in judgment on each other with closed minds, convinced that her own attitude is the right one. Neither is morally right, of course; and neither is entirely wrong. Each is an extreme respresentative of her own generation. Both Granny and modern Miss Millie should be prepared to modify their views in accordance with the correct principles of morality and their application.

III. A *certain conscience* is one that is convinced without any doubt that an action is sinful or not sinful.

EXAMPLE:

Young and attractive Miss Typist is invited by her employer to spend the evening out with him. After carefully weighing the circumstances (his sometimes improper conduct during office hours, what happened on similar previous occasions, etc.) she comes to the definite conclusion that she would be placing herself, for no reason at all, in an occasion of sinning with him. Her conscience definitely tells her that it would be sinful to go out again with him. Miss Typist's conscience is certain.

A certain conscience (moral judgment) must always be obeyed in whatever it commands or forbids. This holds true even if this certain conscience happens to be false. True, God's will as expressed in law is the ultimate guide of our actions; however, we are bound to it and can obey it only when we know its precepts. Thus, conscience, the personal judgment concerning the agreement or disagreement of our actions with the law, is our proximate norm, and must be followed, even when, unwittingly, mistaken. It is according to how we conform our actions to this norm that we will be judged by God.

EXAMPLE:

Robert X read extensively about the issues involved in the Vietnam war. When he was drafted, he refused to serve in the U.S. Army because he was sincerely convinced that American involvement in the war there was unjust. He had formed his conscience definitely and conclusively. Though many people would disagree with his conviction, Robert indeed was obliged to follow his certain conscience.

IV. A *doubtful conscience* is one which leaves a person undecided about the goodness or badness of an act. Living in a complex world can be very puzzling and the problems of conscience will be no less so. All sorts of complicating factors can get in the way of making a clear moral decision.

EXAMPLE:

In the example above, if Robert could not come to any definite conclusion whether or not he could serve in the Army (that is, if he saw reasons which would indicate that it was very wrong for him to serve in the Army under the circumstances and yet he saw reasons which would indicate that it was not, and as a result he could not make up his mind on the matter) he would have had a doubtful conscience.

What are we to do when we are undecided about the goodness or badness of an act, when we have a doubtful conscience?

First of all, we should never get into a frenzy about it. It happens to the best of people, even highly educated ones. True, it is never right to act with a doubtful conscience; thus, if my conscience is wavering and does not come to a definite conclusion that a particular action is sinless, I cannot perform that action until I settle my doubts one way or another. I must refrain from acting until I consult some informed person or reliable book on the matter in question. If I have no opportunity to do this, I must sincerely think the matter out according to the knowledge I have at the time. And only after I have settled my doubts, one way or another, that I may act accordingly. The reason is that if a person acted without making an honest decision about such a case, he would be accepting the possibility of violating what God wants in a moral law, and doing this voluntarily would implicitly be willing what is sinful. For example, if a hunter doubts whether that which he is aiming at is a wild animal or a valuable domesticated creature, privately owned, and shoots anyway, he is guilty of an injustice. Even if what is slain happens to be a wild animal, the hunter is still morally guilty of an unjust act.

PROBABILISM

But what of one who is unable to obtain the needed information and whose doubts still remain? Keep calm, stay cool. There is a practical rule of principle which helps to settle a doubtful conscience. It is known as *probabilism*. It is definitely a safe doctrine to follow, but it may be used only after a reasonable investigation has been made of the matter in question, if, indeed an investigation can be made.

THE PRINCIPLE STATED. *If the lawfulness of an action is doubtful, one may follow the opinion that favors liberty provided he is certain that this opinion is well-founded (even though realizing that the contrary opinion may possibly be true), and provided it involves no risk of causing harm to oneself or to others without necessity.*

An opinion is well-founded if it is based on sufficiently serious reasons to induce a sensible or prudent man to give his assent, though he still realizes that the opposite opinion may be true. In many cases, it is relatively easy to determine, indirectly at least, whether the opinion favoring liberty is well-founded or not, by acting in accord with what is generally done in like cases by practical Catholics. Certainly if the weight of probability outweighs that of improbability, it is quite obvious that opinion is well-founded.

An *opinion favoring liberty* is an opinion which leaves the person free to perform the action, the lawfulness of which is in doubt. For example, I want to go to Holy Communion, but I am not sure whether or not I ate something within the last hour. I have good reasons for thinking that I did; yet I have equally good reasons to think that I did not. The opinion favoring liberty is the one which says that I may go to Communion.

If there is any risk of causing spiritual or temporal harm either to oneself or to others, then we cannot use probabilism. We must then follow the safer course of action.

We shall not go into the proofs for the lawfulness of probabilism, for that is the theologians' business. We only emphasize again that it is definitely a safe course to follow. We may mention, however, that our state of mind, after applying probabilism, differs from a doubtful conscience in that by resorting to probabilism we actually do come to a definite conclusion as to whether or not we may perform the act in question.

Actually, probabilism is only common sense. Here is what a good, solid theologian of yesteryear has to say about probabilism: "In its ultimate analysis, probabilism is common sense; it is a system used in practical doubt by the majority of mankind. People rightly say: 'I am not going to debate all day before acting in doubtful matters; there must be some very obvious way of making up my mind. At all events, if I cannot make up my mind for myself, I will act as some good people act, though many other good people might disapprove.' That practical solution of doubt is common sense, and it is probabilism" (Henry Davis, S.J., *Moral and Pastoral Theology,* New York, Sheed and Ward, 1935, I, 93). So the key to making up one's mind is the common-sense axiom: *If I cannot make up my mind for myself, I will act as some good people act, though many other good people might disapprove.* When all is said and done, probabilism is nothing more complicated than that.

We may use probabilism as many times as the same problem arises in the future, as long as the impossibility of making an investigation remains. Naturally, as soon as the opportunity of making an investigation whereby we can find out the objective answer to our problem presents itself, we must try to find the answer; if we neglect to do so, we can no longer avail ourselves of the use of probabilism. The amount of diligence or effort that we must use to find the answer on such an occasion must be proportionate to the importance of the problem at hand: the graver the problem, the greater must be our diligence. If, after trying our best to obtain the correct answer, our doubts still remain, we may again resort to probabilism.

But remember: we are not allowed to use probabilism if in following the opinion favoring liberty the contemplated action would risk causing grave harm to another (or to oneself) without necessity.

EXAMPLES:

1. Louise borrows her brother's car, which has very poor tires. She knows that they may blow out at any time. Just to see how fast the car will go, Louise speeds up to eighty miles per hour. "The tires will probably not blow out," she says, "so I may drive at any speed." In this case it was unlawful for Louise to use probabilism, because the action involved the risk of causing grave harm to herself without necessity, not to mention the risk of gravely harming others or, worse yet, jeopardizing their very lives.

2. There is no priest around and a baby is dying. Bert, though he could easily get water, baptizes the baby with some liquid in a nearby dish which seems to be, and probably is, water. It was unlawful for Bert to do this (to assume that the baptism would probably be valid, even though there was some doubt about the liquid); in this case Bert without necessity risked grave harm — the loss of heaven — to the baby.

OTHER CLASSIFICATIONS OF CONSCIENCE

We may also speak of conscience as being delicate, lax and scrupulous, depending on the habitual manner in which the person makes his moral judgments.

I. We have a *delicate conscience* if we habitually judge correctly and with prudent attention concerning the acts we are about to perform. We are neither insensitive nor over-sensitive to the circumstances that affect the morality of actions; that is, to any circumstances that make an act sinful or not sinful, more sinful or less sinful. A delicate conscience is actually nothing more than a habitually correct conscience.

A delicate conscience, however, is more than a mere mechanical application of moral laws to one's living. Here we may recall the law of love. A conscience may be correct regarding individual actions but may still be habitually ungenerous to God with self. If a Christian thinks only of what he must do to avoid grave sin, or even any kind of sin, he reveals the mentality of a slave. Merely mechanically applying moral rules to one's living leaves conscience sin-oriented, negative. If, instead, a Christian is imbued with the fundamental love of God and neighbor, he will use the observance of the law as the first stepping-stone to be free, to soar on to the more positive ways of serving God and his fellowman. Being a Catholic will mean not merely Sunday Mass attendance, avoiding birth control or a hamburger on Friday, but rather the willingness to do what he can for God in his family, in his community and in his Church. Instead of merely avoiding quarrels with the neighbors across the street or gossiping about them, he will try to be helpful to them in times of sickness or sorrow. Instead of counting the sins he avoids by his observance of external laws, he will start counting the ways in which he can show his love in the service of God and man. A person with a truly delicate conscience is free to understand the needs of love far above the requirements of external law and tries to act on them. In doing this, he finds his freedom and joy.

II. A person has a *lax conscience* if he is always inclined to judge too negligently as regards the lawfulness of actions; if he is prone to make light of his responsibility, or if for frivolous reasons he sees no sin where there really is sin. He is a minimizer: he easily and habitually excuses himself from guilt when he has no valid reasons for doing so; he "makes small sins out of serious sins" and tends to see no sin at all where normal people recognize venial sin. A lax conscience may also be described as a habitually erroneous conscience.

One's guilt for actions committed under the influence of a lax conscience is to be determined according to the rule governing vincible and invincible ignorance.

An attitude cannot be changed overnight. It has to be done by steps. A lax attitude is no exception. How do we go about changing it? First of all, since a lax conscience is a more or less habitually erroneous one, implying a lack of necessary knowledge, a serious study of moral principles and laws such as this book is a great step forward. Meditating on, and thinking about Christ's values will help form a better attitude. More importantly, since a lax conscience is usually the result of much lukewarmness in the service of God and man, zeal for doing good works must be enkindled. Praying for a change of attitude, of course, is so obviously necessary that it seems a cliché to mention it; so is the fervent, frequent reception of the sacraments. Like the sick man who goes to his doctor for help and listens to his advice, a person with a lax conscience should go to his spiritual doctor — his confessor or spiritual director — and be willing to follow his advice. When he does, recovery of a delicate conscience is well on the way.

III. A person has a *scrupulous conscience* if, influenced by trifling and unsound reasons, he is prone to exaggerate his responsibility to the extent that he often judges as sinful, actions which in reality are not. He is often tortured by doubts that he may be living in mortal sin, or he may be constantly beset with an unfounded (based on feeling rather than on reason), sickening fear of having committed sin. Here we are considering a scrupulous conscience not so much as an isolated act of judgment but rather as a habitual manner of judging.

The scrupulous person is frequently tormented with the awful thought that he may be sinning seriously. If his reason tells him that a certain course of action is sinless, immediately a silly, nagging interior voice tells him that it *may* be sinful or that it *is* sinful. What appears quite harmless to ordinary people still *may* be sinful *for him,* he thinks; but he can't give any good reasons why it should be sinful for him. Something tells him so.

Did he really put out that cigarette? Though he is sure he put it out, the silly little voice keeps on: "It may keep on burning; the sofa was quite near that ashtray; it may burn down the house — a serious matter — yes, you must go back to *make sure.*" He *remembers* how he pressed down the stub until there were no more live ashes. Yet the nagging voice keeps on: "But it may still be burning; you are not really sure; it is a serious matter if you burn the house down, or even the sofa. They aren't yours. . . . A mortal sin." He goes back to make sure simply because he is afraid to flout the nagging "voice in the back of his mind." He confuses conscience with that silly voice. So he has a moment's peace; then something else comes up. Did he give in to those impure thoughts just now? And so on and on. His waking hours are a living nightmare.

Other scrupulous people are forever worried about past confessions; these are judged to be sacrilegious either because of lack of real sorrow or because of having concealed a grave sin, or for some other such reason. This type of person is *not sure.* Hardly is he out of the confessional when his troubles begin: he minutely reexamines his preparation for confession, his examination of conscience, his telling of the sins, the words exchanged with the confessor, the act of contrition, etc. He completely forgets that one cannot make a bad confession unless he is fully aware of the fact that he *deliberately* held back a grave sin or *deliberately* was not sorry, etc.

Mental ailments, as everyone realizes, can be far more torturing than physical suffering. Perhaps no keener mental suffering can be had than that involving conscience. In a word, scrupulous people are suffering souls, really and truly sick. They deserve the love, tenderness and patience which every sick person deserves. To tell them to pull themselves together is useless advice, because that is exactly what they want to do, but don't know how to go about achieving it. Nor is it very helpful to tell the scrupulous that the funny feeling inside is not conscience, because sensibly enough they want to know what it is, if not conscience.

The causes of scruples are legion: some are physical, others psychological, others still are of a purely spiritual nature. In order to cure a person of scruples completely, we must find and remove their cause, a difficult matter, indeed, requiring great sympathy and skill. Advice and remedies of a general nature may cure some cases, not because of the universal applicability of those remedies but because some particular remedy happened to pertain to that particular type of case. Where there are several causes of scrupulosity, then several remedies must be applied.

If the real cause of scruples is physical, the cure must be sought on the physical plane. The most competent person to help in such cases is an experienced physician.

Some people are healthy by nature, others are not. The temperament of some is an easier prey for worries and anxiety than that of others. Those who are unwell often only see the dark side of things; that is why people often suffer from scruples when suffering from shock, from nervous exhaustion, and the strain of overwork. Many, again, are attacked by scruples during adolescence or the change of life.

The doctor will usually prescribe treatment with drugs, rest, sleep, nourishing food, fresh air, etc. The more tranquil and cheerful a patient keeps his mind, the sooner will he find himself cured.

Some of the psychological causes of scruples are: a vivid imagination, predominance of emotion over reason, lack of judgment because, as a child, the person was not allowed to make up his own mind. Sometimes an overly cautious upbringing, especially in the area of sex, will be a very real cause of scruples.

Scruples may also have their origin in the purely spiritual plane: lack of instruction regarding moral principles — what is a sin, what is not; or worse, false ideas of the same; failure to distinguish between temptation and consent; false ideas of God, etc. It is tremendously important that we have correct ideas about God; a person with a severe upbringing may unconsciously have transferred the image of severe parents, strict teachers, or insensitive confessors to God. Such a person would quite naturally form the idea of God as a stern taskmaster, ready to pounce on unsuspecting mortals for every slipup and quick to punish accordingly.

Before anyone can hope to be cured of scruples, he must be convinced, and convinced thoroughly, that conscience is simply sound reasoning, judgment based on good reasons, and that the "nagging voice at the back of one's mind" is merely a phobia, a bogey cropping up from the subconscious.

The following remedy, applied faithfully and perseveringly, cannot fail to set aright many a troubled conscience. It may cure some cases completely; others it may not cure at all, but at least it will stunt the growth of the loathsome, nagging phobia. The scrupulous person should not be afraid to apply these rules ruthlessly to his own case: they are not revolutionary or unorthodox, though they may seem just that to many timid souls. They have been, with God's grace, the most effective remedy many confessors have found to date. We repeat: apply them ruthlessly; every word means what it says and is to be taken literally.

TO CURE SCRUPLES

1. *Take no notice whatever of your doubts:* (Just ignore them.) Treat as absolutely null and void all laws, obligations and prohibitions which are doubtful; and

2. *Regard as doubtful all* laws, obligations and prohibitions which are not as certain to you as it is certain that two and two make four. Therefore:

3. Do without fear whatever at first sight and without examination you do not know to be *certainly* sinful;

4. Do not consider yourself obliged to confess a sin if you have the *least* doubt whether it is mortal or not; and

5. Do not mention in confession a mortal sin which was *perhaps* confessed before, nor repeat a confession which was *perhaps* bad or invalid. (Quoted from *L'Ange Conducteur des Ames Scrupuleuses,* Part I, Chapter I, by R. J. Meyer, S.J., in his work, *The Science of the Saints,* St. Louis, Herder, 1919, I, 193.)

Surely nothing could be more explicit and peremptory! One more thing: some scrupulous persons will still ask, "But how do I really know that I'm doubting?" The best answer is that when you are in doubt whether you are doubting or not, then most assuredly you are doubting!

OTHER SUGGESTIONS TO HELP THE SCRUPULOUS

Of prime importance is the practice of absolute obedience. I know — the confessor may not understand — but then neither does the penitent! Others have been scrupulous but not precisely as this penitent is; that again is only another symptom of scrupulosity; if the scrupulous person feels this way, he should be all the more convinced that he is in need of help. Remember, no one was ever lost through obedience to a confessor or saved by disobedience! God will never hold the penitent responsible should there ever be any error of judgment on the part of the confessor. The penitent must boldly follow the advice given him by the confessor, convinced that by so doing he cannot be committing sin, regardless of how he feels about it.

It is always beneficial to develop one's sense of humor. Looking at the funny side of life will do wonders! Also try for a time, say several weeks, to forget your problems and self-analysis. Anything can wait that long. At the end of that time, refreshed and strengthened, you will be in a better position to tackle your problems once more. And remember: avoid self-pity — forget yourself!

The scrupulous penitent should try to act as other good people act; what is sinless for them is sinless for him, even if he does not see how it can be so. He should never give way to scruples on the plea that it is better to have peace of mind than to continue the battle. The phobia grows stronger with every victory gained over the penitent.

Think often of the goodness and mercy of God. He was, and still is, the friend of all publicans and sinners who are willing to try again. In mankind's history, who was kinder and gentler to the sick and suffering than the Master Himself? Love God much and trust Him. He is still the same God who forgave Mary of Magdala because she loved much. Often think of the story of the prodigal son. The father looked for the return of his sinful son every day and longed for him to come back; when he finally saw him, he ran out on the road to meet him, threw his arms around his neck and kissed him. The Master told this story so that we would not be afraid of Him as a taskmaster but rather think of Him as that loving father with his wayward son. If you are anxious about His forgiveness, think of the nicest, kindest friend you ever had . . . and how understanding such a friend is. Christ is that and much, much more. He loves you without limit with understanding, kindness and compassion despite your failings. He understands your troubles, your bewilderment. No matter what they are, if they are doubts, simply trust Him with them . . . like a child with someone who loves him. Trust and love go together always.

Chapter II

TEMPTATION
AND SIN

To disobey willingly and knowingly one of the laws proceeding directly or indirectly from God is a sin. In paradise Adam and Eve did what God did not want them to do — transgressed a commandment of His; they knew what they were doing, that they were disobeying Him; and no one, not even the serpent, forced them to do it. Thus, they committed sin. Before they sinned, however, there had to be something delightfully appealing to entice them to perform the evil act. There had to be temptation.

TEMPTATION

A soldier cannot merit a reward for bravery unless he has been exposed in the front lines to the perils and dangers of battle, so neither can we prove our loyalty and love to God (and increase our merit for heaven) unless we are tried and tested by temptation. A wise man once put it: "No one can be crowned unless he has conquered; no one can conquer unless he fights; and no one can fight without an enemy. Hence temptation must come."

The word *temptation* itself comes from the Latin word *tentatio,* meaning "a testing" or "trying-out." Temptation is a testing of our obedience to the will of God as it is manifested to us through the moral law and our conscience. God will never permit us to be tempted beyond our strength (1 Cor. 10:13). The more violent the temptation, the stronger His help; the greater the danger, the more potent His grace. That the temptation was too great to resist can never be used as an excuse by anyone.

As we know, temptation does not necessarily lead to sin. Far from it! It may and should lead us to a strengthening of our relationship with God by proving our loyalty and love for Him in overcoming the trial. Friendship is stronger when it has been sorely tested and found faithful. Even on a purely natural plane, we make our will stronger by its constant exercise and thus we shall be better prepared to take a firmer stand against future temptations.

A temptation may be also defined as an incitement to evil proposed to the will.

1. First of all, a *suggestion* to do wrong comes into the mind. To guard our

thoughts is a serious duty; but there are times when we cannot prevent evil suggestions and ideas from intruding, any more than an island in mid-ocean can prevent the waves from lapping its shores.

2. With these thoughts or suggestions we experience *involuntarily* a delight in the possibility of performing the proposed act or enjoying the sinful thoughts. So long as this delight is involuntary, no matter how vehement, it is not a sin.

3. *After we realize* our delight in the possibility of committing the proposed evil, we then either *deliberately* refuse to consent or we give in and consent to this delight itself, or we go still further and decide to perform the suggested evil itself.

The first two steps are only parts of the temptation and are not sinful in the least. Only in the *third step* does sin or victory result. The trial is complete only when there is consent or rejection.

SIN

A practical way of defining sin is this: sin is the deliberate disobeying of God's law. It may smack of legalism but it's another way of saying that we do not want to do what God wants of us. What God wants of us (His will) is revealed to us through the various moral laws: the natural law, divine positive law, Church and civil law. This may not be all God expects of us if we truly love Him, but at least through these laws we know the minimum of what we should do if we are not to offend Him. That's why we also speak of sin as an offense against God. As in any friendship, an offense affects the relationship; if it is really serious, it will end it and friendship will turn into enmity. Our friendship with God is affected in the same way by sin. On the other hand, every time we do something good we please God and our friendship with Him is strengthened and increased. Either way, our acts show what is in our heart.

The true Christian gets a correct insight into the meaning of sin only when face-to-face with the cross of Christ and what sin did to Him there. Because of sin, even today Christ continues to suffer, not personally as He did on Golgotha, but through the Church, His body. Actual suffering is entailed because it involves actual loss. Realizing this will help us to avoid sin in any form, great or small.

FORMAL AND MATERIAL SINS

A *formal* sin is an act by which a law of God is *knowingly* and *freely* disobeyed. This is "sin" as it is commonly known and understood. It always presupposes that we know and realize that we are performing the evil act and that we are freely doing so. If I know a certain book is an extremely obscene one, yet I deliberately read it without a justifying reason, I am committing sin, doing what I know God does not want me to do. This is *formal* sin.

A material sin, on the other hand, is an act by which a law of God is *unknowingly* violated. We cannot break or lessen our friendship with God innocently. Actually it is not a sin in the ordinary sense at all, for there is *no moral guilt* involved; hence it need never cause anxiety and should not even be mentioned in confession. The newly acquired knowledge is to be a norm from that time on.

EXAMPLE:

On a walk through the city park one Sunday afternoon, Jack hears a soap-box orator decrying the miseries of inner-city slums and a collection is in progress. Truly moved by the speech, Jack decides to give all the money he has in his billfold, $36.70. Only after he returns home and listens to the local radio station does he find out that the recipient of his generosity was a well-known society for the repeal of abortion laws in his State.

Jack need not be anxious. His action of promoting the abortion society in this case was free from moral guilt, since it was done unknowingly.

VENIAL AND MORTAL SIN

According to the gravity of the guilt involved, sin (formal sin) is divided into *venial* and *mortal*. Physically, some diseases only weaken bodily strength; others destroy life completely. The same is true spiritually: some sins only weaken or lessen the friendship of God (sanctifying grace), while others completely extinguish it. Differences may arise between friends. If the offense is slight, it does not seriously affect the friendship. If it is grave, it puts an end to the friendship entirely. Venial sin does not seriously affect our friendship with God, but mortal sin extinguishes it completely.

VENIAL SIN

I. *Venial sin* is an act (thought, word or deed) by which a person violates God's law either in (a) slight matter, or (b) in grave matter but without full realization or consent. For example: (a) Irene cheats the grocer of twenty-five cents (her sin is venial because the matter is not grave); and (b) John was slow and hesitant in expelling impure thoughts ... he "half-consented" to them (John's sin is venial because he did not fully consent).

One venial sin may be more sinful than another venial sin. This may be due to the fact that the subject matter is greater or lesser or that the deliberation is full or only imperfect. If Irene cheats the grocer of three dollars, her sin, though venial, would be greater than that if she had cheated him of twenty-five cents. Likewise if, let us say, Patsy with full deliberation and reflection writes an insulting note to her teacher, her venial sin would be greater than that if she wrote the note in a fit of anger, not fully realizing at the moment the import of the insulting words.

Although venial sin is slight in comparison to mortal sin, we must never forget that Christ suffered for our venial sins as well as for our mortal sins. Venial sin does not hurt Him (through the Church, His body) as much as mortal sin but it hurts Him nonetheless and our friendship with Him is lessened.

Even apart from this consideration, we must remember too that those who make light of venial sin soon fall into grave sin. "Avoid small sins," says St.

John Chrysostom, "for they will grow into great sins." The Scriptures admonish us with similar warnings. An illness may be slight at first, but it often becomes serious, then fatal, if neglected. The devil (he does exist, the Scriptures are very clear on this) is very careful not to tempt us to great sins at first. He knows the laws of human psychology well: mortal sin involves the total orientation of the person, and man does not ordinarily make such a drastic change by just one isolated action; rather, the change begins to happen gradually in the person through a number of smaller and less important actions — through these our friendship with God begins to cool, to lessen. So the devil begins by persuading us that it is quite a small matter to steal trifles, to tell a little lie, to practice trifling familiarities with persons of the opposite sex. When he succeeds in calming our conscience about these small faults, he tempts us to greater ones, ensnaring us more and more with his wiles; finally, when our conscience is sufficiently calloused, he leads us to the frightful excess of mortal sin.

A Christian who habitually excuses himself with, "It's only a venial sin," does not seem to understand what sincere love of God demands. He is ever skirting around the outer edges of friendship, trying to stretch the relationship to the breaking point without actually severing it. These are not the actions of a heart full of love! Love is rather interested in the thousand and one things which will strengthen, deepen the friendship, concerned only how it can be increased. Love is self-effacing, always desirous of doing the wishes, not merely the commands, of the beloved. God asks many things of us; some of these He commands but He wants us to fulfill these commands out of love not because of threats. If threats alone move us to do what He commands, we have the mentality of a slave; but if we are eager to do as much as we can for Him out of love we are truly His children . . . with the happiness and freedom that children of God deserve. That's why He asked us to regard Him, not as Master, but as *Abba* ("Father").

MORTAL OR GRAVE SIN

No words can adequately describe the tragedy that is mortal or grave sin. Theologians try. And they express it in very different ways. The varying expressions describe not different realities but only the various ways of looking at the same things. Chances are if a hundred people are asked to tell what they saw at an accident they will give a hundred different views. In the same way theologians will vary in their attempts to tell us about mortal sin. All of them are right too. They merely give us different views.

Some describe mortal sin as a complete rejection of God: by mortal sin man prefers a passing pleasure, convenience or thing to God; he chooses to do what he wants instead of what God wants, even though sometimes this rejection consists in running away from doing what he knows he should do. Others have described mortal sin as the destruction of sanctifying grace in the soul or perhaps more clearly as the killing of the life of God in the soul (even the word *mortal* comes from the Latin *mors,* meaning "death"). In truth, sanctifying grace is the life of God in our soul and through mortal sin this life ceases to exist in us; that is why we say a soul "in mortal sin" is dead, though the soul itself does not cease to exist. Of all our qualities as human beings, the life of God in our soul (sanctifying grace) is what makes us resemble God the most. This God-likeness is destroyed by mortal sin and, after dying in such a state, there is nothing belonging to God in that soul, so it never attains God and heaven.

Still other theologians, emphasizing the communitarian aspects of sin, explain mortal sin as a separation or a division, not simply between the sinner and God, but also between man and the Church of Christ: by mortal sin man cuts himself off from Christ and His people. He not only disrupts union with God but also with the family of God. Mortal sin seriously hurts the Church, the body of Christ, and through His body, Christ Himself. This is the reason why the Sacrament of Penance is necessary: to restore us to the unity of God, true (though we can do this by a perfect act of sorrow), but also through an act of the Church (absolution) to restore us to the unity of the People of God.

More recently theologians began describing mortal sin as the complete breaking-off of our relationship, our friendship with God, just as some older theologians used to stress that mortal sin makes us enemies of God. Friends, perhaps, can cease to be friends without becoming enemies but the basic idea they try to express is this: through mortal sin we deliberately and completely reject God in preference to what we want. Some modern theologians, without any real proof, go further and insist that, since mortal sin involves the total orientation of the person, it can *never* be just one isolated action; they even berate preachers and teachers for teaching that one mortal sin can send a person to hell regardless of the good such a person has done in life. These moderns seem to forget that a friend sometimes does turn into an enemy by one serious, deliberate act against friend, e.g., to save his own life before a gauleiter or commissar he betrays his friend. What happens to his total orientation in such a case? He would like to save his friend too but, under the circumstances, does not. A man might plead that when he willfully commits fornication he really does not want to lose the friendship of God, much less to become God's enemy. When Peter denied Christ, he wanted to stay Christ's friend too (it would seem that his total orientation toward Christ could not have turned completely around), yet he committed a serious sin by his act of denial. The point is that we can indeed reject God by one serious, deliberate act, that is, we can commit mortal sin by one act. Another thing, Christ did not reject him but he rejected Christ by his denial. God never changes in His relationship to us, He does not reject us, but we change in our relationship to Him — we reject Him when we sin mortally. In serious matters, by deliberately choosing something else than God we show by our act what is really in our heart.

By now it should be clear that mortal sin, as the old catechism put it, is a serious offense against God. Or if we particularize it further, a mortal sin is an act (thinking, speaking or deed) by which a person deliberately disobeys God's law in a serious matter. This definition, though somewhat legalistic, is important to help us understand that an act can be mortally sinful only if three conditions are present: (a) serious matter; (b) sufficient realization; and (c) full consent ("deliberately" means with sufficient realization and consent). If one of these is missing, we can be consoled that we have not offended God seriously, i.e., we have not committed mortal sin.

A. By *serious matter* here we mean that the act itself is a serious violation of God's law or the law of the Church; for example, idolatry, murder, stealing hundreds of dollars, etc. The seriousness of matter is interpreted for each individual by his conscience, rightly formed. In other words, the individual person has the obligation to learn which sins are in reality serious (from God's point of view) and which sins not as seriously wrong; so his conscience must be based on right knowledge. We may learn that a sin is serious from the Scriptures (e.g., Gal. 5:19-21; 1 Cor. 6:9-10, etc.); from the general teachings of the Fathers, Doctors and theologians of the Church; and from the specific law — doctrinal, moral and disciplinary — laid down for our instruction and guidance by the Church, which is endowed by God with full power to teach and govern the faithful.

The average person learns about the sinfulness of certain actions from his parents, teachers, and his parish priests. Often the nature of the action itself may clearly show us that the act is serious (e.g., anything that causes grave harm to God, the Church, the State, our neighbor, or to ourselves).

Because mortal sin deprives man of eternal life and delivers him, if unrepentant, to eternal damnation, human sympathy and compassion instinctively lead us to hope that men are not really guilty of the many serious sins they commit. Many "new moralists" reduce the number of mortal sins committed in the world by diminishing the objective binding force of the moral law or even abolishing it in certain very difficult situations. Others, again, claim that no moral law has any absolute value and in certain situations a man may act for the sake of love against moral principles and laws — if it helps self-fulfillment and expresses our love of neighbor. In other words, a person in certain situations can do anything, they claim, as long as he has the right intention or if he does it out of love. That is not God's brand of morality. When the Scriptures list the sinful actions for which the sinner will not inherit heaven (Gal. 5:19-21), they do not say that a man may do such things provided he does them out of love, self-fulfillment, or some other similar reason. God, through St. Paul, unequivocally states: "I warn you now, as I warned you before: those who behave like this will not inherit the kingdom of God" (Gal. 5:21). Period! The same holds true of the vices, listed in the Scriptures, which exclude a man from heaven (1 Cor. 6:9-10). These are facts and no amount of wishful thinking will change them.

The Christians of the early centuries, when led to the chopping block, found themselves in as difficult a situation as anything we can offer today. They were terrified, like we would have been. Most of them would have gladly saved themselves and their families if they had not believed in the absolute value of moral law. Even those who weakened and denied God did not attempt to deny the objective binding force of moral law. They did not appeal to any higher law of love (love of neighbor, their children and self) to excuse themselves precisely because they knew that they should have done in love *what truth demanded.*

Whatever happened to the Scriptural maxim: "The fear of the Lord is the beginning of wisdom" (Prv. 1:7)? There were ages, true, in the history of Christianity when the fear of hellfire lay too heavily on man. Excessive emphasis on fear and soul-searching can sink into morbidity, into a kind of spiritual hypochondria. But, heavens! Ours is no such age! Ours is an age of indulgence, permissiveness and softness. What is worse, some are smug in calling this permissiveness by another name: love, self-fulfillment. The modern declaration of "God is love" is turned into a thoroughly permissive "God the Chum," properly instructed by Freud, Dewey and the hosts who followed them into convincing us that God is too indulgent to punish much of anything — even though half the world is being kicked to death or starved by the other half. If we succumb to this line of thinking, we are blind leading the blind, spiritual fools who refuse to face the facts.

Christian love is the willingness to sacrifice oneself to whatever God and His truth want of us, not what we want. Hell is part of the nature of things, though thoroughly unpleasant to face, just as much as are the multiple deaths in airplane accidents caused by the law of gravity. The idea of a retributive Providence is almost blasphemous to the ears of "enlightened, progressive, modern man," even though the injunction to fear God is one thing beyond dispute in God's Scriptures.

Eternal hellfire does not mean entrapment of the guiltless. God is also just. Only the truly guilty will ever be damned. The justice of God means that such punishment will befall only those richly deserving of it, those fully responsible for their seriously sinful acts. This means that even in serious matters a person must *know* and *sufficiently (fully) realize* the grave sinfulness of the act when he does it.

B. *Sufficient realization.* "Sufficient" is a relative term, but sufficient realization, as commonly accepted by the Church's moralists, means the attention or deliberation that a person would normally give to a fairly important business deal (e.g., buying a suit, an overcoat, etc.). Though this deliberation or attention is far from being one hundred percent perfect, one doesn't just make such business deals lightly or absent-mindedly. We may safely say that sufficient realization or deliberation is not had (consequently, no grave guilt) when actions are performed by one half-asleep, greatly distracted, or delirious. In these states the person may be vaguely aware that he is doing something sinful, but still does not realize that it is *mortally sinful.*

EXAMPLE:

Without doing anything, before falling asleep, which would directly or indirectly cause pollution, John is half-awake when he experiences the pleasure of pollution during the night and does not make an effort to resist it. John may be guilty of venial sin but not of mortal sin, because being half-awake he was in a semiconscious state and, therefore, he was only half-conscious of what was taking place (did not have sufficient realization). Also, being in a semiconscious state, he could not have been capable of full and deliberate consent; in such a state a person is capable of partial consent only.

C. *Full consent.* The dread threshold of grave sin is not crossed unless a person consents fully to the evil act (thought, word, deed) even in serious matters — and this, despite clear knowledge and sufficient realization. In other words, no matter how clear one's knowledge and realization of a mortally sinful act may be, if one does not consent fully to it, he does not sin gravely. For example, even though one plainly knows that the unchaste or blasphemous thoughts which have come to his mind are matter for grave sin, he commits no sin (even though the thoughts just do not seem to go away) provided he tried his best to dispel them. The same is true of the emotions. Feelings of deadly revenge may well up in the heart of anyone, but as long as he does not want them, there is no consent and, hence, no grave guilt. The determination to sin must never be confused with the pleasure one experiences when such thoughts present themselves. As was pointed out before, this is part of the temptation. Only when the fight is given up and consent given is sin committed.

DETERMINING GUILT WHEN TEMPTED

It should be clear by now that in judging the guilt or sinfulness of our thoughts, words, or actions, we must always keep clearly in mind the three things that must necessarily be present before a grave sin is committed (sufficient realization, full consent and serious matter). This is important especially with regard to sins against the Sixth and Ninth Commandments, because in such matters sufficient reflection or consent is often lacking.

Those in doubt about consenting should not pay any attention to their feelings, but should look only to their intellectual conviction in forming a judgment. Feelings of uneasiness and alarm should be dispelled at once as they may very easily lead to a false conclusion of grave guilt. This is particularly true of those leaning toward scrupulosity, since they constantly seem to confuse their natural anxiety with remorse of conscience. Much has already been said about doubts concerning consent in the preceding chapter on scrupulous conscience; more will be found in the final chapter.

A person may be besieged repeatedly by feelings of hatred and revenge or by impure images, desires and suggestions; but if he does not want them in his mind or does not realize their presence or sinfulness, he does not sin at all. If, *after* becoming aware of their *presence and sinfulness,* he consents fully and entirely, deliberately taking pleasure in them, he sins grievously; if he rejects them, he commits no sin but performs an act of virtue; *if he does not know or doubts whether* he had full consent and realization, he may not have committed any sin at all or perhaps only a venial sin; certainly he did not sin gravely. A wise old confessor once compared full consent (and realization) and "half-consent" (and partial realization) to an elephant and a mouse: "If there is a mouse in the room with us, we may not be sure of its presence and thereby doubts may arise, but if there is an elephant with us we will certainly know it."

Certainly, if *one* of the following circumstances is true regarding one's case, the realization or consent is imperfect, and therefore no mortal sin was committed:

1. If a person was occupied and distracted with another matter and only lightly and in passing noticed that the thoughts, etc., were evil.

2. If one was half asleep or half-delirious when the evil act (thought,

word, or deed) was performed. The general rule is: unless one is *fully* awake he hasn't sufficient self-control to commit a grave sin. Hence, whenever a person sincerely doubts whether he was fully awake or not, or whether he consented fully or not, he may reasonably presume that he is not seriously guilty. We are always allowed the "benefit of the doubt" in such instances.

3. If, after the act (thought, word, or deed) one scarcely remembers what has happened.

4. If, reflecting on what has been happening, one is immediately anxious and saddened and turns from the evil.

5. *If one hesitates momentarily;* he would fain relish somewhat the forbidden pleasure, but he is loath to offend God, and after a moment's hesitation he repels the temptation.

6. If a person resists the thoughts or desires in a half-hearted way; he resists but only in a feeble, indolent manner, putting up a sort of half-resistance which implies half-consent.

7. Finally, anyone who has a sincere doubt about yielding and who ordinarily leads a good life or, at any rate, generally overcomes temptations against the particular virtue about which he is now in doubt, may presume he has not sinned gravely.

We are never bound to confess any "doubtful sins," nor is one obliged to abstain from Holy Communion in such cases. One should make an act of perfect contrition and leave the rest up to God. Naturally, those who prefer to confess such sins, may do so. Is it advisable to confess doubtful sins? That depends. If a person finds himself anxious about such "sins" or if he finds himself frequently confessing such doubtful matter, then it is better that he refrain from confessing such sins; otherwise, scrupulosity may develop.

On the other hand, if a person does not get himself "worked up" or rarely finds himself confessing "doubtful sins," then it is advisable, not obligatory, to include them in the next confession.

Do people who have a lax conscience enjoy the same benefit of a doubt? Yes, if lax persons really and sincerely doubt, they are allowed the same benefit of the doubt that normal people enjoy. Some moralists hesitate to allow this, but it is really a matter of sincerity and honesty. One's confessor is the best judge in such cases, for the lax are strongly inclined to minimize their guilt when it ought to be rather clear to them.

OTHER CIRCUMSTANCES WHICH LESSEN GUILT

Certain circumstances or obstacles may impair the *knowledge (realization)* or *free will (consent)* of the person performing the evil act (thinking, speaking, or action) and thus proportionately lessen or may even entirely free him from guilt. These obstacles are five: *ignorance, violence, fear, passion* and *habit.* To help us know how to judge the extent of guilt involved under these circumstances, we shall examine each.

I. IGNORANCE, as we commonly understand it, is the lack of essential (or necessary) knowledge about some particular thing; in other words, we cannot realize we are doing wrong or the extent of it if we do not know something is wrong or how wrong. There is one type of ignorance which a person cannot dispel, either because he is not aware of a certain obligation, or because, even if he does realize it, he cannot dispel it in the circumstances in which he finds himself (e.g., not having any books to consult on the subject or being far from anyone who could enlighten him on the matter). This kind of ignorance is called *invincible* because it cannot be overcome. *One is not responsible for one's acts performed in invincible ignorance; consequently he is not guilty of any sin.* The same is true if a person does not know the object of his act: for example, if I am shooting at something which I think without a shadow of a doubt is an animal but in reality it happens to be a man (I did not know the object).

Anxiety concerning actions a person has performed in the past, not knowing their sinful character, is to be dispelled immediately; otherwise, scrupulosity may develop. When one discovers that something which he has been doing in the past, no matter how frequently, is sinful (mortally or venially) he does not have to confess these past actions. Not having known the sinfulness of such actions, he was not guilty of any sin. The knowledge discovered is to be the norm of conduct from that time on.

EXAMPLE:

Ted, an unmarried young man, in reading **To Settle Your Conscience,** *learns that a certain type of kissing is seriously sinful. Ted has done that type of kissing in the past, thinking it was venially sinful. Ted's new knowledge does not make these past sins mortal ones for him; one's guilt is judged according to the knowledge he has at the time of the action, unless, of course, he is vincibly ignorant. Ted has therefore no obligation to confess this past matter of kissing, since only mortal sins must be confessed.*

Vincible ignorance is ignorance which can be cleared up if a person makes sufficient effort to do so. It is called vincible because it can be overcome (from the Latin *vincere* — "to overcome," "to conquer").

How much effort are we expected to make? Though all of us are expected to move ever onward toward a fuller realization of Christian life, common sense will tell us that our efforts should be proportionate to the seriousness of the moral matter in question. If the matter is small and inconsequential, our efforts need not be strenuous nor time-consuming. In serious matters, however, we are expected to make serious efforts. This sense of proportion can be seen in the business world: in buying a loaf of bread most of us will not spend much time comparing prices at the various grocers; usually we will expend a little more time and effort in buying a hat; however, in buying a car we will make really serious efforts and spend considerable time to find out where we can make the best deal. Effort-wise we must do no less regarding our spiritual obligations.

What if a proportionate effort is not made to clear up a serious moral matter? If one makes *some but not enough effort* to clear up a serious matter before doing it, then his guilt is adjudged as somewhat diminished on that account but not enough to excuse such a person from serious guilt. In ordinary layman's language, the guilt is lessened somewhat but "not enough to make a gravely sinful action become venially sinful for that person." The same holds true if no effort at all is made because of laziness or some other insufficient reason. On the other hand, a person's guilt is not diminished in the least, if a person deliberately makes no effort to clear up something in order that he may not be bound by what he would find out. This type of ignorance is really pretended; it is deliberately not wanting to know.

Of course, it is understood that in insignificant matters one does not commit a grave sin by acting under vincible ignorance — that is, when performing an action which he knows is not gravely sinful but doubts whether or not such an action is completely sinless.

II. VIOLENCE is external force exerted on a person in order to make him do something against his will. Others can sometimes force us to perform an action against our will, but in no way can we ever be forced to consent internally to that action or pleasure. In other words, our will can never be forced, though our actions may be. Naturally we are not guilty of any sin if we do not consent internally to the forced action and if we offer external resistance as best we can. External resistance may be omitted if we see that it would be useless and ineffective; however, if scandal or proximate danger of internal consent would result because of nonresistance then we must resist.

EXAMPLES:

1. A young Czech Catholic is physically forced by the Communist secret police to step on a consecrated host. He resists vigorously but to no avail. He is in no way culpable.

2. Waldo and Marge are parked on a lonely country road. Waldo begins to indulge in sinful petting with her. Marge knows that it would be useless to resist and that she cannot get help, yet she feels that she may consent to the sinful pleasure if she does not struggle. Hence her resistance is not only useful but obligatory.

In case resistance could prove effective if we would put up greater opposition than we are doing at the moment, but the extra effort is *not* made, the guilt is lessened but not taken away. The same holds true if one offers sufficient resistance externally while consenting internally to the forced act.

EXAMPLES:

1. Agatha's suitor is becoming highly excited and she knows his evil intention. Their car is parked behind that of another couple whom Agatha knows well. Agatha struggles somewhat against her suitor's brute force but not enough. Furthermore, she could have effectively stopped him by screaming. By not offering the stronger resistance which she knew would have been effective, she is judged to have consented to the evil act; her guilt, however, is not as grave as it would have been had no force been used, although it is still considered grave.

2. Caroline is forced to sin with Russell. Physically she resists as best she can (so that she would not be considered an "easy mark"), but internally she consents to the evil act. Her sin is presumed grave though not as grievous as it would have been had violence not been present.

Note: Agatha and Caroline, of course, could be without serious guilt because of other reasons, e.g., their consent may not have been full or sufficient to impute grave guilt, etc.

III. FEAR is the mental anxiety caused by some threatening danger. The danger is not necessarily physical harm threatened to the one who fears; it may be loss of reputation, of riches, or some other similar misfortune. A person may also have fear because the danger threatens other people, his parents, relatives, friends or acquaintances. Actions performed because of fear, whether that fear be grave or slight, real or purely imaginary, are still truly voluntary. Hence, if evil, they are truly culpable; if good, they are meritorious; thus, in the early persecutions, the fear of death was not considered as an excuse for apostasy. Nor does common opinion excuse a soldier's cowardice or desertion for fear of death on the battlefield.

EXAMPLE:

Erwin gets thoroughly intoxicated with his companions because he is afraid that they would think him a sissy if he refused. Erwin is still considered seriously guilty of his act, though his guilt may be slightly lessened if his fear was great.

On the other hand, fear does excite the mind so that judgment is easily distorted and the freedom of choice impeded. The greater and more overwhelming the fear, the less moral guilt. It is difficult, of course, to judge just how much a person's actions are influenced by grave fear. Only God can do that. Certainly if the fear is so great that it deprives one of the use of reason for the moment, actions performed during such moments would not be truly voluntary and so would not be culpable. But such cases seem rare.

IV. PASSION or CONCUPISCENCE, the instinctive tendency in a person to do something which at the moment seems desirable, may also lessen guilt. Emotion and feelings are other names for passion. Some of the passions are anger, fear, love, hatred, joy, sorrow and aversion. Under love we include the sexual appetite. In trying to determine the guilt of actions performed under the influence of passion, we must distinguish between the two types of passion: *antecedent* and *consequent*.

A. *Antecedent passion* is that which comes before or precedes the consent of the will (the spontaneous surge of anger, hatred, the sexual appetite, and so forth). This spontaneous surge of passion up to the point of consent of the will is involuntary and thus not sinful; in fact, if consent is not given, it affords occasion for merit. If consent is given, antecedent passion lessens the guilt of the action performed under its influence, in proportion to the degree that the person is hindered in his use of reason by the intensity of that passion. A completely normal person may be put under considerable pressure from passion, concupiscence or emotion but in practice it is often difficult to determine whether or not the guilt is diminished enough to excuse from grave sin in serious matters. One must, in such cases, leave the judgment up to God. To ensure peace of mind one may confess the sin and explain his doubt about the guilt because of the vehemence of the passion.

We should emphasize, however, that a person must never expose himself without adequate reason to the danger of arousing passion, and he must do what he can to resist his passionate disposition; otherwise, he is considered to be willing the passion indirectly and, hence, culpable.

B. *Consequent passion* is passion which follows an act of the will and is either freely consented to or is deliberately aroused. Passion is deliberately aroused if one *consciously and willfully* fosters the "surge of passion" which has arisen spontaneously or if one purposely stimulates his passions by such actions as reading immoral literature, dwelling upon an injustice suffered, etc. The guilt of the ensuing acts performed because of the vehemence of consequent passion is not diminished. The reason for this is that the person, by free act of the will, arouses or encourages the consequent passion which causes the resulting actions; he is therefore guilty of those actions. If one directly wills the cause of something, he also wills the result.

EXAMPLE:

Clement deliberately reflects on the insult he received from John, in order to get angry enough to start a fight; he knows that John does not stand much of a chance against him and thus he can easily avenge himself. Clement's guilt in the fight to which his consequent passion leads him is not diminished in the least.

V. HABIT is a permanent disposition, acquired by repeated acts, which makes it easy for one to perform similar actions. A habit may be good or bad. If good, it is a virtue; if bad, a vice. Examples of evil habits are the vices of impurity, cursing, drinking and blaspheming.

A person who *earnestly and sincerely* strives to correct the habit does not sin in performing the evil act *by force of habit without advertence* to its sinful character. This would apply, obviously, to habits of cursing, swearing and the like, but it may also apply to the habit of impurity, especially regarding momentary touches, etc. In regard to any habit the malice of an evil act performed with advertence but by reason of that habit, is lessened somewhat, provided that the person is sincerely trying to overcome the vice. On the other hand, if an evil habit is freely permitted to continue after it has been recognized as evil, the guilt of the evil acts committed is not considered diminished.

MORE ABOUT PASSION AND HABIT

Of all human judgments the most difficult is assessing the culpability of acts performed under severe stress of passion or habit. In many instances, it is impossible for humans to judge; only God can with accuracy. We can, however, offer some guidelines which will indicate whether we are too lenient or too harsh in judging ourselves guilty of serious sin under such circumstances.

Guideline I: *Psychologically normal individuals are ordinarily capable of sinning mortally.* We mention this because some people deny this; they have the exaggerated idea that a formal mortal sin is nearly impossible to commit under considerable emotional stress, passion or concupiscence. Others hold that formal mortal sin hardly ever takes place. Such people judge far too leniently. This does not square with the ordinary teaching and practice of the Church down through the ages: psychologically normal people, though it seems harsh to say so, can and do commit many formal mortal sins. Formal mortal sin is by no means a rarity in this world, even though passion and/or habit may lessen their guilt somewhat.

Guideline II: *God assures us that His grace is always sufficient for us to avoid formal mortal sin;* He will not let us be tempted beyond our strength (1 Cor. 10:11-13). Again those who forget this tend to judge themselves too leniently. Fidelity to the teachings of Christ may sometimes demand heroic sacrifices. Failure to live up to them can mean serious guilt for us because God provides special help for special difficulties.

This does not mean, however, that in some instances a person who cooperates with God's help will be preserved from material mortal sin due to overwhelming interior pressure of passion or habit. In other words, passion and habit may sometimes be so great that a person does something forbidden under pain of mortal sin (material mortal sin) and yet may not be mortally guilty of that act (formal mortal sin). Here we refer to guilt in cases involving deeply ingrained habits, addictive urges, "irresistible" or "compulsive" impulses.

Every priest has met with sincere penitents who admit having had clear knowledge and realization of a gravely sinful action which they were doing but still equally sincerely and firmly plead that they had little or no power to resist. Furthermore, psychiatrists tend to agree with such claims.

Without going into the philosophical and theological discussions about these matters, we can say that a person may have clear abstract knowledge and realization of a mortally sinful act but under the "overwhelming" influence of habit and passion he may not be able to evaluate sufficiently during that time to be guilty of serious sin, that is, he may not be able to realize and appreciate the real significance of his sin. A man with a long and inveterate habit of masturbation, for example, will generally go on doing it, even if he fully believes in severe injury to health which he had been told will ensue. The much less tangible idea of spiritual harm will probably restrain him less. At a time like that he seems to be unable to evaluate the moral weight of what he is doing. The sexual urge is so completely dominant that his action does not seem to him to be anything gravely contrary to the will of God or contrary to his otherwise ordinary desire of not separating himself from God. So all-absorbing can the object of desire or pleasure be for a person that it narrows his consciousness to a kind of hypnotic fascination and thus can exclude any realistic appraisal of the alternatives to that pleasure or desire; in such case mortal guilt (mortal sin) can be presumed absent.

We can say too that a sudden onslaught of passion that takes a person unawares can be presumed as insufficient deliberation or realization and therefore no mortal guilt.

Sometimes during the struggle with temptation a person can't believe that it is he who is thus acting. It seems to him, "It can't be me doing this; it's another person," etc. Such fantastic ideas show that a person is not himself and are indications against grave guilt.

In trying to assess the mortal guilt or lack of it in actions performed due to deeply ingrained habits, addictive urges, "irresistible" or "compulsive" impulses, etc., our attention should be focused on the sufficient consent of the will. The phrase "irresistible impulse," despite its popularity on TV in criminal cases, can be misleading. If we take the phrase to mean a sudden and overpowering outburst either of sex, rage, or the appetite for alcoholic drink, the suddenness of these "impulses" would exclude deliberation or at least the kind of sufficient deliberation whereby one would be guilty of serious sin.

If by "irresistible impulse" we mean a compulsive, continuing obsessive fascination or attraction — which does not usually exclude all advertence (realization) to the malice of the act performed — the problem is much more complicated and the guilt much more difficult to assess. Perhaps a better way to describe this condition would be as a continuing, compulsive urge which affects the mind with greater or lesser force and with greater or lesser frequency. To say that a compulsive drinker commits a formal mortal sin every time he gets thoroughly intoxicated would not only be uncharitable but incorrect; simply because he can refrain from getting intoxicated on some occasions such as the funeral of his son, the wedding of his daughter, or after he joined the A.A. is no proof that he can, if he wants to, refrain from intoxication on all occasions, or that he was not a compulsive drinker in the first place.

An intensive, compulsive urge may be counteracted by other factors, e.g., the overriding conviction of the need to stay sober at the funeral of his son. A habitual masturbator does not yield to his extremely intensive urges in the presence of other people but that is not to say that the urge is not compulsive to the extent that he is not mortally guilty when he is alone. The point is that the intensive urge is indeed counteracted sufficiently by other factors, in this case, the presence of other people. Furthermore, the same individual may have urges that may be compulsive one day and not compulsive another day.

Again, without going into the philosophical, psychological and theological discussions of such problems, we shall try to be practical and offer some guidelines for assessing guilt in such circumstances.

Guideline I. If a person addicted to an evil habit (drink, drugs, masturbation, etc.) is sincerely and honestly convinced that he could not have resisted, he may presume that he was not guilty of sin on that occasion. If a person doubts whether he could have really resisted or not, it still does not indicate conclusively that he has sinned gravely. Therefore:

Guideline II. A person with a severe habit, that is, one of long duration and inveterate frequency, can presume that grave guilt is absent in individual lapses if he doubts whether or not he could have resisted and is seriously trying to overcome the habit. This guideline is especially consoling to persons with addictive personalities, those who are much more prone to form enslaving habits, whether physiological or psychological, than others. Such persons quickly develop addiction to alcohol, drugs, or any habit that is pleasing to the senses (e.g., masturbation). When such more or less pathological habits occur, there is good reason for asserting that grave guilt is absent in individual lapses despite the struggles to resist.

Good theology never equates the freedom of a man with inveterate habits against any virtue with one who may have experienced occasional temptations. A person struggling to overcome an inveterate habit is never quite "normal" in the sense of psychological-moral freedom. This was recognized by St. Augustine when he wrote: "God does not impose impossible things, but by giving His command, He admonishes you to do what you can and to pray for what you cannot do (yet)."

Hence, some of the best theologians offer yet another guideline:

Guideline III. A person honestly striving to overcome a bad habit of sin is not sinning gravely at all if his action results from the habit rather than from a weakening of purpose to amend. This guideline may be an important first step in the struggle to overcome any addiction or habit: it will do much to alleviate the feelings of hopelessness and morbid guilt induced by past experience of continual defeat. The fact that a struggling man can believe he is still in God's grace, despite his obvious habitual weakness, gives him courage not to give up his efforts. He will tend to view God as a friend, a friend who understands and cares.

CONQUERING BAD HABITS

Evil habits may be formed easily but extremely difficult to break. The more a person gives himself up to sin, the stronger the habit becomes and so the harder will it be to overcome.

To conquer an inveterate evil habit one needs the mighty help of God, His grace. We cannot do it alone. Even if the individual wants to quit the habit, he still needs God's help. But His help is with us even before we ask. However, when we continually plead for it through prayer and the sacraments, He will give us more and more help. Habit must be overcome by habit, day by day. This requires long, strenuous exertion of the will, especially at the beginning. It may take years before final victory is achieved. After every lapse it may seem hopeless to struggle on; that's human. Still, no matter how disheartened we may feel, we should get up, stumble on, try again as if our failure never happened. It is much more important to try again than it is to recriminate against oneself or to be remorseful after a fall. Besides, if a person keeps on praying, doing his best to beat the habit and doing more in areas where he is not burdened with the evil habit, he is indeed God's friend, in His grace. Of that he can be sure. For him the sin rather consists in giving up the struggle.

Chapter III

OCCASIONS
OF SIN

In fighting yellow fever Dr. Walter Reed saw it would be useless to try to control the disease without discovering its cause or source, and then removing that source. So with any illness.

After a bout of sickness, a patient would hardly be wise to expose himself again to whatever brought on that illness, especially if the disease is contagious. If he does, chances are he will have a relapse. Sin is something like a contagious disease. In fighting against it we too should find out and remove, or at least, avoid, whatever leads to sin: this we call an occasion of sin.

More particularly an occasion of sin is any person, place, or thing which is likely to lead *us* into sin. It means *us,* not Billy, Jane, or Sue. The same occasion may never have led them to sin and maybe never will, but for us it has proved otherwise. Not everybody gets sick by being exposed to a contagious disease and not everybody will sin by being exposed to the occasions of sin. Some do, but others do not. Another thing, when we say that an occasion is likely to lead us into sin, we mean that there is danger of actually consenting to sin and not merely the danger of having a temptation. Now dangers differ. Some are naturally more serious than others and so the obligation of avoiding the former is greater. What we should do is honestly to gauge our strength in relation to the forces tempting us. In order to prudently determine the risk involved, we must distinguish between the two types of occasions leading to sin: the *remote* and the *proximate.*

REMOTE OCCASIONS OF SIN

Remote occasions of sin are any circumstances which may possibly, but most likely will not, lead one to sin. These are called *remote* either because they are of such a nature that an ordinary person most probably will not sin or because the individual himself knows from experience that he generally (the majority of times) does not sin as a result of their influence. Such occasions are very numerous and exist everywhere in the world or in our environment: reading ordinary newspapers and magazines, coming into contact with people of the opposite sex at work or recreation, etc.

We are not obliged to avoid remote occasions of sin, because in the first place it would be impossible to do so and still continue living normally in this world; then, too, the danger of sinning is slight and can easily be overcome.

EXAMPLE:

Roger knows from experience that, in going out with Irene, about eight out of ten times he does not sin with her. Irene is considered a remote occasion of sin for him, and so Roger does not have to avoid Irene's company. If, however, Roger knows that they sin every time they park on a lonely road, then he is seriously obliged to avoid parking in such places, since this would constitute a proximate occasion of sin for them.

We can be much too negative in viewing the world or our environment as possible occasions of sin. Rather we should consider them a challenge to our mission as Christians. A truly Christian attitude about the world and our own environment is one of gratitude and of responsibility. Learning to appreciate the blessings of the world around us, of our environment, will induce us to accept greater responsibility for it. Each of us should at least once in a while count our environmental blessings, that is, weigh the reasons why we should be grateful, such as being born into our particular family, brought up in a particular city, neighborhood, school, parish, etc. If we are really grateful and appreciative, we will generally try to do something for them.

A man who appreciates the world around him will instinctively wish to better it. For a Christian this means trying to raise its spiritual level. This attitude of responsibility, born of gratitude, will inevitably also change our outlook on occasions of sin: the things around us which might have constituted dangers or occasions of sin become incentives to further progress in responsibility as Christians. We will not only hold our ground but will become leaders and shapers of opinion. We will be the salt of the earth, the light of the world.

This, of course, presupposes a certain amount of immunity against the ills and dangers of the world. We can properly immunize ourselves through closer personal union with Christ and His Church. We must become Christians of strong conviction and prayer before we can bring these to a stricken society. In fact, before we can give anything spiritual to anyone anywhere, we must have it first ourselves and have it abundantly. Only then can we come in contact with the varied diseases of sin in the world and come away healthy, more than ever immune. If, however, our locale be so polluted or if we ourselves are still shaky from prior falls, then obviously we are not strong enough for direct involvement and our strategy should be one of flight.

PROXIMATE OCCASIONS OF SIN

Proximate occasions of sin are circumstances which *generally lead one into sin* either because they are, in themselves, so stimulating that the ordinary person is almost certain to sin when confronted by them (e.g., attending pornographic films or plays, reading erotic books) or because the individual himself knows from experience that he will generally fall as a result of the influence of these circumstances.

Circumstances considered as proximate occasions of sin for almost everyone are: burlesque shows, plays in which the actors are nude or very nearly so, in fact, any nude adult of the opposite sex or pictures of the same, erotic books, films, etc. There are, however, some individuals who for one reason or another would not be led into sin by such circumstances; hence, even these circumstances would not constitute proximate occasions for *those individuals*.

A person may know from experience that even though some circumstances are usually not proximate occasions for most people, they are such for him. A tavern or barroom is not usually a proximate occasion for most people, but for the alcoholic it is; one person cannot take a single glass of beer without going on to become roaringly drunk; another can. Certain kinds of dances, though they may be perfectly legitimate for most persons, may be a proximate occasion for an individual if he knows that they usually cause him to consent to sin. One man cannot lapse into the mildest familiarities with a woman without rushing into sin; another will find little or no temptation in such slightly unbecoming conduct.

As we have said, an occasion in which an individual *generally* sins is called proximate. Now, whether a certain set of circumstances will lead us into sin may be either *merely probable* or *morally certain*.

1. If it is *merely probable* that certain circumstances would lead one to mortal sin, he is not obliged under pain of grievous sin to avoid them. Thus, a person who judges that such and such circumstances would probably not with overwhelming likelihood occasion his falling into mortal sin, does not have to avoid such occasions under pain of serious sin. In such a case, one would be guilty of *venial sin* in exposing himself to such an occasion needlessly or without any reason, but he would not sin gravely, for he is not exposing himself to what will almost inevitably lead him into mortal sin.

EXAMPLE:

Gertrude has gone several times to a fraternity house party at which she happens to be the only Catholic. On each occasion, the attitude of the other guests has influenced her to miss Sunday Mass. Another invitation comes from the same group, and she accepts. She commits at least a venial sin of imprudence in accepting the invitation.

2. If it is *morally certain* that one will sin mortally as a result of exposing himself to some particular occasion, then he is bound gravely to avoid it. Moral certainty means that a person is sure, despite the fact that once in a while the expected result did not take place. Everyone is seriously obliged to avoid whatever he knows will surely lead him into grave sin.

EXAMPLE:

Every time Mr. Brown, who is not an alcoholic, goes out with his old college

chums, he gets thoroughly intoxicated. On Saturday night he again deliber-
ately goes out with them, even though he realizes that he will certainly become
intoxicated again. Mr. Brown is seriously obliged to avoid going out with these
particular friends, unless he can strengthen himself enough to render such an
occasion remote.

In confessing the resulting sin, one need not mention the proximate occasion connected with it, since resulting sins always include their proximate occasion and every preparatory circumstance.

As we know, there lies a wide zone between the two extremes (proximate
and remote), which might be termed *intermediate* danger (or occasion). This
would be the case if we cannot say that a certain set of circumstances are proximate occasions for us, yet neither can we say that the danger of sin is
thoroughly remote; the danger is somewhere between the two. We frequently
but not generally fall into serious sin as its result. There is no sin in exposing
ourselves to such an "intermediate" danger if we have a proportionate reason
for doing so; if we haven't, we sin venially. This is simply another way of stating that a certain set of circumstances will *probably* lead us into sin.

MORE ABOUT PROXIMATE OCCASIONS

But what of one who is unable, through necessity, to avoid or give up a
proximate occasion of sin? When we say that "one is unable," we mean that he
cannot avoid it at all or he can do it only with grave inconvenience (or difficulty) or, perhaps, with great danger of ruining his reputation, social accept-
ance, etc. Theologians call this a *necessary proximate occasion.* In such cases
the occasion must be made remote or "intermediate" either by strengthening
oneself spiritually (by prayer, the sacraments, etc.) or by directly lessening the
influence of the occasion (by avoiding the chance of being alone with another,
by guarding the eyes, of discontinuing intimate familiarity, and so on).

EXAMPLES:

1. Doctor Jones finds that in the practice of his profession he always suc-
cumbs to impure thoughts when handling certain types of cases. He needs the
money derived therefrom for the support of his large family and so cannot give
up handling these cases; besides, there is no other doctor in his locality to han-
dle them. Doctor Jones is bound to make this necessary proximate occasion less
dangerous by using means to minimize and resist the temptations as outlined
above.

2. Walter and Dorothy are keeping company and are to be married shortly.
Unfortunately, nearly every time they go out they sin. Since this (company-
keeping with prospect of early marriage) is considered a necessary occasion,
they are not obliged to avoid each other's company; but they must avoid the
particular circumstances which always end in their sinning: parking on lonely
roads, being alone with each other at home, etc.

Chapter IV

WHAT CHANGES AN ACT'S GOODNESS OR BADNESS

A deliberate (human) act is morally good or morally bad, depending on whether it conforms or does not conform to the norm of morality as expressed in *law* and *conscience*. In general, *law* is the external objective rule of conduct; *conscience,* the internal subjective rule by which the individual person applies the external law to his own actions. This is sometimes easier said than done, for living in a highly organized society can be very complicated. Some of the problems facing us today have never been met before. In trying to unravel them we have to consider the factors which can completely change the goodness or badness of any deliberate act.

Just what makes a deliberate act, good or bad? If we analyze a deliberate act, we find three elements or parts that go to make up the morality (the goodness or badness) of every such act. They are: (I) *the object of the act;* (II) *the circumstances accompanying the act;* and (III) *the motive prompting the act.*

I. *The object of an act* is that which the act of its very nature tends to effect. It must not be confused with the motive or purpose which prompts the act. The object of a murderer's act is the strangulation of his victim, but the motive or purpose prompting that strangulation could be one of several: to avenge himself, to silence the victim, to obtain insurance benefits, to receive an inheritance, etc. The object of an act of impurity is the unlawful stimulation of the sex organs, but the purpose prompting it is the enjoyment of the pleasure derived from that stimulation.

The object of an act, if it conforms to the norms of morality mentioned above, is good; if it does not conform, it is sinful. In some instances the object by its very nature is evil and thereby is never allowed. Hating God, stealing, lying, blaspheming, calumniating, are by their nature evil and so, if knowingly and freely performed, are always sinful. No conceivable circumstance or situation could ever justify such actions. But taking another's goods, doing heavy work on Sunday, or cutting off a leg, can be either good or bad, depending on the purpose for which the act is performed. To take a different example: if strangling an assailant is the only immediate means of defending one's own life, then it is in conformity with the norms of morality and so is good; if done for a purpose which disagrees with the norms of morality, it is evil. If the act were by its nature evil, it could under no circumstances ever be lawful and good.

Considered in the abstract, acts such as eating, running, walking, are not directed by their nature toward a good or a bad end; they are indifferent. The doer of this kind of action can direct his acts to either end by his intention or purpose. If his intention is good, the act is good; if his intention is bad, the act is bad.

EXAMPLE:

Dan is reading a book. This act by its nature is indifferent. If Dan is reading in order to arouse and enjoy sexual pleasure, his act of reading is evil; his evil intention makes it so. If Dan is reading in order to improve his mind or to gain useful knowledge, his action is good because his intention is good.

II. *The circumstances accompanying the act* are those accidental conditions which may completely change the morality of an act. We saw above that a circumstance (necessary self-defense) could change the ordinarily very sinful act of strangulation into a lawful and good act. Work is usually good and necessary, but to work *on Sunday* without a good reason would be adding a circumstance which would make the action sinful. Cutting off a man's leg to *save his life* is a good act because the circumstance (saving his life) makes it good; but to do it *unnecessarily* or *in a fight* would be sinful because of the circumstance.

Circumstances may therefore change: (1) a good action into a bad one, e.g., laborious and unnecessary work *on Sunday*; (2) a venially sinful act into a seriously sinful one, e.g., stealing an equivalent of a half day's wage *from a totally destitute widow*; (3) a mortally sinful act into a venially sinful one, e.g., stealing twenty dollars *from a millionaire*; (4) may add new badness to an already bad act, e.g., killing or striking *a bishop*; (5) may change an indifferent act into an evil act or a good act, e.g., taking a dog *into church during Mass* (evil, irreverence) or walking the dog *in a park because its sick owner cannot* (good, a little act of kindness). In all these cases the circumstances change the morality of the actions; but, as we shall see, the intention is also necessarily bound up with their morality.

III. *The motive prompting the act* (the intention) is the reason for which the person undertakes the act. It is that which induces one to perform the act, the purpose; for instance, a man strangles his wife *to obtain insurance benefits*. We saw above how the intention affected the indifferent act of Dan's reading.

Quite obviously, if one or more of the three elements (object, circumstance and motive) are evil the whole action is morally evil. I cannot steal twenty dollars to give to charity. My motive is excellent, but the object is evil; hence my whole action would be evil. Thus, prayer is an act in itself good and holy but if a nurse were to go to the hospital chapel and pray, instead of caring for a critically ill patient assigned to her while on duty, her act would be bad no matter how good her motive. In this case the *circumstance* (the neglect of duty accompanying the act) is the evil factor which makes the whole act iniquitous or morally bad.

An action is morally good if all of the three elements are *essentially good.* It may happen sometimes that something venially sinful is accidentally connected with one of these elements; but this would not change the basic goodness of that element; for example, Mary goes to Communion in order to fulfill her Easter duty, but in so doing she also yields to vanity and "shows off" her new coat. Her motive includes a venial fault of vanity, but this does not change the basic goodness of her motive, the fulfilling of her Easter duty.

If, in order to have an entirely good act, none of these three elements can be evil, it follows that "sinning for a good cause" (the end justifying the means) is never allowed. "Sinning for a good cause" simply means that the motive (the good cause) is good but that the object (sinning) is evil; hence, it is never permitted.

The same is true of the various forms of situation ethics. In general, situation ethics (the "new morality") boils down usually to "sinning for a good cause" and allowing it! After all, proponents of situation ethics would have a person in certain situations *for the sake of love* (seeking one's self-fulfillment or expressing love for neighbor — the good motive or cause) act even in a way opposed to the general moral principles (the object of the act, or sinning). A good intention or motive can never make adultery, premarital sex, rape or publicly disowning God sinless, because the object of such acts is evil. Remember, *none* of the three elements or factors constituting a deliberate act can be evil if the act is to be good. In other words, if one or more of the three elements are evil the whole act is morally evil (objectively).

PRINCIPLE OF DOUBLE EFFECT

What happens if an action results in two effects, one morally good, the other evil? Are we allowed to do it? During World War II, for example, it was necessary to bomb a large munitions factory. In bombing the factory many innocent people living nearby would surely be killed. Was it morally lawful?

In this case, one effect — the destruction of the enemy's munitions factory — was a morally lawful one; but at the same time the killing of many innocent civilians was another effect — an evil one — which would also necessarily result. The commanding officer knew that he was directly willing the destruction of an important factory, but still he would be indirectly permitting the deaths of many innocent victims if he gave the order to bomb. Though the latter was only an incidental result of the effect directly willed, yet it was actually willed in a lesser degree.

To solve problems such as this and others like it which may occur in an ordinary person's life is quite involved. Still, there are principles which will help us solve them.

First of all, we must clearly understand what is meant by *directly willing* an effect and *indirectly willing* one. A man wills something *directly* if he chooses it for its own sake or as a means of accomplishing something else, e.g., Peter deliberately kills his wife in order to obtain the insurance benefits, or Abe murders his wife because he detests her. Both Peter and Abe *directly* will to kill their wives.

A thing is willed *indirectly* if it is not chosen for itself but is only permitted because of its inseparable connection with another thing which is directly willed: for instance, Doctor Durnan removes a patient's cancerous vocal chords to save the patient's life. Doctor Durnan knows that in saving the man's life he will deprive him of speech permanently. Saving the man's life is the thing directly willed. The permanent loss of speech is the thing indirectly willed or permitted, and this, because of its intimate connection with the directly willed effect; otherwise, neither Doctor Durnan nor the patient would want the loss of speech.

To perform an act which has a good and an evil effect is lawful only if the following four conditions are verified:

1. The action itself from which the double effect results must be good or at least morally indifferent.

2. The good effect must be intended directly, and not the evil effect.

3. The good effect must not be produced by the evil effect.

4. There must be a proportionate reason for permitting the foreseen evil to result.

If one of these conditions is missing, it is unlawful to perform such an act.

EXPLANATION OF THE CONDITIONS

I. *The action itself from which the double effect results must be good or at least indifferent.* Thus actions which by their very nature are evil — lying, blaspheming, etc. — would not fulfill this condition.

EXAMPLE:

Joe commits perjury to save his friend from a possible jail sentence, though another man is thereby convicted. Joe was not justified in his action of perjury because lying by its nature is evil and so is never permitted regardless of the excellent motive prompting the act.

II. *The good effect must be intended directly, and not the evil effect.* If a person directly intended the evil effect, he would have an evil intention, and an evil intention always corrupts any act. The intention of the person performing the act with the double effect must be directed exclusively to the good effect; the evil effect must only be permitted to happen because of its inseparable connection with the good effect. Therefore, one who desires both the good and the evil effect to occur would not be fulfilling this condition. Such would also be the case if the good effect were obtained by means of the evil effect.

EXAMPLES:

1. Catherine, who has a large family already, must either have an operation performed or take an equally expensive drug to save her life. Each remedy would result in saving her life; but the operation would render her incapable of ever having any more children, while the medicine would not have this bad effect. Catherine chooses the operation because this would solve the problem of birth control which she and her husband had been considering. Obviously, Catherine directly intends both effects and so does not fulfill condition II (the good effect must be intended directly, and not the evil effect). The operation with its double effect is thereby sinful.

2. Judy, trapped in a locked room by an insane man who attacks her with a carving knife, jumps through an open window to the lawn below in order to avoid a terrible death by stabbing. In jumping she clearly realized that her fall might be fatal. It was. She died instantly of a broken neck.

Her action was not immoral (suicidal). Judy did not wish to be killed in the fall. Leaping from the window was merely the act of withdrawing from the assailant. She wished only to avoid the stabbing and did not will her death. Thus, she directly intended the good effect (avoiding death by stabbing) and not the evil effect (death by her fall).

III. *The good effect must not be produced by the evil effect.* Should the good effect be produced by the evil effect, then evidently the evil effect must first be directly willed as an evil means — something which, of course, can never be justified by the good purpose (the good effect). This is, again, "sinning for a good cause," which is never lawful.

EXAMPLE:

After being raped, Jane, an unmarried young woman, is found to be with child. To avoid disgrace Jane contemplates abortion. This is strictly forbidden, for she would be procuring the good effect (avoiding disgrace) by means of the evil effect — killing an unborn child!

IV. *There must be a proportionate reason for permitting the foreseen evil to result.* Naturally, we are forbidden to risk harm to ourselves and others without necessity — even disregarding for the moment the law of charity, reason and common sense tell us this is so. By "proportionate" is meant that if the evil effect is slight, the reason for permitting it to occur need only be a slight one; but if the effect is grave, then the reason must also be grave.

CASES OF 'DOUBLE EFFECT'

CASE I. In the case mentioned earlier in this chapter, the officer ordered the bombing of the munitions factory even though, secondarily, it resulted in the killing of many innocent people.

Condition 1. In fighting a just war, the action of destroying an enemy munitions factory is not evil by nature.

Condition 2. The good effect (destruction of the factory, which is the lessening of the enemy's strength) is directly willed, and not the evil effect (the killing of innocent people).

Condition 3. The good effect (destruction of the factory) is not produced by the evil effect (the killing of people); for even if by some stroke of fortune the people were not killed the good effect would still follow.

Condition 4. There is a proportionate reason — that is, the delivering of a serious, damaging blow to the enemy in a just war.

Hence the bombing was lawful in this case.

CASE II. Doctor Durnan removes a patient's cancerous vocal chords in order to save the patient's life.

Condition 1. Doctor Durnan's action of removing the diseased organ is not an action which is evil by nature; it is, in fact, an act of mercy.

Condition 2. The good effect (saving the patient's life) is directly intended, and not the bad effect (loss of the power of speech).

Condition 3. The good effect (saving the patient's life) is not produced by the bad effect (loss of speech), but by the removal of a diseased organ.

Condition 4. There is a proportionate reason — the saving of a life.

The operation is therefore lawful and good.

CASE III. Leona, a pregnant woman, has to take a medicine which is necessary for saving her life, but it is known that this medicine will also expel the living fetus from her womb. Is Leona allowed to take the medicine?

Condition 1. The action itself (taking the medicine) is not evil by nature, but is lawful and good (a means of self-preservation).

Condition 2. The good effect (saving her own life) is directly intended, and not the evil effect (expulsion of the living fetus).

Condition 3. The good effect (saving her own life) is not produced by the bad effect (expulsion of the living fetus), for even if the fetus should happen to survive, the good effect would follow.

Condition 4. There is a proportionate reason; a life is saved.

As the case stands, it would be lawful for Leona to take the medicine. It should be noted, however, that the case would not be lawful, if one of the following were true:

A. *If the bad effect* (expulsion of the living fetus) *were also desired* — e.g., for economic reasons, to save a reputation, etc. — for then the intention would corrupt the whole act, and condition number 2 would not be fulfilled, as both effects are intended.

B. *If the expulsion of the living fetus* thereby produced the good effect — e.g., if the mother would die had the fetus been allowed to live and develop — for then condition number 3 would not be fulfilled.

C. *If the living fetus were directly killed* by poison, cutting, crushing, etc., for then the action itself (directly killing the fetus, tantamount to murder) would be evil. Hence, condition number 1 would not be fulfilled.

Complicated? You bet! Cases of double effect can be very confusing to the ordinary man or woman. Since such cases usually involve possible harm to others or to oneself, a person cannot act when doubting the fulfillment of any of the conditions; hence, expert advice is imperative.

Chapter V

COOPERATION IN ANOTHER'S SIN

Sometimes it happens a person is doing something in itself sinless but it helps another to sin; such a person is cooperating in another's sin. A bartender, for example, in selling drinks does nothing wrong in itself; he may even be performing a public service but in selling drinks to a man certain to get thoroughly intoxicated, the bartender does indeed "help" him to get drunk. He is cooperating in another's sinful action.

Cooperation, in the moral sense, means acting jointly with another in the same sinful action or supplying him with what is helpful in performing that sinful action. Cooperation may take on many forms: joining in someone's praise for the so-called benefits of abortion, supplying another with a gun with which to commit murder, selling pornographic books or magazines, etc. The list could go on and on. Acting jointly does not always mean that we physically help in the sinful act; after all, a man hiring someone else to do something sinful may not physically help one iota in the actual commission of that act but he is just as guilty as the one who does it. A man who hires someone to commit murder, for example, will not usually help a bit with the actual commission of the crime but he is just as guilty as the actual murderer.

Our society is a highly organized one: from family to the city or town in which we live, to county, to state, to nation; from the shop (office, etc.) in which we work, to the corporation which may own it, to the corporate conglomerate which in turn controls it. How responsible are we for their corporate acts? When they engage in dishonest acts, when they advocate abortion, euthanasia or some other evil against God's law, how guilty are we personally? We are part of them and therefore, in a sense, cooperate in their evil acts. What if my city practices unfair housing because of race? Since such acts are remote and our part in them minimal, they may not seem burning issues to us but, then, neither did the gassing of the Jews in Nazi Germany to the average German.

But getting closer to home: if I work in a factory manufacturing toys which are dangerous, highly inflammable, or toys that easily come apart and may gouge, gash, or maim an innocent child — how do I judge the guilt of my cooperative act? If I work in a used car-lot and sell cars with faulty brakes to unsuspecting customers? If I am a mechanic in a garage and my boss tells me to replace parts needlessly or to charge for parts which were not replaced? And if I refuse, I may get fired, which I can ill afford. What am I to do? Can I cooperate? What is my guilt if I do?

Questions such as these demand answers; the answers may not be easy. Complex questions of cooperation need complex solutions; hence, we must make several important though rather complicated distinctions and examine the corresponding moral principles applicable to each distinction.

Basic to gauging accurately the guilt of cooperation in another's sinful action is the distinction between *formal* and *merely material* cooperation. Just remembering this important difference will answer many questions of cooperation.

I. *Formal cooperation in another's sin means taking part in the external, sinful deed of another and at the same time approving his evil intention.* "Taking part in" means actually participating in some way in the act itself. It does not mean doing something merely preparatory to the sinful act or merely connected with it (this would be material cooperation). The "external act" may be one evil by nature (lying, blaspheming, calumniating, etc.) or it may be one indifferent by nature but the circumstances, its object, or the intention make it evil (e.g., reading with an evil intention, doing unnecessary servile work *on Sunday,);* in these cases, if the one cooperating with the external evil act also intends the evil, then he is *formally* cooperating.

For example, a friend happens to be preparing an extremely insulting and uncharitable speech against Mr. X. Since I do not like Mr. X either, I help my friend prepare the vitriolic speech by typing it, correcting the mistakes in grammar and using my influence with the radio censors to have nothing "cut" from the speech. I am formally cooperating in my friend's sinful act (delivering an uncharitable speech).

Formal cooperation is always sinful. Besides being a sin against charity, it is also a sin against the particular virtue which the cooperative, evil act violates. Thus in the above example, I sin not only against charity but also against honesty if the speech contains lies, and against justice if the speech unjustly ruins the enemy's reputation. A cooperative act such as adultery violates charity, chastity and justice.

EXAMPLE:

Dr. X is interning at a large city hospital where abortions are legal under state law. Soon he is posted to surgery to assist Dr. Z whose workload includes many abortions. In order to come to some mutual understanding before going into the operating theater, Dr. X tells Dr. Z that, in conscience, he cannot help him by actually participating in any sinful operations, such as abortions, because this would constitute formal cooperation on his part. The most he can do is to prepare the patient for the operation, administer the anesthetic, hand the instruments to him, suture and bandage any wounds if necessary. Is Dr. X right?

Yes, very definitely. First of all, actually participating in performing abor-

tions and other such gravely sinful operations (e.g., eugenic sterilization, fe-ticide, etc.) is indeed formal cooperation and, hence, seriously forbidden (mor-tally sinful). No reason can ever justify it.

Preparing the patient for such operations, handing the instruments, etc., is not formal but material cooperation and may be done without sin provided there is serious reason . . . in the case of the intern, there is, since it may jeop-ardize his career if he even refused to cooperate materially.

The same may be said for nurses: under no circumstances can they cooper-ate formally, i.e., participating in the actual performance of such sinful opera-tions. If possible, nurses should refuse to be present at such operations; how-ever, they may assist at such operations (by proffering instruments, etc., to the surgeon) if they have grave reason. One of the following reasons is considered grave enough: losing her job at that particular hospital and the inability to get another without difficulty; losing her position in that particular hospital where she can get special courses, training, etc., and the inability to get such courses at another hospital willing to hire her; being forced to leave her present train-ing school and relocating in a distant city to attend another. Of course, we presuppose that in so materially cooperating they in no way approve of such operations.

It may happen sometimes that a nurse could easily get another position elsewhere but she does not want to lose it in a particular hospital where she can help many patients spiritually, patients who otherwise would receive little if any spiritual attention. In such cases, material cooperation is also justified if by her refusal to do so would threaten her present position.

II. *Material cooperation in another's sin means helping another perform his sinful action by an act (a) not sinful by its nature (indifferent) and (b) without ap-proving the other's wrongdoing.* Thus it happened that Joseph, a Negro boy, materially cooperated with a Southern lynching party in the murder of his friend, John. Joseph was forced to provide gasoline, matches and rope for the lynching under the threat that he would be lynched together with John if he refused to cooperate. Knowing that the leaders meant every word they said, Joseph complied with their demands.

Was his action sinless, i.e., a morally lawful one? Before we give the an-swer and the principles applying to *material cooperation,* we must clearly un-derstand why material cooperation may at times be permitted.

We see from the definition that the materially cooperative act, by which a person assists the wrongdoer, must not be sinful in itself (in the above case, the giving of gasoline, matches, etc., to another is not sinful in itself; however, Joseph could not help actually set the victim on fire, for this would be formal cooperation). Also, the one materially cooperating must neither desire nor approve the sinful use for which the object of his assistance will be used. Though the cooperator knows beforehand that someone will commit sin by the act with which he is materially cooperating, yet his obligation of preventing this sinful act is not one of justice but of charity. Since charity never binds any-one to a burden disproportionate to the good which will result, it follows that, generally speaking, material cooperation with another's evil act is permitted provided one has a proportionate reason for so cooperating. A "proportionate reason" is one whose good results at least balance the evil effects of the cooperation. We must consider how great is our cooperative act as well as how closely this cooperative act is connected with the principal sinful action. The following principles, therefore, must also be applied to each case:

1. Only an *extremely grave reason* would make permissible a cooperative act which is very proximately connected with the *principal, gravely sinful action.* Thus, in robberies (in banks, stores, bars, etc.) the employees or anyone there may collect the money, put it in bags, tie up the nonparticipants, even take the money out of customers' pockets, etc., if so ordered by the robber.

2. A *grave reason* would permit a *less proximate* cooperative act, that is, an act whose connection with the principal, gravely sinful action cannot be said to be really close and yet cannot be said to be really remote either.

EXAMPLE:

Rudolf needs money badly and a job. The only work he can find is that of clerking in a drugstore in which he must also sell contraceptives and some pornographic magazines. Can he take the job?

Yes, he may accept the position, since he has a grave reason (great need of money) and cannot find another job. In the future, however, Rudolf must be on the lookout for another job, one in which he would not have to be a material cooperator in the sinful acts of others.

Sometimes it is difficult to judge, to weigh and balance the close connection of the material cooperation with the principal act and the proportionate gravity of our reason for doing it. All we can do in such cases is to try to judge honestly and sincerely — and then decide accordingly. Not even the experts, the theologians, will agree exactly on some questions of cooperation, so we need not be surprised if we find some solutions difficult to assess. The balance between the gravity of the reasons justifying the material cooperation of the intern and nurses, for instance, illustrates the type of proportion necessary. To summarize: the greater the connection and the possible consequences of our cooperative act the greater our reason must be for doing it.

3. A *slight reason permits a remotely cooperative act.* In the case of a worker in a factory making dangerous toys which may easily maim children, the cooperation is remote; hence, a slight reason would justify such work. In fact, the difficulty he would meet in attempting to change company policy, etc., for the better, would excuse him from trying, especially since parents have the primary obligation in seeing to their children's safety. We are, of course, discussing the minimum obligation on the part of such workers; choosing the better part would be trying to convince the company to make safe toys — also perhaps tipping off the public media, newspapers, etc., about such dangers. The effectiveness of such efforts will always depend on the circumstances, not the least of which are the persuasive powers of the worker in question. Usually corporations are very sensitive to adverse public opinion and will quickly react to its possibility. The point is that, instead of any hyper-rigorous stance to con-

demn with smug horror every kind of material cooperation, we should take more positive action by attempting to change that part of the world around us for the better. This is what we mean, after all, by truly Christian responsibility and applying it in every field of endeavor, whether in politics, civil service, communications, social welfare, etc.

4. Material cooperation is *never allowed if one's material assistance is given to an action gravely injurious to the common good;* in serious matters the common good is always greater than the private good. The lesser good (private good) must always yield to the greater good (common good) because the good effects redounding to the benefit of a private good can never balance the resulting evil effects to the common good, always the greater of the two.

EXAMPLE:

Ned can get a very good job by contributing $500 to help elect a Communist candidate for governor. Because Ned's contribution would help in a state of affairs gravely injurious to the common good, it is not allowed.

5. In the case where the cooperative action materially helps in the production of a sinful action gravely injurious to an innocent third person, material cooperation is permitted *only if a refusal would bring the one cooperating injury equal to that done to the innocent person.* In the above case of the Southern lynching party, the Negro boy, John, is threatened with grave harm (death); charity requires his friend, Joseph, to prevent that injury if he is at all able. But Joseph's attempt to prevent that harm (refusal to supply the gasoline, rope, etc.) would only cause equal injury to himself, and charity always allows one to provide for one's own safety first. As the case stands, Joseph's material cooperation was sinless.

SPECIAL EXAMPLES OF COOPERATION

After considering all the principles regarding material cooperation, one conclusion stands out: questions of material cooperation are complicated! Confused? Perhaps some problems may be answered more clearly in considering the special cases of cooperation in which the experts have applied the necessary principles for us. Though the solutions presented here can be altered by different sets of circumstances, they do illustrate the application of universal principles which are always valid. The only other thing to keep in mind is this: the proposed solutions are concerned only with the morality of cooperation and not with the element of scandal which may result in any given case; naturally, if scandal would result, actions otherwise lawful would be forbidden (cf. Fifth Commandment, scandal).

1. Cooperation of Businessmen

Drinking. Bartenders, cocktail-lounge hostesses, tavern keepers and others employed in a similar capacity may serve alcoholic drinks to guests in general, even though they know that some usually drink too much; they are seriously obliged not to serve intoxicating drinks to anyone who will obviously become intoxicated or to one who already is, unless there is grave reason, that is, to avoid fighting, cursing or foul language, danger of hostility, and the like. They must be careful never to encourage patrons "who have had enough" to take still another drink (even if the drink is "on the house"), since they may easily induce others to the sin of intoxication (inducing another to drunkenness is formal cooperation); it is gravely sinful if the person thus induced will become so drunk that he will lose the use of his reason.

Treating Others to Drink. Anyone who "treats" others who have had enough cannot be excused from formal cooperation, since he is in effect inducing others to the sin of drunkenness; the gravity of sinful cooperation depends on how drunk the other person gets; if the latter gets completely intoxicated, the cooperator's guilt can be serious.

2. Cooperation of Motel and Hotel Operators

Motel and hotel operators, apartment-house operators, etc., must use reasonable precautions to "run a clean house." If they rent rooms or apartments to others for purposes which are quite obviously sinful (e.g., prostitution, adultery, anti-Catholic propaganda, homosexuality, etc.), they become material cooperators and usually cannot be excused from serious sin. Reasonable care is all that is expected. The benefit of the doubt is always in favor of the customer, of course. Excessively harsh demands "for proof" will only drive innocent customers away.

3. Merchants and Store Personnel

Businessmen and store personnel may sell articles, the misuse of which they foresee in a general way, such as dice, cards, drugs, alcohol, etc. This holds true of any article that may be classified "indifferent," i.e., anything which may be used in a good way morally, although it can also be abused morally or put to sinful uses. Generally speaking, salesclerks and merchants have no obligation to investigate the possible moral abuse of their merchandise once it is in the customers' possession. Selling such articles, however, to customers who, *it is certain,* will abuse them requires a grave reason (loss of profit is not sufficient).

Style-shop owners and merchants who openly provide and sell "peeka-boo" dresses, "see-through" dresses and other indecent clothing cannot be excused from serious sin; these are not "indifferent" articles, but inducements to sin. Salesclerks, to keep their job, may sell such clothing to those who ask for such clothes but may never advise customers to purchase them nor to praise them.

4. Employees, Office Help, Cooperating in Sins of Employers

Office help may make copies of accounts which will be injurious to others if their employers order them to do so, and they may even draft such statements themselves under orders and for a very good reason (e.g., danger of loss of job). Clerks in drugstores, in order to keep their jobs, may sell contraceptives to those who ask for them, but may never advise customers to purchase these. Taxi drivers may drive those who ask to be conveyed to houses of ill-repute, since their refusal would mean loss of business for themselves and since they cannot prevent the sin anyway; however, they may not direct inquirers to such places (since such help is considered to make the sin itself possible).

Personal servants (maids, butlers, chauffeurs, etc.) are permitted to carry out their usual personal duties, though these services may be perverted to evil ends by their employer. By reason of their employment therefore they may serve drinks if requested, even if they know that the employer will become intoxicated; thus also, employees, when ordered, may purchase or procure immoral literature (books, magazines, films, etc.) for their employers. They may also (but without volunteering) drive their employer, or his letters or gifts, to persons with whom he has illicit relations, and they may admit such persons into their employer's house, serve meals, make up the guest rooms, etc. In none of these cases, of course, may the cooperating person give internal consent to another's sin, nor feign pleasure over it.

5. Narcotics Traffic

The judgment of theologians is extremely severe regarding all forms of deliberate cooperation in the traffic of narcotics. Even the pathetic pleas of the drug addict do not justify cooperation in this vicious trade. The only possible exception would be the danger of death in the case of an addict's too sudden withdrawal; but usually hospitals, where proper treatment is obtainable, are within easy reach.

6. Cooperation in Immoral Press

The publishing, printing, or editing of books, magazines, or newspapers opposed to faith or morals is formal cooperation and therefore forbidden; hence, participants in such firms, i.e., publishers, editors, managers, members of directive boards as well as their advertisers are formal cooperators and nothing justifies such serious cooperation. In firms which only occasionally publish immoral writing (the bulk of their publications are wholesome) such individuals, if they had no decision-making voice (e.g., they were outvoted in the board meeting) and are opposed to it are not guilty of any sinful cooperation. Threat of resignation may be obligatory if it could prevent the firm from taking on excessively immoral matter to print.

To proofread or set type is allowed only for a very grave reason (such as not being able to make a living otherwise), since this would be proximate material cooperation. A lesser reason would justify (for a time) working in such places, operating the presses, mixing the ink, feeding the paper, etc., unless the firm's work is devoted entirely to the production of pornography and other immoral literature. One may sell paper, machinery, and other similar types of equipment to such establishments for the sake of profit because this is only remotely cooperating. One may sell professedly immoral literature only to avert great harm (e.g., loss of position), as this is a form of proximate material cooperation. A grave reason, such as being a great advantage to one's business, etc., permits one to subscribe to such papers. To buy a copy occasionally to see what one's competitors have to say or sell would only be remote cooperation and thereby this reason, morally classified as unimportant, would justify it.

7. Cooperating in Immoral Shows and Dances

To take part in, arrange, conduct, finance, or to invite others to pornographic shows, films and erotic dances is gravely unlawful. To do the same in regard to dances or shows only slightly indecent is venially sinful. Some grave reason, such as the inability to find other employment, would excuse musicians who play at immoral dances or shows; otherwise, they cannot be excused from gravely sinful cooperation. Repairmen and others who keep such theaters and halls in condition are excused for a less weighty reason, since they are only remotely cooperating. Those who must be on duty as policemen or watchmen are excused for the same reason; however, they have the same obligation of not putting themselves in the proximate occasion of serious sin as everybody else.

Judgment is very severe regarding owners of movie theaters who book immoral films; they are formal cooperators in the sins of the moviegoers by seducing them to sin and giving scandal through this seduction.

8. Armed Forces Personnel

Many servicemen are disturbed in conscience regarding the distribution of contraceptive packages, euphemistically called "hygienic safeguards." The armed forces of many countries require servicemen going on leave to accept a contraceptive package; some even make the leave dependent on it. In such cases, the personnel assigned to the distribution have relatively little choice in the matter and their assignment is sufficient reason (for what may be termed material cooperation) for merely passing out the articles. Going on leave is sufficient reason for the serviceman to do no more than mechanically accepting the articles. All this may be regarded as material procedure connected with leaving the base and so there is no obligation to protest the procedure. (The case is different with those responsible for introducing such a practice; such are formal cooperators in the sins which may be or will be committed.)

Servicemen may never salve their conscience by pleading that they are following orders in killing clearly innocent persons or cooperating in the mass murder of innocents by deliberately bombing residential areas; such are guilty of formal cooperation in murder.

9. Cooperation in Politics

May I seek office in a political party whose platform includes legislative

proposals opposed to faith or morals, e.g., legalizing abortions and sterilization, "liberalizing" divorce laws, etc.? Grave guilt of formal cooperation in sin
may be incurred if party discipline will force me to support legislation opposed
to faith or morals. There is no formal cooperation, however, if party policy
leaves each member free to oppose any such program both within the party
and within the assembly (senate, house of representatives, parliament, etc.). If
the latter is true (and no scandal results), influential positions within such a
party and officials elected under the same party banner may actually make of
their positions real Christian apostolates — in order to use such positions of influence to counter the evil proposals more effectively and to change the party's
policies for the better.

CAUTION: Members of legislative bodies who *merely* vote in favor of
legislation opposed to faith or morals are formal cooperators in sin. If such a
member has no other alternative than evil, he must choose the lesser of two
evils; however, he must voice his honest convictions in the matter, which in
democratic countries is usually not difficult.

10. Voting

Sometimes citizens may be faced with moral problems in voting. Voting
for a party or a candidate representing anti-Christian or immoral principles is
forbidden: the ballot itself represents approval and support for such principles
(and is therefore formal cooperation in evil). Often, however, the situation is
not quite so simple. At times, politics being what they are, a voter has no real
choice between two evils: all parties may have something in their platforms
inimical to faith or morals. In such cases, the Christian voter must shun what
he considers the greater of two evils; usually, all things considered, he should
vote for the party or candidate whom he judges least hostile to Christian principles. Abstention from voting entirely may sometimes be fine but often it may
result in a greater evil, tipping the scales in favor of the party or candidate most
hostile to Christian principles. It is sadly true, as experience has shown, that
many advocates of evil — advocates of legalized abortion, euthanasia, "more
liberalized" divorce laws, Communists, etc. — are the most zealous in getting
out to vote.

Chapter VI

OBLIGATIONS ARISING OUT OF CHARITY

Charity is that virtue which disposes our will to love God above everything else for His own sake and to love our neighbor as ourselves for love of God.

OBLIGATIONS TOWARD GOD

The principal object of charity-love is God Himself. Him we must love before and above all things. It is called "the greatest and the first commandment" by Christ Himself (Mt. 22:38). This love is obviously not a matter of emotions but of the will, wanting to do whatever He wants. This is a commandment. God does not say, "I suggest you do this." God does not say, "I advise you to do this," or "I hope you do this." God says, "I *command* you to do this." Nothing else counts in this life or in the life to come unless we have obeyed this one great command. We show our love to Him essentially when we seek His will and do it. That is why, through St. Paul, God told us, "Love is always patient and kind; it is never jealous; love is never boastful or conceited; it is never rude or selfish; it does not take offense, and is not resentful. Love takes no pleasure in other people's sins but delights in the truth; it is always ready to excuse, to trust, to hope, and to endure whatever comes" (1 Cor. 13:4-7).

God loves each one of us with a love so intense that it is absolutely immeasurable. Loving God for His own sake simply means loving God for the "qualities" which render Him lovable, that is, His loving-kindness, His compassion, His goodness, understanding, etc., without any limitations. In our relationship with people we instinctively feel drawn to a person who loves us and does much for us; God's love for each of us personally is infinite, without limits of any kind. Put together all human love, present, past and future, and it would not even be a fraction of the smallest degree we can imagine, compared to God's love for us (if, indeed, we attempt to compare it).

The signs of His love are everywhere. In the blade of grass, in the laughter and innocence of children, in the smile of anyone we love, in their touch; the majesty of the sunset reflects His love for us, the sparkle of a cool drink of water, the kindness of our neighbors, the concern of our friends, the tenderness of our family, all the goods things of earth mirror it — because from all eternity He thought of us and created all things for us. It is only because we do not recognize these signs of His love that we are not moved.

The human heart is inclined to love and to overflow with love. It is made that way. Most of us succeed in loving His creatures for their lovable qualities, yet do not succeed in adequately loving the Creator of these creatures — all their lovable qualities are what makes them God-like, are merely a pale reflection of His perfections. He is so lovable that He is Love itself. The human heart yearns for Him in such a way that it will never be satisfied except in loving Him. True, love for God is supernatural (above nature) and so requires grace, but this is never refused to the sincere. God made it easier for us to fulfill this, the greatest commandment, by sending His Son to us, so that we have something tangible on which to focus our love, a Person who is God, yet a man like ourselves.

Generous without limit, God rewards us for loving Him. He will forgive all sins, no matter how many or how great; for only an act of love to Him — for only one "I love you, Lord," from the heart, sincerely said (in effect, perfect contrition, perfect love) — is enough to win forgiveness for anything. We have only to will it; emotion, to repeat, need not enter into the act at all. Really, heaven is within easy reach! True, we have to submit all of our unconfessed serious sins to the "power of the keys" in the Sacrament of Penance; still, if we should die without being able to confess, an act of perfect love for God would save us.

In fact, whenever we doubt whether we are in God's friendship, in the state of grace, we should immediately make an act of love or perfect contrition. We are not obliged to confess doubtful sins, but we are obliged by God (divine law) to remain in His love and, indeed, to follow the way that makes us more certain of God's friendship; this is possible at any time through an act of love for Him. Confession is only obligatory if we know with moral certainty that we have sinned gravely, but an act of love, or an act of contrition, extends also to doubtful sin.

After God, we must love ourselves, not with the unregulated love that is synonymous with pride and egoism but with a regulated self-love: that is, by striving to save our own soul and by using the means necessary to do this. All modern inferences to the contrary, we must never prefer our neighbor to ourselves in the matter of salvation. The wise old proverb, "Charity begins at home," is not meaningless. When Christ said, "You must love your neighbor as yourself" (Mt. 22:39), He meant what He said, "as yourself"; after taking care of yourself in the matter of salvation, then take care of your neighbor as you have taken care of yourself. Because the right kind of self-love is confused with the unregulated, egocentric type, it is all too often represented as something vicious and contrary to the love of God!

EXAMPLE:

Rita and Laura are both employed in the same office. Laura, a non-Catholic, asks Rita to accompany her on her date so that her boyfriend will not be able to take any liberties with her. Rita, being a good Catholic, is glad to help.

After a time they always double-date and all seems to work out well. In a few months, however, Rita notices that, though she always has a good time with Laura and her "set," her own attitude toward religion and morals is quite obviously becoming purely materialistic. So she tells Laura that she must stop accompanying her, since her own spiritual well-being comes first. After trying vainly to dissuade Laura also from her spiritually dangerous associations, Rita sticks to her decision even though she knows that now very probably her friend will be seduced.

Rita acted rightly in this matter.

OBLIGATIONS TOWARD OUR NEIGHBOR

As the Lord carefully pointed out, love of God is only a part of the precept of charity. Our love must extend to everyone in need, even to our enemies. Charity, however, demands that those most closely bound to us must be helped first if in need. Thus, those related to us by blood, friendship, religion, or nationality are to be given preference to others in similar need.

But how much of a sacrifice are we to make in order to help our neighbor in need? In general, the greater the need, the greater must our sacrifice be. More specifically, to know the actual sacrifice required of us, we must understand the types of need or necessity that may arise.

I. A person is said to be in *extreme spiritual necessity* if he cannot at all, or can only with extreme difficulty, avoid eternal damnation without someone else's help. We must help a person in extreme spiritual necessity, even to the extent of risking our own life, property, social standing, etc. We need not, however, *risk our life* if there is no certain hope that such a person will be saved by our help. Our assistance and risk of losing any temporal good need only be proportionate to the hope of saving such a person. The obligation ceases either if others are present who can and will lend their help, or if the salvation of a number of others would be endangered by our help.

EXAMPLES:

1. Deborah, Mr. Kindman's secretary, is desperate. One afternoon she buys poison and is about to take it when Mr. Kindman walks in. He snatches the poison away and tries to comfort her. Since he knows that she has no relatives or close friends and that he is almost the only person she trusts, he thinks he can persuade her to give up the idea of ending her life. He knows that charity obliges him to help another in extreme spiritual need.

So he asks her to spend the afternoon and evening with him at the country club, where they can talk the whole thing over. He does this, although his absence at just this time will probably cost him a valuable business contract. The next day Mr. Kindman and his wife invite Deborah to spend the weekend with them in a neighboring city in order to provide some much-needed recreation and diversion for her.

Their kindness gives Deborah new hope and all ends well. Mr. Kindman has done his duty (assisting his neighbor in need when there is no one else to extend help). There might have been some other way in which he could have equally helped, but he was obliged to assist somehow, even at the sacrifice of his own temporal good (in this case a valuable business contract).

2. By accident Ellen learns that her young unmarried sister Clementine, now estranged from the family and living in a distant city, is about to marry a divorced man. Ellen knows that it will be difficult to make the journey to her sister and that she will meet with dreaded antagonism. Still, she feels that her appeal to her sister may have its effect in causing Clementine to reconsider the serious results of her contemplated act.

If Ellen thinks she may be able to do any good by discussing the situation personally with her sister and if there is no one else close to Clementine to do so, she is obliged to make the attempt.

II. Our neighbor is in *extreme temporal necessity* if he is in immediate danger of losing his life or if he can scarcely escape a grave, permanent evil, such as lifelong imprisonment or invalidism unless he is helped. A person in extreme temporal necessity must be helped even at great inconvenience to ourselves, but not at the risk of our life. Our convenience, quite naturally, is never preferable to our neighbor's life.

EXAMPLE:

Out for a stroll one late November morning, twenty-year-old Earl Curly-head, hears screams for help. A little boy has fallen off a bridge and is drowning (extreme temporal necessity). Earl rushes to the scene just as the boy goes under. Earl, an expert swimmer, wonders whether he is obliged to jump into the icy waters to save him.

Yes, he is, for it would only cost him great inconvenience, that of jumping into icy water and, perhaps, some sickness. The obligation is a serious one.

III. Our neighbor is in *grave spiritual necessity*, if he is in danger of losing his faith or virtue (and thereby his soul possibly) and can only overcome this danger with great difficulty. We are obliged to help such a person insofar as possible without serious inconvenience to ourselves.

EXAMPLE:

Mr. Shoe, living on the same block with Mr. Lace, walks to work and back. Lately Mr. Shoe has been stopping at Charlie's Bar on the way home and not infrequently comes home drunk. The temptation to stop at the bar is getting the best of him. Mr. Lace notices this and, since he himself works in the same plant, he decides to give Mr. Shoe a lift in his car every evening. This will help Mr. Shoe avoid the danger of losing the virtue of sobriety (grave spiritual necessity). He does this despite the fact that he has to wait for Mr. Shoe five minutes every day. Mr. Lace fulfills his obligation of charity in this case; and, though waiting five minutes a day is an inconvenience and taking his car to work, it is not a serious one.

IV. A person is said to be in *grave temporal necessity* if he is threatened with the danger of losing some temporal good, such as wealth, social standing, authority, liberty by imprisonment of not too long duration, or something else of great value but less than life itself. We are not obliged by charity to help a person in grave temporal necessity if it would cost us serious inconvenience.

EXAMPLE:
Alice is trying her best to make the monthly installments on her new car. Two months go by and she just doesn't make them. Since the local bank refuses to lend her any more money, she asks Gertrude, her roommate at college, to lend her a hundred dollars so that she will be able to make the payments. Gertrude could actually lend her that amount (and she knows that Alice would definitely pay it back the following summer), yet this would cause her much inconvenience. She would even have to forego some meals if she lends the money. Is she obliged in charity to do so?

No, because in getting her roommate out of grave temporal necessity (losing her car to the finance company), she herself would be put to serious inconvenience.

Though not at all obliged, we may give up a great spiritual good (but not something necessary for salvation) for the sake of another's spiritual or temporal welfare; e.g., a person may postpone entry into religious life or expose himself to a remote or "intermediate" danger of sin.

Sometimes charity may not oblige us to help, but justice, piety, duty, or authority do; thus, policemen, priests, soldiers, employed physicians, and others, in virtue of their occupation or duty, are obliged to risk their lives where ordinary people would only be bound to inconvenience themselves seriously. Similarly, parents must gravely inconvenience themselves for their children if these cannot otherwise avoid losing their life, health, faith, or virtue, whereas other people would not have the obligation of seriously inconveniencing themselves to help.

Here again we have outlined only the minimal obligations of charity towards God and man, not the thousand and one ways which true love finds to express itself — and is never satisfied that it has done enough. The ways of love are endless. Through a thousand ordeals love will not cease. Though fire burns and waves engulf, love is not quenched. Love kisses the hand that hurts. Love sits and weeps with a friend bereaved, feeds the hungry though it has not wherewith to feed itself. Love gives the glass of cold water, speaks the comforting word, offers the encouraging smile, the touch of an understanding look. Love clothes the poor though it shivers itself from the cold. Love holds the hand of a sick child through a hundred sleepless nights. Burdens all, but burdens made light through love of God and man.

Chapter VII

THE TEN COMMANDMENTS: INTRODUCTION

Since the Ten Commandments are substantially a codification of the natural law imprinted on the heart of every man, they bind all men: Catholics, Protestants, Jews, Mohammedans, Hindus and even atheists. What man would no longer read in his own heart, God spelled out in the Commandments to Moses on Mount Sinai. They are called the Commandments *of God* because *He* is their author. They are also known as the Decalogue (from the Greek words *deka,* meaning "ten" and *logos* meaning "speech" or "word").

The following precepts constituted the Jewish Decalogue given on Mount Sinai (the Protestants also follow this particular arrangement): (1) the command to worship the true God only, and no other god; (2) the prohibition against the worship of graven images; (3) the prohibition of taking the Lord's name in vain; (4) the command to keep the Sabbath holy; (5) the command to honor one's parents; and the forbidding (6) of murder; (7) of adultery; (8) of stealing; (9) of bearing false witness, and (10) of coveting the goods and the wife of another (Ex. 20:1-17). Catholic interpretation of textual difficulties resulted in a slight rearrangement of order. The second Commandment, prohibiting the worship of images, was joined to the First; the Tenth Commandment was divided into two distinct commands. In order to commemorate the day of the Lord's Resurrection, His rising from the dead being the greatest proof of His divinity and His victory over sin and death, the Church has changed the command to keep holy the Sabbath into sanctifying Sunday. Finally, the principal feasts of the Jews were replaced with the great Christian feasts.

The external form of government and the special system of religion with its rituals, ablutions and various kinds of sacrifice were prescribed by God in the Mosaic Law to prefigure the mysteries of the Christian faith. After the coming of Christ the Messiah, the need for prefiguring and foreshadowing (and the obligations to perform these prefiguring rituals) ceased to exist. But the Decalogue was not and cannot ever be abrogated because it is an explicit enunciation of the natural law. It holds true today as it did before the time of Christ.

Apart from the primary motive of doing in love what God wants us to do, our own interests demand that we get to know and observe the commands of

God — our happiness depends on it, happiness in this life and in the life to come. Each of the Commandments enunciates some dictate of the natural law, a law based on the very nature of things, the way things were made, the way we were made. Disobedience to the Commandments brings injury to ourselves and to the human race, sometimes with long-lasting, disastrous consequences. Nature will not be mocked.

Historically, even the most primitive peoples had codes of morality drawn up for self-protection. Insofar as these codes did not coincide with the teachings of the Commandments, they failed to accomplish their object. In one way or another the results of permissiveness are always devastating. Twentieth-century society is no exception. What modern man refuses to expiate in church, he does on the psychiatric couch, on his streets through violence, in his home through marital miseries and divorce, through drug addiction. Down through history, when man had forgotten the commands of God regarding his relationship with the Almighty, the heavy hand of his superstitions crushed his spirit more than the most excessive fear of his Lord ever could. The fright of his man-made gods, almost always pitiless and unfeeling, engendered a terror that was white-hot. The Greeks had a word for it: *phikodestatos,* literally, "what makes one's hair stand on end"! In comparison, the fear of the God of Israel and Moses was mild indeed. Some of man's gods would not be propitiated unless human blood was shed, human sacrifices offered, thousands and thousands of them through the years.

Some codes permitted infanticide and abortion, with the result that countless little lives were snuffed out — prelude to the downfall of many a nation. Whenever the sanctity of human life, defended by the Fifth Commandment, had been forgotten, the slaughter reached proportions that boggle the imagination. History repeated itself in our own century.

The Sixth and Ninth Commandments protect family life, the foundation stone of society. When this foundation is broken, society disintegrates. This the Soviets discovered in only a few years. After the Revolution everything was free and easy, in the spirit of the newly found Soviet freedom and democracy. The Kremlin's change of heart came about not from moral or religious motives but from the purely natural consequences of a policy that disregarded the sanctity and protection of family life and marriage. During the early years of the Soviet regime, the means for contraception were made easily available even in certain department stores in Moscow; now their purchase is relatively difficult, compared to that in the West. Abortions have again been made illegal and can only be procured under medical auspices, governed by strict Soviet law. Divorce laws in force now in Russia are extremely severe by our legal standards. In fact, the obstacles to divorce seem to be prohibitive for most Soviet citizens; that is why there are fewer divorces than in the United States. The State subsidizes large families; spinsters and bachelors are taxed. The title "Motherhood Glory" is awarded to mothers of seven to nine children, and those who have ten or more are named "Heroine Mothers;" whereas before, the Soviet press, in speaking of another government's measures to encourage large families, branded it as "a debasement of women to the role of brood mares!" There is no hypocritical fear of any population explosion. You will find no chapters of the "Zero Population" organization in the Soviet Union! Soviet movies and dramas are perhaps the cleanest on earth; pornography is virtually nonexistent. Why? Because the Soviet government saw what permissiveness, promiscuity and moral decadence can do to their people, to their nation.

In contrast, the moral decline of the "privileged" nations of the Western world, supposedly Christian, is alarming. We are committing spiritual suicide precisely in the measure by which we are forgetting the natural law as enunciated in the commandments of God. We are glutting ourselves on license and calling it freedom. Passion, weakness and malice still warp man's interpretation of the natural law and the infallible code of morals in the Ten Commandments. Like the pagans of old, we are perverting our very reason in the process. Pornography, promiscuity and adultery are encouraged under the guise of self-expression and self-fulfillment; dishonesty in high and low places, as "shrewd deals and sophistication"; legalization of abortion as mercy and compassion; divorce as humane consideration, etc., etc., etc.

Are we happy and contented? At peace with ourselves? Let's take a walk down through the streets of a Stockholm, a Detroit, a New York (if we can indeed walk down Detroit or New York streets without danger to life and limb!): do we see much laughter, much joy, much happiness? Sweden with its decades of permissive society has one of the highest suicide rates in the world. As a nation we are not too far behind. Is this the symptom of a happy society?

Happy people are not escapists, yet we wrestle as never before with the gigantic problems of drug addiction, of alcoholism and nervous disorders. Why do we gulp down the tons of tranquilizers yearly? Why are our psychiatrists' couches full? Because as a people we are happy and contented? Crimes in the streets, crimes in business, in our homes — is it because we as a nation are poor, underprivileged? Labor troubles, race problems, or Vietnam have not divided our nation and our society; it is our disdainful disregard of God's commandments that has caused the divisiveness. Disobedience to the commandments of God always has its price and we are merely beginning to pay it. It will get progressively worse in time. In eternity, it has not begun.

The fear of the Lord is the beginning of wisdom. We seem to have lost both. If the pagan Romans were inexcusable for their excesses (Rom. 1:20ff.), Christian man is incalculably more.

THE COMMANDMENTS IN THE CHRISTIAN CONTEXT

The presentation of moral obligations is by no means the most important consideration for the Christian. Obey the Commandments we must, whether out of love or out of fear of the consequences, but obey them we must if we are to fulfill the minimum requirements set by God for happiness in this life and in the life to come. Christ insisted on it (Mt. 19:16-19, Mk. 10:17-19, Lk. 18:18-20). He came not to abrogate the Law and the Prophets but to fulfill them. He did it by giving us His Gospel as the chief norm of our lives. Account, therefore, must be taken of the Commandments but within the framework of the New Testament, of Christ's great law of love and the spirit of the Sermon on the Mount.

Our response accordingly must be the spirit of love with which we Christians should meet our obligations, should do what God wants us to; otherwise, our observance of the law is dead, lacking the quickening spirit which vivifies. How do I love Thee? Count not the ways! Only then will we not be "forced" into obeying. Only then we shall be free, as the children of God should be.

Chapter VIII

THE FIRST
COMMANDMENT

"I am Yahweh your God who brought you out of the land of Egypt, out of the house of slavery. You shall have no gods except me. You shall not make yourself a carved image or any likeness of anything in heaven or on earth beneath or in the waters under the earth; you shall not bow down to them or serve them" (Ex. 20:2-5).

Worshiping God basically means acknowledging His excellence and our dependence on Him. Man gives religious worship to his Creator in three ways: by *sacrifice, adoration* and *prayer*.

SACRIFICE

In the New Law, the worship of God as prescribed by the First Commandment demands the offering of the Eucharistic Sacrifice. The faithful fulfill their obligation in this regard by participating in the Sacrifice on the days prescribed by the Church (on Sundays and holydays of obligation). But the compelling love of Christ and His Church invites all the People of God to do more: to assist at other liturgical services and this by an ever-increasing participation in their celebration. After all, the work of our redemption is ever being applied to us through the liturgy, especially through the Eucharistic Sacrifice.

"To accomplish so great a work," says Vatican II, "Christ is always present in His Church, especially in her liturgical celebrations. He is present in the sacrifice of the Mass, not only in the person of His minister, 'the same one now offering, through the ministry of priests, who formerly offered Himself on the cross,' but especially under the Eucharistic species. By His power He is present in the sacraments, so that when a man baptizes, it is really Christ Himself who baptizes. He is present in His word, since it is He Himself who speaks when the holy Scriptures are read in the church. He is present, finally, when the Church prays and sings, for He promised: 'Where two or three are gathered together for my sake, there am I in the midst of them.' " (See *Constitution on the Sacred Liturgy*, Chapter I, 7.)

Though the spiritual life is not confined to participation in the liturgy and the Eucharistic Sacrifice, the glorification of God and our own sanctification is best achieved through them. In order that the liturgy may produce its full effect, not only must the faithful take part in it *knowingly, actively* and *fruitfully* but they must come to it with *proper disposition.*

Certainly the faithful should, according to their ability and talent, try to learn the sacred rites and take part in them wholeheartedly. Fortunately, since Vatican II, the forms of divine worship are more meaningful and better adapted to the understanding of the faithful. The more perfect their knowledge, the better they are able to participate in all liturgical celebrations by means of acclamations, responses, psalmody, antiphons and songs, as well as by actions, gestures and bodily attitudes. This is the right and the duty of the faithful by reason of their baptism, as "a chosen race, a royal priesthood, a holy nation, a purchased people" (1 Pt. 2:9; cf. 2:4-5). (See *Constitution on the Sacred Liturgy,* Chapter I, 14.)

Under *proper dispositions* of the faithful we may understand that their thoughts match their words and that they cooperate with divine grace, lest they receive it in vain (cf. 2 Cor. 6:1). Proper dispositions for liturgical worship also include the submissive use of what is being provided by the Church whose first concern in reforming her liturgy was the welfare of her children. Liturgical services pertain to the whole body of the Church and are the worship of the entire Christian community. Individuals, therefore, should conform to the group as organized by the Church and should submit to the forms and directives governing the whole body. As an individual member, one does not have the right to try making his personal likes or dislikes, his preferences or prejudices, the standard for community ceremonial. Corrosive criticism quickly kills the spirit of the liturgy. Certainly interior experience of religion will vary to a certain degree with each individual, but patience, understanding and love should underlie all our observations in these matters.

ADORATION AND PRAYER

Any act showing honor and subjection to God because of His infinite perfections and supreme dominion over all things is *adoration.* Since man does not consist of soul alone but is a composite of both soul and body and both are God's works, he must, then, if his acts of adoration be complete, employ both body and soul to make such acts; his acts of adoration, therefore, must be *internal* (acts of the mind and will) and *external* (outward, exterior acts).

External tokens of reverence such as vocal prayer, kneeling, striking the breast, folding the hands, and the like, not only edify our neighbor, but also give public evidence, or witness, of our submission to God as Lord. Furthermore, such acts tend to help us foster interior devotion and drive away distractions. Just as the other sentiments of the soul — love or hatred, joy or sorrow, fear or hope — instinctively tend to show themselves outwardly on our facial features, in gestures and in our whole exterior, so our repentance, gratitude, faith and our other religious sentiments tend toward exterior manifestation.

God, the all-knowing, does not need these outward signs of reverence. Since He sees the intention and inner dispositions of the worshiper and since these external ceremonies during private prayer are only a means to an end (e.g., to intensify interior devotion), the external acts may, and indeed should, be omitted if they prove a hindrance to interior worship. Thus, if we are really tired, we would do well to sit when praying; if we find we can pray more devoutly standing, sitting, or walking, we should do so, by all means. To weary ourselves with protracted kneeling is unwise if it occasions distractions. After all, it is the heart that prays, that is, what is most spiritual in us, and if we add certain bodily postures, words and external marks of devotion to what is really the essence of prayer, we are only adding the "trimmings" to an already beautiful gift to God. All these trimmings of themselves mean nothing, and are pleasing to God only insofar as they express the sentiments of the soul.

EXAMPLE:

Jane, an overworked wife and mother, finds she can't set aside too much time for prayer but that she can "talk" with God easily while mopping the floors and dusting.
Beautiful!

ECUMENISM

Promoting the restoration of unity among all Christians was one of the main concerns of Vatican II. Even before then, many people of good will, Catholic and non-Catholic, have felt the impulse of grace to work and long for the restoration of unity among all Christians. This movement, whether organized or not, was called ecumenical. The Second Vatican Council gave it new dimensions and impetus.

In the words of Vatican II, "Catholics must assuredly be concerned for their separated brethren, praying for them, keeping them informed about the Church, making the first approaches towards them. But their primary duty is to make an honest and careful appraisal of whatever needs to be renewed and achieved in the Catholic household itself, in order that its life may bear witness more loyally and luminously to the teachings and ordinances which have been handed down from Christ through the apostles.

"For although the Catholic Church has been endowed with all divinely revealed truth and with all means of grace, her members fail to live by them with all the fervor they should. As a result, the radiance of the Church's face shines less brightly in the eyes of our separated brethren and of the world at large, and the growth of God's kingdom is retarded. Every Catholic must therefore aim at Christian perfection (cf. Jas. 1:4; Rom. 12:1-2) and, each according to his station, play his part so that the Church, which bears in her own body the humility and dying of Jesus (cf. 2 Cor. 4:10; Phil. 2:5-8), may daily be more purified and renewed, against the day when Christ will present her to Himself in all her glory, without spot or wrinkle (cf. Eph. 5:27)." (See *Decree on Ecumenism,* Chapter I, 4.)

The *primary duty* of a Catholic towards ecumenism, therefore, is self-renewal and spiritual purification, so that one's whole life may bear witness to the true faith of Christ. Secondly, concern for our separated brethren must also include: (a) praying for them, (b) keeping them informed about the true Church, and (c) making the first approaches towards them.

Ecumenical Prayer Services Encouraged. Generally speaking, common prayer services for unity are not only permitted but are definitely encouraged. "Such prayers in common," the Fathers of Vatican II emphasize, "are certainly a very effective means of petitioning for the grace of unity, and they are a genuine expression of the ties which even now bind Catholics to their separated brethren. 'For where two or three are gathered together for my sake, there am I in the midst of them' (Mt. 18:20)." (See *Decree on Ecumenism,* Chapter II, 8.)

Before Vatican II, the Lord's Prayer (Our Father) was commonly used for prayer at ecumenical assemblies. Now, much more is deemed appropriate for Catholics at such interfaith gatherings: joining in Psalms, full Bible services or "vigils," and spontaneous prayer. As early as December 4, 1965, Pope Paul set an example at an interfaith prayer service for unity at the Basilica of St. Paul Outside the Walls, where he assisted with Protestant, Catholic and Orthodox members of the clergy in a reading of Scriptural lessons.

More intimate participation in the divine services, such as inviting non-Catholic ministers to assist in the celebration of Mass or the sacraments (e.g., marriages, baptisms, etc.), must ultimately be guided by what the local bishop permits. Assuredly, the local bishop will follow, as he must, whatever has been determined by the Holy See or by the respective National Bishops' Conference.

CONDUCT INCOMPATIBLE WITH PRAYER

When we talk to God we pray, even though this "talking" be purely mental. In a restricted sense, prayer means a request (from the Latin *prex, precis* — a "request" or "entreaty") made to God that He grant something to us. In a wide sense, prayer may express praise, thanksgiving, sorrow for sin, and so forth. Some standard formulas for prayer, such as the Our Father, include all these aspects.

When we pray, we should not occupy ourselves with actions that are incompatible with reasonable concentration on our prayer such as writing, reading, counting, or carrying on a conversation with another person. Actions which prevent us from applying our mind to an attempted prayer can themselves be sanctified by offering them to God and doing them for Him. Actions thus sanctified, even the most mundane, then become beautiful acts of love to Him. We can also momentarily pause during such "incompatible actions" and mentally say an aspiration such as, "Jesus, my God, I love You above all things," or simply the name, "Jesus."

EXAMPLE:

George is stockboy in a supermarket. Since he can't keep his mind on his business and still concentrate on any long prayer, he makes it a practice to say mentally an ejaculation every time he finishes replenishing a different kind of product on the shelves.

An excellent practice.

During other actions we are able to give sufficient thought to praying and at the same time perform the actions themselves. Thus, we can say the Rosary while driving a car or tractor, riding on a bus, dressing, washing, and so on (we do not have to hold the Rosary beads in our hand while thus occupied). If our attention happens to wander to other things or if we get distracted by something without our realizing it, we need not worry. God is pleased despite our involuntary distractions.

We are guilty of some irreverence toward God if deliberately and without reason we let our mind wander and still continue reciting the prayers with our lips. We certainly would be judged disrespectful if we were deliberately to let our mind wander while conversing with, say, the President or a State governor. No less can be said of our conversation with God. We are not guilty of distraction, however, if we break off a non-obligatory prayer and occupy ourselves with something else. Why? Because we did not have to begin such a prayer and so we do not have to continue it.

EXAMPLES:

1. Angela and Mathilda are saying the Rosary while walking along a trail. Angela just doesn't seem to be able to keep her mind on the prayers; try as she may, she doesn't even say one Hail Mary without her mind wandering. Mathilda, on the other hand, has no trouble at all in meditating on the mysteries; only during the last few minutes of the Rosary, she finds her mind thinking of the nice new boy in school. And she deliberately goes on thinking of the new classmate.

Every time Angela turned her thoughts back to the prayers, she performed an act of virtue; but Mathilda, though she meditated very well during all but the last minutes of the Rosary, sinned (venially) by irreverence when she deliberately let her mind stay with the "nice new boy" at school.

2. In the example above, if, for instance, Angela and Mathilda see their new classmate coming toward them, they can without any scruple discontinue saying the Rosary and engage in conversation with him.

TWO KINDS OF PRAYER

Prayer may be of two kinds, *vocal* and *mental.*

1. *Vocal prayer* is "talking" with God or with the saints and is expressed in words. The word "vocal" may suggest the emission of sound, but sound is not necessary as long as the words are formed with the tongue (and with the lips if necessary for the pronunciation of certain words). To gain the various indulgences, we are required to pray vocally; for example, if an indulgence is to be gained on condition that one say an Our Father, Hail Mary and Glory be to the Father, these must be said vocally (in the sense explained above).

Still, one may *alternate* with another person in saying the prescribed prayers or mentally follow while another recites them. In order to gain the indulgences attached to aspirations or ejaculations (e.g., "My God and my All!"; "O God, be merciful to me the sinner," etc.), we need only recite these prayers *mentally.* Some moderns are "de-emphasizing" indulgences since Vatican II, but the Church has never officially changed its stand on indulgences; they are still as valid as ever.

Mutes can gain the various indulgences either by mental recitation, by sign language, or merely by mentally reading the prescribed prayers. They can gain indulgences attached to public prayers, if together with the other faithful they devoutly raise their hearts to God.

2. *Mental prayer* is the raising up of our minds and hearts to God without pronouncing any words. A very good practice, this "chatting" with God as we would with a dear friend, telling Him of our problems, big or small, our troubles and heartaches, of our joys and successes — little things that happen, that Susie got a new hat, that we have this pain in our shoulder — we do that to friends, don't we? Loved ones like assurances of affection and esteem; so does the Lord. We can talk with Him about anything and everything, anytime, just as we do with friends and loved ones.

Many times we can just lovingly think about Him or His interests without trying to formulate any words. Some simply like to love with their hearts, somewhat as human lovers do when they are happy merely to be in the presence of one another.

Others, again, like to enkindle their love for Christ by imagining themselves sitting at His feet, or reclining their head on His lap. It is the heart that prays, after all, and it can pray alone, without words, either expressed or mental. Thoughts are formed in the mind before they can be clothed with words. That is the best kind of prayer. Words would only be bothersome at such times, for they would have to be sought after and rejected one after another until some are found to express our thought.

One young man, extremely fond of symphonic music, uses it to express his love for God and makes it into a form of prayer by imagining, for instance, that the harmonic swells are mutual surges of love between his heart and God's. When the soft, sweet strains of the violins come, he thinks of them not as a diminution but as a more beautiful type of love; the staccato parts, he says, are shafts of intense love from God, darting, penetrating deep into his heart; the sad, heavy music, suggestive of complete desolation of soul, represents to him his sorrow and sadness over offending God by sin, while the light, joyful music suggests the joy experienced in returning to his Father's house; in the intense finales with their ecstatic reverberations, swells and sweeps, God as it were, clasps and enfolds him in His infinite love. Every mood, every interpretive nuance is something enabling him to love God the more. Years ago, Francis of Assisi used the harmonic beauty of nature in order to draw closer to God. Every created thing radiated love of God, a sign of God's love and concern for this humble servant until he fairly overflowed with divine romance. Even death (Sister Death, he called it) he welcomed with open arms because it was from his Beloved.

THE OBLIGATORY PRAYERS OF PENANCE

Prayers imposed as a penance by the priest in confession should be said with as much fervor as possible since these are very effective in taking away the temporal punishment (punishment in purgatory, etc.) due to our sins. A single prayer said devoutly as part of our penance will perhaps take away more punishment than dozens of others not prescribed as a penance.

Since actual attention to the words said is not necessary for the essence of prayer, a person fulfills his penance even though he is *voluntarily* distracted when saying them; such distraction is evidently a venial sin, however. (Here we are concerned with absolute essentials, not with what is desirable. Actual attention to the words we say is not essential, for our words [including our posture, gestures, etc.] do not cease to be an appeal to God, though of course we must strive also for actual attention.)We should never repeat the penance, since repetition easily leads to scrupulosity and makes prayer burdensome, even distasteful. This holds true for any prayer which is repeated just because one "feels" that he had not said it devoutly enough. Some needlessly torture themselves in repeating their prayers simply because they are seldom satisfied with the way they have said them; such people may spend forty minutes saying the Rosary; others repeat a prayer three or four times before they feel they have said it devoutly enough. Children, especially, should be taught never to repeat any of their prayers. Sometimes their whole outlook on prayer can be changed by this instruction. Young minds are impressionable to life as it daily unfurls new vistas before them: early over-insistence on attention in prayer sometimes leaves some of them with the impression that prayers are to be repeated until well-nigh perfectly recited, with protracted attention on each and every word. Gentle persuasion to the contrary may have lifelong effects. St. Thérèse, the Little Flower, during her childhood period of scrupulosity used to repeat her night prayers late into the night. Only God and she know how much effort and energy it cost her to break this habit.

EXAMPLE:

After confession Mrs. Learnall begins the ten Hail Marys she received as penance. Just them Mrs. Knowhow walks in wearing a gay new hat and kneels in front of Mrs. Learnall. Immediately Mrs. Learnall's mind is caught up with imaginings of the stylist who designed such dashing headgear, the quality of the rose-colored material, the smart angle of the feathers. Before she realizes it, her fingers are on the last bead of the Rosary she uses to count off the Hail Marys. She is not obliged to repeat the prayers, for she has fulfilled her penance.

AVOIDING USELESS DETAILS IN PETITIONS

Some, again, in making their petitions known to God, feel that they have to state every minute detail so that they will not be misunderstood by God or that He will take advantage of some "loophole" and, hence, leave their petition unanswered. Children especially may be prone to do this. Such meticulous distress is not only useless to the efficacy of their prayer but is positively detrimental to a healthy outlook on prayer in general. Children should be assured that God never "takes advantage of loopholes" because He loves them with a Father's love and cares with a mother's care. He will definitely not misunderstand because our needs are present to Him before we open our mouth. He sees our intentions as soon as they form in our heart. No need ever to be anxious about explaining our wants sufficiently to Him. If sometimes He does not give what we ask, it's because He loves us so much that He will not give us anything harmful even though we beg Him! Instead, He will substitute even better things, greater benefits. Besides, if we love God, we will trust Him completely.

IS IT A SIN TO MISS MORNING AND NIGHT PRAYERS?

God never said that we must pray each morning, night, or before and after each meal, but Christians have always done it. Certainly these are the most convenient times for formal prayer and, likely, if one does not pray then, he will not pray at all.

To omit these prayers, even knowingly and willfully, is in itself not a sin. But if a Christian should neglect them habitually for days and days on end (and does not pray at all), he would be guilty of venial sin on the score that he is spiritually careless and running the risk of falling into sin. Going for very long periods without praying at all is a matter for serious sin because divine precept obliges frequent prayer.

We are not obliged to say Grace openly at meals in restaurants. Praying openly, however, is one of the little ways in which we bear witness to the truth of what we believe — and not hiding our light under a bushel.

PRAYER AND FAITH

Christ said, "Watch therefore and pray." He meant it. A man who loves will understand that. Lovers are constantly watching for opportunities, for the slightest needs of their beloved. Failing that, a lover *asks* what he should do. And only a man who habitually seeks God's guidance through prayer will know exactly what God wants of him. True, there are the commandments but true love is not satisfied merely with keeping these, just as lovers are not satisfied merely in doing their duty to each other but want to do more. Only prayer and love can make a man sensitive to the opportunities, the chances of doing good in any, even the most unlikely, situation.

True Christian living is a process of perpetual action and reaction: love and prayer inspiring deeds, deeds strengthening love and prayer.

Chapter IX

FIRST COMMANDMENT: THINGS FORBIDDEN

A Christian is guilty of false worship if he mingles religious errors and deception with his worship of the true God. Catholics, though little realizing it perhaps, do take part in false worship by describing or publishing miracles, visions, private revelations, or "prophecies" which are known as untrue; also by causing false relics to be venerated. Guilt, of course, is incurred only when such persons know that the facts are otherwise, i.e., that the miracles, visions, etc., are fabrications. Besides being sins against truth, these practices are wrong because they cause others to suspect our faith of error and make real witnessing to our faith unbelievable. In short they make Catholics look ridiculous.

Though guilt in such practices can be gravely sinful, it usually is venially sinful because of the person's ignorance or simplicity or because the matter itself is insignificant (e.g., to recount once a fabricated miracle would be a small matter). Sometimes the "zealots" who do these things are entirely free from all fault because of their simplicity and total ignorance.

EXAMPLE:

In order to appear important before her classmates, Linda, a high-school girl, shows them a few drops of dried blood on a handkerchief and claims that it is a relic of St. Thérèse.

There is venial matter here: that of lying and of fabricating a false relic.

WORSHIP RENDERED TO FALSE GODS

The First Commandment does more than command man to recognize and worship the true God; it forbids him to render worship to anyone or anything else, to make false gods out of mere creatures or created things.

I. IDOLATRY

In idolatry, worship which should be given to God alone is given to a creature. Ancient Egyptians worshiped animals: the cat, the crocodile, the hawk and particularly "Apis" (a black bull with a white scar on its forehead). Pagan Slavs worshiped "giants" which they believed existed in lakes and rivers, as well as animals. In lands where celestial bodies shine more brilliantly than in northern climes, the ancients regarded the sun, moon and various constellations of stars as gods; they also worshiped fire which they thought was the source of all light. The ancient Greeks and Romans worshiped statues and images, signifying the various deities; in representing some deities (e.g., Venus and Bacchus) as the patrons of vice, they thought they were honoring these gods by indulging in their respective vices. St. Paul tells us (1 Cor. 10:20) this worship of false divinities was nothing less than the service of the devils, for Satan was the animating spirit of this idolatry.

While the idolatry of pagans might be excused to some extent on account of ignorance, idolatry is always seriously sinful for Christians, whether practiced privately or publicly (there is added gravity when publicly practiced). To perform the external actions of worshiping an idol even without believing or consenting interiorly to the false worship is seriously sinful. This holds true even if the action is done to avoid death or some other great loss. Christians by the hundreds of thousands preferred death rather than yield even to feigned idolatry.

EXAMPLE:

James, overcome with emotion, whispers to Rosy that he adores her. Later he begins to scruple whether he had committed the sin of idolatry.

This term is merely a form of endearment usually whispered by ardent lovers in their more foolish moments, and it is not intended to be idolatrous; hence it is not sinful!

DO CATHOLICS WORSHIP GRAVEN IMAGES?

In the age of ecumenism, fewer and fewer good Protestants think that Catholics "worship" or "pray to" statues and holy pictures. They are better informed than in Grandma's day when denials to the contrary were countered with remarks such as: "Yes, but I have heard them singing hymns to the images and banners of their Blessed Virgin in outdoor processions," then for good measure, adding, "and besides, I've seen them praying before the statues themselves; you can't deny that!" It never seemed to cross their minds that one can kneel before a statue in prayer and pray not to the statue but to the person represented by it.

Nor did it seem incongruous to Grandfather's Protestant friends in knowingly smiling at him when he tipped his hat in passing a Catholic church — on the way to Memorial Day ceremonies — and a few minutes later proudly lifting their own hats before Lincoln's statue, then solemnly laying a wreath at the cenotaph, and wiping away an emotional tear when saluting the flag!

In our day the problem generally is not misunderstanding but a question of importance, of evaluation. Our non-Catholic friends simply are not convinced that statues, holy pictures and crucifixes are all that helpful as an aid to more fervent prayer. Judging from the starkness of some churches in the post-Vatican II era, more and more of our Catholic friends seem to agree. Still, the Second Vatican Council maintained: "The practice of placing sacred images in churches so that they may be venerated by the faithful is to be firmly maintained" *(Constitution on the Sacred Liturgy,* Chapter VII, 125). But it wisely added: "Nevertheless, their number should be moderate and their relative location should reflect right order. Otherwise they may create confusion among the Christian people and promote a faulty sense of devotion" *(Constitution on the Sacred Liturgy).* The underlying reason given was: "To the extent that these works aim exclusively at turning men's thoughts to God persuasively and devoutly, they are dedicated to God and to the cause of His greater honor and glory" *(Constitution on the Sacred Liturgy,* Chapter VII, 122).

Modern psychology has demonstrated what the Church has always known that nothing brings home a truth more vividly than pictures or images. A picture is worth a thousand words. Visual education is based on this idea. This is why textbooks are filled with pictures, why magazine articles are illustrated by them, why advertisers exploit them to the nth degree.

The meaning of a picture to the human heart can be unfathomable: the touching pathos of a dead lover's picture, evoking lovely memories; the picture of a son just killed in a car accident, lovingly kissed and pressed to a mother's agonized heart; the picture of a devoted wife tenderly caressed by a prisoner of war. To those who love, pictures are filled with evocative meanings. That is why Catholics often express their love for Christ by reverently kissing the crucifix, why they have pictures of Christ and His friends in their homes along with pictures of their own friends and loved ones. At home or in church most people can pray only with difficulty or not at all when they have the Sunday comic strip before them; they can pray better if it is removed; they can pray still better if a lovely statue or image of Christ is substituted.

This in no way contradicts the First Commandment. The Hebrew phrase often translated as "to make a graven image" or "carved image" actually signified "to make an idol." The modern Confraternity of Christian Doctrine edition of the Bible uses this latter expression. And the Commandment's closing words, "you shall not bow down to them or serve them," render unequivocally clear that what God forbids is the making of images intended as gods.

True, any image as such was a danger to the faith of the ancient Israelites, living amid idolaters whom they were plainly prone to imitate — and did, on occasion. But it is equally clear that God did not forbid images in themselves. After poisonous snakes attacked the complaining Israelites in the desert — a form of punishment for their complaints — God commanded Moses to heal those who were repentant *by making a bronze serpent* and holding it up before them. Again, the Ark of Covenant, center of Jewish worship, was sheltered between *graven things made at God's own direction.* Among the instructions for building the first great temple was the requirement that two cherubim be made (of beaten gold) for the two ends of the propitiatory: these were to be turned toward each other but their faces were to look toward the propitiatory itself and their wings spread over it (Ex. 25:18-20). Thus, these images were to be in the very "Holy of Holies."

That the early Christians understood and rightly used sacred images and pictures is a matter of historical record. Some of the earliest date back to the second century. Reflecting the Church's Fathers, St. Basil wrote: "I venerate the holy apostles, prophets and martyrs . . . I reverently kiss their images, for apostolic tradition does not prohibit their use, but rather sanctions the custom of placing them in the churches." We still do it.

II. FORMS OF SUPERSTITION

In Deuteronomy, God reiterates some of the prohibitions of the First Commandment as a warning to the Jews: "There must never be anyone among you who makes his son or daughter pass through fire, who practices divination, who is a soothsayer, augur or sorcerer, who uses charms, consults ghosts or spirits, or calls up the dead. For the man who does these things is destestable to Yahweh your God. . . ." Superstition, or attributing to a creature a perfection or power that belongs to God alone, is a kind of counterfeit faith, a form of divine worship given to a creature; therefore, it is forbidden by the First Commandment.

Ultimately, superstition is worship rendered to the devil; it is an invocation addressed directly or indirectly to him with the hope of obtaining effects that are beyond human power, of obtaining certain effects by means known to be inadequate or of gaining knowledge of occult or "future" events, which humans are incapable of attaining under natural circumstances. The malice of the sin is not diminished by the fact that the appeal to such powers has been fruitless.

Apart from idolatry, there are four general types of superstition: the relatively rare *black magic* and *sorcery;* the two somewhat common types, *vain observance* and the various forms of *divination,* fortunetelling (including phrenology, palmistry and crystal gazing), astrology, planchette writing, the ouija board, spiritism and dream omens.

BLACK MAGIC AND SORCERY

Not to be confused with *black magic* is natural magic, which consists of performing extraordinary or astonishing feats by purely natural means (done through skill, suppleness of body, or simply by using knowledge of certain physical laws). All of us have seen this kind of "magic" performed at parties, social gatherings and fairs. Natural magic is a wholesome recreation and not at all forbidden.

EXAMPLE:

At a lively cocktail party Mr. Whodidit performs some amazing sleight-of-hand tricks. Among other things, he makes coins disappear, then pulls them out of the host's sleeves and ears; he puts Mrs. O'Grady's silk handkerchief into a desk drawer, then pulls it out of the shy Mr. Slim's pocket!
There is no question of sin here but merely natural skill.

Black magic, on the other hand, is the art of producing effects which surpass natural forces by express or tacit aid of the devil. This was probably the type of magic practiced by Jannes and Jambres, magicians of the Egyptian Pharaoh, when they imitated the miracles of Moses (cf. Ex. 7:11).

Allied to black magic is *sorcery,* the diabolical art of casting spells, thus causing sickness either to man or beast by a spirit of revengeful hatred. Where black magic seeks to reap advantages, honor, or riches for oneself, sorcery attempts to inflict harm on others. So grave is this sin that Old Testament law punished it with death; needless to add, it is still a grave sin to attempt to practice black magic and sorcery or to seek its aid.

Modern man scoffs at such "nonsense" as belief in the devil. But disbelief will not make him cease to exist or disappear. Of course, the devil of the picture book, with horns, tail and pitchfork, is ridiculous but Satan actually does exist. We have too many passages from Scriptures asserting it. And to seek his aid is still horribly possible (2 Thes. 2:7 ff.). It may be mysterious but there is a spirit of evil at work in our world. God works in our world but so does the spirit of evil — the devil. Don't ever forget it. You can call him by any name you like. All the evil going on in our world cannot be explained unless we understand a spiritual force back of it, called the devil, to which Jesus referred time after time.

We may be used to thinking of black magic, sorcery or Satanism as practices only of the ancients, of the primitive tribes as Juju in West Africa, or Voodoo in Haiti, yet fascination with the occult is making a comeback in many, modern industrialized parts of the world. In Japan the new religion of Soka Gakkai which mocks every basic Christian belief has trebled its membership to over six million *families* since 1960. In England and the United States, witchcraft is surfacing. In 1969 a school was opened in Essex for would-be witches; the same year Aston University's student paper reported that the Psychical Research Society had been closed down when Satanism infiltrated it. In San Francisco the First Satanic "Church" has been founded. Evidence is mounting that more and more people are dabbling in serious witchcraft and other sinister activities — not only by way-out people, but by businessmen, civil servants, housewives, etc.

The practice of Satanism, sorcery and black magic can hardly be a moral problem for Catholics here but excessive fear of its effects can be. Such fear undermines filial trust in God's power and His providential protection. The Church is fully aware of the power of the evil spirit and his accomplices among men, as the rites of exorcism reveal, but she puts her trust entirely and unreservedly in the power and love of God. So should we. Without divine permission, the devil can harm no one. Superstition lies in the belief that the maledictions, enchantments and execrations of sorcery are infallible instruments of themselves, that of their own vile power they can bring harm to others. This simply is not true. The devil can do his evil work only if God permits him, either to prove a person's virtue — in which case God supplies special graces to resist — or where sin has already cleared the way. In any case, a false dread of the power of the evil spirit is unwarranted for the ordinary Christian.

A worse danger facing the faithful is their unwarranted suspicion of others regarding the "black arts." Rash judgments concerning others in this area are just as sinful as in any other.

VAIN OBSERVANCE

What most people simply call "superstitious practices" really consists in *vain observance,* that is, the use of evidently inadequate means to produce some definite desired effect. There are many such practices: spitting on three pebbles, turning around, taking three steps and throwing the pebbles over the left shoulder in order to get rid of warts; carrying a rabbit's foot (or any kind of amulet or charm) in the belief that it will bring good luck; believing that crossing the street on the same block within the same hour will bring bad luck; believing that beginning an important enterprise on Friday, especially on Friday the thirteenth, will mean a complete failure of that undertaking, etc. The list could be extended for pages, because many foolish superstitions are widespread, even international.

In order to judge the sinfulness involved in these various superstitions, we shall divide them into (1) *positive practices* and (2) *negative practices.*

1. A person indulges in *positive superstitious practices* if he *does* (not merely omits doing) something to produce a particular desired effect by means known to be inadequate; that is, he does something to obtain some benefit, such as *wearing* or *carrying* about a rabbit's foot (charms, amulets, horseshoes, etc.) *to ward off evil* (the benefit); *dipping* three coals in water with three pieces of bread to *cure* a baby of colic (the benefit), etc. Such practices are really implicit invocations to the devil for aid, even though the person protests against the influence of the evil one; for the desired effect cannot be obtained by these means either from God or from nature — which leaves but one alternative power left capable of accomplishing the effect — the devil.

A person who believes and seriously expects the desired effect to follow *infallibly* when he performs such foolish actions would sin gravely. We must keep in mind, however, that many people are not to be judged guilty of serious sin because, in their simplicity or ignorance, they do not realize the malice of their act or because they fail to understand how utterly impossible it is for the means to produce the desired results by purely natural means. If these acts are done in jest, they are, of course, not sinful at all. If a person has some but little faith in these practices (he "somewhat" believes in them), he would sin venially if he performs them.

EXAMPLE:

Three elderly spinsters, Mabel, Gable and Ella, want very much to get married. While on a trip to Ireland, they are told that if each hops on one leg around the Blarney Castle, she will get married within the year! So the would-be Juliets decide to try.

Now Mabel doesn't believe a word of this but goes just for the laughs; Gable thinks that there may be something to it and so she goes in order not to lose out . . ." just in case"; credulous Ella, on the other hand, takes the whole thing very seriously and is firmly convinced that the result (that she will get married within a year) will definitely follow if she hops around the castle.

Presupposing that each knew the principles of judging the morality of her own contemplated action (the act in conjunction with the amount of credence in its "efficacy"), Mabel commits no sin, Gable a venial sin, while Ella would be considered to have sinned gravely by her action if all the other factors for grave guilt were present.

If there is a possibility that the effect is the result of some unknown powers of nature, one is permitted to use such means provided he protests against any diabolical influence. Such a protestation does not have to be made if one is certain that the effect is produced by some natural cause or power even though these natural powers are little known; for example, the use of the divining rod for locating veins of metal or water.

EXAMPLE:

In order to find the best place where he can sink a well, Mr. Brown wants to use the divining rod.

He may do so without sin and he does not even have to make a protest against the interference of the devil.

2. A person indulges in *negative practices* if, because of fear caused by superstition, he *avoids* some circumstances or *omits* doing something in order to avoid "bad luck"; in other words, if, prompted by superstition, he desists from some action because he fears that something detrimental will befall him otherwise; for example, if he *avoids* walking under a ladder so that he will not have "bad luck," or if he does not continue along the same street or road because he saw a black cat cross it but takes another route instead in order that some misfortune will not befall him.

Most people following these negative observances experience a sort of vague fear or uneasiness if they deliberately defy them; they would regretfully reproach themselves if something did happen. Being of a nervous temperament, perhaps, they prefer to avoid anything that would cause them uneasiness.

Indulging in such negative observances solely because of one's nervous disposition or simplicity is considered no sin at all. If slight belief is had in them, as generally seems to be the case, then it would be venially sinful to indulge in them. But to permit one's whole life to be dominated by these silly practices would be an indication that such a person is actually very serious about them and hence would be a matter for grave sin. All this presupposes that such a person has been duly instructed about such practices.

LEGITIMATE PRACTICES

Legitimate Catholic practices and customs should not be confused with superstitions. To wear medals, scapulars, crucifixes and other such articles of devotion is not superstitious because our trust is not put in the pieces of metal or wood as bearers of some supposed magical power but in the one in whose honor we wear such things. When I wear a blessed crucifix, I do not expect the engraved piece of metal to protect me but Christ whom I am honoring. When I make a novena, I do not hope to obtain my favor by any magic supposedly connected with the number nine (which happens to be the number of days during which a novena is usually made) but I do hope that the one in whose honor I made the novena will help me obtain my request, especially since I had to put in extra effort not to miss a day.

Such pious practices can, however, be used superstitiously too. Hoping to cure a sore hand by making the sign of the cross over it is an act of deep and reverent worship given to the Holy Trinity, if the trust is put in God for the cure; on the other hand, it will be an act of superstition if the trust is put in the mere observance. Hence the internal attitude of the individual is the deciding factor.

DIVINATION

Divination is invoking the help of the devil, either tacitly or in expressed words in order to learn unknown or secret things, especially the hidden things of the future. We can never obtain knowledge of the *free future* by natural means. By *expressed words* is meant that the devil is directly addressed and asked for help in definite and explicit words, such as: "Satan, tell me whether I shall be killed if I go on this bombing mission." Very few people today are so foolish, ignorant or evil-minded as to appeal thus to the father of lies. *Tacitly* invoking the help of Satan means any attempt to learn occult or future things by means which are naturally inadequate for imparting such information — by such means as gazing into a pool of blood, a crystal ball, or tea leaves, etc. Here the aid of God's archenemy is not sought directly in express and definite words; but the appeal is made implicitly by the means mentioned above, means which by nature are incapable of giving one such knowledge. Neither can God reasonably be expected to supply enlightenment under such ridiculous circumstances; hence there is only one other left to whom the appeal is necessarily directed, the devil.

Knowledge in itself is a good thing, but to obtain it from God's worst enemy is wrong; to do so is an insult to God. That it is offensive to God to seek such knowledge from the evil one we know from God Himself: "If a man has recourse to the spirits of the dead or to magicians, to prostitute himself by following them, I shall set my face against that man and outlaw him from his people" (Lv. 20:6). Also, in Chapter I of 2 Kings, God punished Ahaziah, one of the kings of Israel, with death because he sent messengers to inquire of Baalzebub, the god of Ekron, whether he would recover from his sickbed.

Furthermore, *only God knows with certainty the future actions that depend on man's free will;* this is a divine attribute. When a person appeals to the devil for such knowledge, he is in effect ascribing to a creature a power belonging to God alone. True, since the devil is an extremely clever being (a fallen angel no less) as well as a shrewd guesser, he can conjecture the future far better than we. Sometimes we can predict the future to a high degree of probability: by merely piecing together certain facts and, with the help of certain other facts known to us, we can form a highly probable, logical conclusion. Past experience will also tell us much about the future. Since Oshwell easily learned seven languages fluently, for example, we can foretell that he will not have much trouble in learning the eighth. If we know human nature well, we can predict what kind of people will probably succeed in what professions, or how certain types of people will react to certain remarks, insults, words of encouragement, and kindness. The devil, since he is far more intelligent than we, can predict quite startling facts at times. In all cases the predictions, however, will be only *probably* correct; in no sense of the word will they ever be certain. This, briefly, explains how in some instances apparently hidden knowledge of events (past, present and future) has been given to those who resorted to various kinds of divination. This may also explain the reason behind the widespread growth of many forms of divination in this century, both for foretelling the future and for diagnosing disease — aside from the fact that as religion decays, superstition and pseudo-cults thrive.

In any case, the Scriptural warning still holds valid: "If a prophet or a dreamer of dreams arises among you and offers to do a sign or a wonder for you, and the sign or wonder comes about; and if he then says to you, 'Come, then, let us follow other gods (whom you have not known) and serve them,' you are not to listen to the words of that prophet or to the dreams of that dreamer" (Dt. 13:2f.).

KINDS OF DIVINATION: SINFULNESS OF EACH

Instead of giving the general principles regarding the sinfulness of the various types of divination en masse, we shall try, for greater clarity, to describe the more common types individually and give the corresponding principles of morality applicable to each.

Fortunetelling is the attempt to discover for another "the good or bad luck" which will befall him. One of the most popular forms of fortunetelling seems to be crystal gazing; that is, the fortuneteller (usually a woman) uses some means, such as a crystal ball, a mirror, a pool of blood or ink on her palm, or some other similar object to "help her peer beyond the mortal veils separating her from the world of secret knowledge and hidden events." Tea leaves are another means frequently used.

No doubt most fortunetellers are shrewd frauds. Many just guess the future and do not pretend to do more; they do it to amuse their "clients." But others really take their "profession" seriously and actually believe in their own "marvelous" and "secret" powers.

Often fortunetellers cleverly word their statements in such a way that they will be true no matter what happens.

Another technique employed by fortunetellers to instill confidence in their "secret powers" is to tell the client something of his past which would naturally be unknown to the fortuneteller (unless the latter had assistants to gather such information, the devil may come into the picture in such cases). Many times, however, the fortuneteller cleverly makes such grand pronouncements as: "I see you experienced sorrow at the death of a loved one, someone close to you . . ." (by middle age or over, who hasn't?); or "There was a large fire, you were afraid, a fire close to your family . . ." (again, in the normal course of events, every adult has had several such experiences). Often the client, without realizing it, will supply the details himself by stating: "Yes, there was once a fire, the neighbor's barn burned down, etc., etc. . . ."

Another reason why so many people still seem to believe in fortunetellers is this: anything that happens to be correctly foretold is broadcast far and wide, while the legions of incidents which never materialize are never mentioned. Who wants to mention his foolishness in consulting a fortuneteller when the prediction proves false! Chances are, when one talks to another person about fortunetelling, he will usually recount only the things that proved true and not the many things that proved false. In this way, we hear many of the instances which happen to be correctly predicted; but, on the other hand, none of the many, many false predictions. So, naturally, a slight credence in fortunetelling may easily be developed.

The objective sinfulness of consulting a fortuneteller depends on a number of circumstances: (a) it is mortally sinful for a person to have his fortune told if he is serious about it and seriously believes the predictions; (b) a grave sin of cooperation may be committed even if one is not serious about it but consults a fortuneteller who is serious about it — that is, a fortuneteller who really believes in her "powers," as, for example, may happen in consulting a gypsy; (c) a venial sin is committed if a person only slightly believes in the forecast and the fortuneteller is not serious about it. This last is generally the case today, since most fortunetellers are merely professional fakers interested only in their pay; and, for the most part, clients visiting them do so for the sake of either diversion or curiosity, but with some belief in their powers.

Many people will protest that they haven't even a slight belief in the fortuneteller's powers — and they still persist in paying good money to have their fortunes told? If they do not give fortunetellers any credit for the mysterious knowledge, why don't they hand over their money to their brother or husband and ask him to reveal their future? Surely, for a dollar or two, a husband could and would only be too happy to tell them the same bizarre, impossible things that the weird-looking professional faker tells them.

EXAMPLE:

One evening while Betty and Ned, two young adults, are visiting an amusement park, they come across a fortuneteller's booth. Bubbling with curiosity, they decide to have their fortunes told. They think that a fortuneteller in a place like this is most unlikely to believe seriously in her powers of accurately predicting the future.

Having satisfied their curiosity, both laugh the whole thing off, but they still have a vague feeling that some of the predictions may be true. As the case stands, there is matter here for venial sin; however, serious guilt could have been incurred had they been serious about the affair.

Of course, if a person really does not have any faith in the fortuneteller's powers and goes only for the "fun of it" or for a pastime, there is no sin involved (it is understood that the fortuneteller is not serious about it either). Thus, at social gatherings, or church fairs, having a fortune told or telling fortunes is an innocent amusement; the same holds true for the fortunetelling done by means of the small cards which are issued from some scales and penny slot machines, in fortune cookies, etc.

Phrenology is the study of the shape and bumps of the skull in order to learn the intellectual or sensual tendencies of a person. While it is not sinful to believe that one may be inclined to act in the manner indicated by the "findings" of phrenology, it is sinful to hold that one is doomed to what these bumps are supposed to show.

EXAMPLE:

The new roomer across the hall, a phrenologist, tells John that he has a great liking for art, literature and good music; that he enjoys good food and usually overeats; and that he is by nature very intelligent but is usually too lazy to study.

John admits that he has these tendencies to a very pronounced degree; however, he refuses to believe that he cannot act otherwise than according to these predispositions.

There is nothing wrong in John's admission and belief that phrenology did actually indicate his natural tendencies. The sin would lie in believing that he could not do other than what the bumps indicated.

Palmistry (sometimes called *chiromancy*) is the art of telling fortunes, of judging character or aptitudes by studying the palm of the hand. Psychologists and psychiatrists tell us that our whole physique and physical makeup have some relation to our temperament and inclinations; but to say, as the palmists insist, that such small portions of the body as the lines of the palm of the hand indicate one's character, temperament, inclination and aptitude is absurd.

The palmists, however, do not stop here; they go on to assert that a "current of unseen life" goes through the palm by way of the index finger, supposedly distributing a "subtile force" throughout the body! The whole idea seems ridiculous: how could such things as the lines of our palm indicate our wealth, political power, etc.?

At any rate, palmistry is not sinful if it merely attempts to analyze one's character, temperament, or inclinations; however, if it attempts to foretell the free future, it is sinful. We judge this sinfulness in the same way as that of fortunetelling.

Astrology, more correctly called *judicial astrology,* is the pseudoscience which aims to foretell a person's future by the study of the influence of the stars, and especially the five planets longest known to man — Mercury, Venus, Mars, Jupiter and Saturn (these were known to man from the dawn of recorded history). It should not be confused with *natural astrology;* the latter, a purely natural science, is concerned primarily with predicting the weather by observing the position of the moon, planets and stars. Astrological predictions for the whole year are given in weather almanacs and on some calendars. Such forecasts are usually the result of many years' observations of the weather in the particular regions, and of atmospheric calculations on the presumed influence on the weather exerted by the various heavenly bodies. The planets' influence on the earth's weather conditions may be great. To believe in these weather predictions or to be influenced in planting one's crops according to their calculations is not at all sinful.

EXAMPLE:

According to the current weather almanac, Mr. Jones notices that the last week of May is the best time to plant this year's potato crop. He may follow this opinion without any sin whatever.

Judicial astrology, on the other hand, is sinful because it professes to foretell one's free future. Judicial astrologers make their predictions according to certain fixed rules dependent upon the "controlling position" of the stars at the time of one's birth.

The calculations necessary to settle these positions are called "casting the horoscope," for which a diagram of the heavens is used. This diagram is divided into twelve equal parts or "houses," and these in turn into "cardinal houses" (or "anguli") and "cadent houses" (or "succeeding houses"), each of which refers to life, personal property, consanguinity, children, jewels, dignities, success, misfortune, etc. The seven planets (not up-dated since the discovery of other planets), divided into "day stars" and "night stars," also vary in their meanings. After the diagram is made, the astrologer proceeds to read and analyze the person's future as it is supposedly influenced by such learned-sounding, mysterious things as "cyclical movements," "star rays," "planetary or stellar vibrations," etc. The jargon is just another technique used to deceive the gullible and to hide the falsity of astrologers' meaningless, obscure predictions. But gullibility apparently is not lacking even among the most cultured and civilized, for in the United States alone over ten million Americans seek the services of astrologers.

Astrologers hold the fatalistic view that our fate was sealed by the stars at the moment of our birth, when we first began to breathe the air, which is "filled with tremendous forces"; according to them, it makes no difference how much we try to do or avoid this or that thing; our efforts will be in vain because our fate is predetermined. To be born, to get married, or to make other important decisions under an auspicious sign of the zodiac or when certain constellations are overhead, they tell us, is of the greatest importance. God does not enter the picture at all as our guiding, loving Father and protector. God even seems to be incapable of helping us, according to their belief; if, for instance, we happen to be born under the inauspicious influence of the planet Saturn, we are doomed to a life of affliction, adversity and financial difficulties "cast" by this planet.

Modern scientific astronomy sharply repudiates current astrology and relegates it to a vitiated astral cult. For one thing the system of seven planets is outdated after the discovery of other planets. For another, the twelve signs of the zodiac are merely an arbitrary ensemble of stars separated from one another by vast worlds of space, so they are not even cosmic unities much less real and effective unities. Furthermore, these signs had been established for the various seasons of the year according to the astronomical observations of the ancients; today they are no longer in accord with the corresponding constellations, for they are progressively displaced in their relation to the seasons (i.e., the relative correspondence of the zodiac signs/seasons/constellations, though valid for about the middle of the second century, is not valid for today). In other words, this part of astrology's whole system limps by about eighteen centuries! (As a result, the disharmony is so great today that a person, say, born under the sign of the ram would in reality fall under the stars of the pisces at his birth, not under the ram; still astrologers put him under the ram!)

Finally, astrologers must answer two very important scientific questions: how can the millionfold influences of uncounted stars and their ever-changing constellations be even approximately measured? And then, what rational reason can they give for ascribing the influence affecting a person's whole life precisely to one constellation when there are so many?

At any rate, consulting an astrologer, the reading of the horoscope for others, and spreading its literature are all matters for grave sin.

PLANCHETTE WRITING

A planchette is a small board supported on casters at two points and a vertically set pencil at a third point. A person rests his fingers lightly on this little board while assuming a relaxed position and putting himself into a listless, lethargic state with a pliable and ready-to-follow-suggestions state of mind. Soon, if all is done according to directions, the board will begin to move, supposedly by itself and will write unintelligibly. By and by it will write legibly, impart "messages" and answer questions.

The habit of planchette writing, once a person begins, is easily acquired, for most people are strongly attracted by the mysterious. Indulging frequently in planchette writing has proven for many people to be productive of nerve exhaustion and neurosis; for others, a weakening of will power.

Aside from cases of fraud or intentional moving of the planchette, what causes the planchette to move at all, much less to write out messages? It may be the operation of the subconscious mind (that is, the hidden storehouse of past experience and knowledge); this would probably be the case if the messages and answers are actually in the subconscious or conscious memory. Then, too, one's own mental imaginings as well as mental telepathy from another may be the explanation for knowledge previously unknown to that person. Chance guessing or coincidence may also be taken into consideration. If these do not explain the planchette's movements at given times, then preternatural influence must be the explanation.

Though not always sinful, planchette writing is always to be discouraged, by all means. It is sinful in any of the following cases:

1. It is a matter of grave sin if one expects the messages or answers will be obtained from the departed (e.g., from a dead relative) or from demons, or if one asks questions about the free future, or hopes that these messages and answers will pertain to the free future (e.g., will the Red Wings win the Grey Cup this year and, if so, by how many points?).

2. When one asks questions about the secret past of others or wishes messages that will be concerned with someone else's secret past, it is then: (a) a matter for grave sin if one asks or wants to find out a *secret, mortally sinful past action of another* (e.g., has my husband committed adultery?); but, (b) venially sinful if it concerns *another's venially sinful action of the past* (e.g., did Susie lie to me when she claimed she passed her Algebra test?).

3. Indulging in planchette writing is not sinful provided one's purpose is sinless and if one asks and wishes that the messages and answers be drawn from his conscious or subconscious knowledge or from the knowledge which can be acquired at that moment by mental telepathy (e.g., how many brothers and sisters has my hostess?).

THE OUIJA BOARD

Similar to planchette writing is the use of the ouija board. The ouija board is a flat board marked with various signs as well as with the alphabet; it is used with a planchette to obtain mediumistic messages or answers to the questions asked. The planchette used in conjunction with the ouija board is slightly different from the ordinary planchette mentioned above: this planchette is like a small, heart-shaped, three-legged table, the third leg of which is not a pencil but only a pointer. When the sitters (or sitter) rest their fingers on the planchette, it moves about and points out the various letters or numbers marked on the ouija board and thus spells out the answers to questions asked by a bystander.

The causes of the planchette's movements are the same presumably as those in ordinary planchette writing. The morality of using the ouija board is judged according to the same principles.

SPIRITISM

Though spiritism (necromancy) as well as most of the subjects already treated under the First Commandment would not come under the title of "ordinary moral difficulties" of practical Catholics, yet the faithful should know the morality of such practices and be on their guard not to get foolishly involved in such "arts." They are certain to meet with the temptation to indulge in these practices, since there has been a marked rise in all forms of the occult within the last several decades. The People of God are bound to meet many who believe in such things and will probably invite them to participate.

Spiritism is the practice in which an attempt is made to communicate with the spirits of the departed or the spirits of the other world. The practice of spiritism is very ancient. Already widespread among Israel's neighbors at the time the Book of Deuteronomy was written, God commanded: "There must never be anyone among you who . . . consults ghosts or spirits, or calls up the dead" (Dt. 18:10ff.). The cult as we know it today originated in 1848, at Hydesville, Wayne county, New York, where Mr. and Mrs. Fox and their two daughters, Margaret and Katherine, heard mysterious raps on the walls of their farmhouse. After establishing a code, the raps, said to have been made by the spirit of a peddler murdered in the house years before, usually gave correct answers to such specific questions as "How many people are here now?" or "What are the dates of their birth?"

The Fox sisters developed their "talents" and became wealthy therefrom. By 1866 (eighteen years after the first raps at Hydesville were heard) they claimed five million devotees. Notoriously active in spreading the cult, both sisters held séances here and abroad, yet both died in destitution.

After more than a century of such communications, nothing substantial or infallible has been added to man's knowledge of the afterlife and no discernible benefits have been conferred upon the human race. From the beginning the spirits promised a new dawn of hope and peace for the world; the world would be fashioned anew; mourning for the dead and fear of death would vanish. Naturally, nothing came of all this. As one well-known author pointed out, even up to the very outbreak of hostilities in 1939 the spirits were promising *no war!*

Religious beliefs when expounded through such transmitters generally disagree with the teachings of orthodox Christianity. Communications obtained through the agency of human mediums are invariably contradictory.

As a general rule, the answers given by the "spirits" echo the wishes and prejudices of those consulting the mediums. Usually the "spirits" say nothing against religion if devout sitters are present at the séance; in fact, if Catholics are present, many times they will tell them to pray and to frequent the Sacraments. On the other hand, to an audience known to be without strong moral principles, the "spirits" often give approval to outright lasciviousness. Aside from the many cases of fraud, Satan seems to have a part in many spiritistic séances: the evil, insidious doctrines, the heresies, the contradictions which the spirits teach certainly indicate nothing but an evil mind at work.

In order to foster interest and credence in spiritism the "spirits" will generally, at the first few séances, urge a pious audience to do good, to pray much, and to practice their religion; but before long, they insinuate doubts and suggest that all religion is superstition, except for what they teach, such as life after death being a continued progress from sphere to sphere of light and happiness. Revealed doctrines are attacked by such questions: "Why does your religion teach you that there is an everlasting hell? How could an all-merciful God punish man forever with fire no matter what he may have done? Why should a certain number of Hail Marys have such mysterious power?" Thus, the sitters' faith is attacked and weakened. In the end the doubting mind is captured and revealed religion is abandoned for the new, consoling religion taught by the spirits, a religion in which hell is simply nonexistent and the next life is seen as a place of plentiful amusements similar to but more intense than those enjoyed on earth; all of this, of course, leads to sensuality and loose morals.

In short, spiritism leads many to the loss of faith, a dissolute life, the ruin of physical health, and sometimes to insanity and suicide. These are facts, not conjecture. Besides, what is to be gained from seeing tables moving without human aid, or hearing hoarse whisperings through collapsible aluminum tubes or witnessing weird forms take shape from a substance called ectoplasm? Then, too, upon competent investigation many spiritistic séances frequently have been found to be fraudulent.

Though much, perhaps most, spiritistic phenomena can be explained as very artfully executed deceit, we should not jump to the conclusion that all spiritism is a fake or is due to the machinations of evil forces. The Church has made no such pronouncements; so neither should we. But, because the Church suspects that diabolical agencies may intervene in many of the manifestations which occur, she commands the faithful to leave such powerful potential occasions of danger alone. The Church has officially condemned spiritistic practices and attendance at spiritistic séances. We are forbidden to attend séances even though we take no part in the proceedings and are present only out of curiosity. The prohibitions expressly include the cases in which the object of attending a séance is to communicate only with *good spirits*. For scientific research, passive attendance at séances is allowed if special permission is obtained from the bishop.

It is gravely sinful for a Catholic to attend a spiritistic séance without ecclesiastical permission.

MENTAL TELEPATHY

Mental telepathy or presumed thought transference is the communication of impressions from one mind to another by means other than the ordinary channels of sense, that is, without speech, gestures, writing, etc. It may be something like a "mental radio." Mental telepathy is usually divided into two types: the first is brought about by conscious effort (usually referred to simply as *mental telepathy*); and the second is communication occurring spontaneously — the spontaneous "seeing" of events beyond the range of ordinary vision (called *clairvoyance*); for example, I "see" my friend drowning in a place hundreds of miles away.

Many of these "visions" can be given very natural and even prosaic explanations. Neither type of mental telepathy has been incontrovertibly proven. Some psychologists claim to have established proof; others are not convinced. Since no real evidence proves or disproves these strange phenomena and since we are still unaware of many of nature's forces, we should at present attribute the forces behind such manifestations to purely natural causes and not to preternatural influences. It is entirely possible that humans possess an undeveloped but natural faculty of telepathy, the use of which would in no way be sinful. At any rate, we may without sin experiment with mental telepathy or attempt to transfer ideas and impressions by mental effort.

EXAMPLES:

1. One Sunday afternoon, Mrs. Smith is quietly dozing in a rocking chair.

Suddenly she is startled by a strange feeling of suffocation, and the picture of her son lying on a floor in a dark small room flashes across her mind.

Now she is convinced that her son, a prisoner in North Vietnam, was choked to death at that very moment. Though she may be in error as to the fact, there is nothing sinful in believing it.

2. Ted and Ned, both interested in mental telepathy, decide to try some experiments with it. Ted is to go into the adjoining room and concentrate on any number between one and twenty; in the meantime Ned is to put his mind into a receptive state by trying not to think at all. Just then Ned's sister walks in and insists that it is gravely sinful to go through the experiment.

She is wrong. It is completely sinless.

BELIEF IN DREAMS

Much doubt still exists about the exact causes and origin of dreams. Ordinarily, dreams seem to arise from natural causes, such as overeating, an upset stomach, some recent vivid occurrence, overworked nerves, worries, the last thing we have thought of before falling asleep, pressure on the back of the head exerted by the pillow, etc. The devil, since he can influence our imagination, may possibly be able to influence our dreams too. Obviously, dreams arising from natural causes as well as those coming from the devil cannot give us knowledge of the free future; and to believe that they can is pure superstition.

Does God choose to send certain dreams? Many of the saints tell us that they were thus favored. Holy Scripture in several passages also mentions God speaking to some in a dream. But how are we to know if a particular dream is from God and not from other sources? First of all, if God ever chooses to make something known to us in a dream, He would certainly make us realize it; that is for sure. Still there are other indications to help us decide whether a dream is from God or not. Thus we know that God would not send us dreams which would not influence us toward good or dreams that would either induce us to sin or leave us undisposed to serve Him.

Any dream which suggests something unworthy or something entirely inconsequential as coming from God also originates obviously from some other source. For instance, I know my dream is not from God if I dream that I should cheat Mrs. Goodheart because I suspect she shoplifted in my store. My sister dreamed that an angel told her to wear her hat at a certain tilt every time she goes to the movies. Cousin Jake dreamed about heaven where all the garden gates were painted white so that the termites would not get at them! Such dreams also are obviously not from God.

As to other dreams, it depends: sometimes it may be superstitious to credit them; at other times it may not be. There may be some connection between a dream and a forthcoming event because of the mysteries of mental telepathy, or the elusive influence of mind upon mind and soul upon soul; hence, to believe in such a connection in a particular case would not be superstitious. Say, for instance, I dreamed last night that my rich Aunt Sara was coming to visit me and was going to give me two thousand dollars. Upon awaking this morning and reflecting upon my dream, I feel inclined to believe that Aunt

Sara is really coming to give me two thousand dollars, even though I haven't seen her for years. This would not be superstition, because her resolution of paying me a visit and giving me two thousand dollars might in some way have been transmitted to my mind, thus affecting my dream.

Now and then it happens that people, shortly after having dreamed of a friend from whom they have not heard for a long time, surprisingly enough do meet or receive a letter from that friend; the connection between such a dream and the forthcoming visit or reception of a letter may possibly be explained by mental telepathy.

On the other hand, it would be sinful to act according to "omens" indicated in dreams which cannot be explained by mental telepathy or which are not clearly from God. For then one would either put credence in a superstitious practice (if the dream were of natural origin), or one would implicitly be worshiping Satan (if the dream were from the devil). How sinful is it? To be influenced *at times in little things* by such dreams is a venial sin; for instance, to take a bus to work instead of driving because one dreamed that he got into an accident while on the way to work in his own car. It would, however, be matter for serious sin *to habitually guide one's life* by this kind of "omen," for such conduct would show that one put really serious credence in the dreams.

IRRELIGION

Irreligion is a positive irreverence to (a dishonoring of) God, either directly, to God Himself, or indirectly, through His saints or persons and things consecrated to Him. A person may be guilty of sins of irreligion against the First Commandment by *tempting God,* by *sacrilege* and by *simony*.

I. *Tempting God* is any act or omission by which a person puts to the test one of God's perfections (His love, mercy, power, etc.) without good reason. We can *explicitly* tempt God by doing, omitting, or asking something of God in order to ascertain whether He possesses a certain power and whether He would here and now use that power. This kind of conduct is a direct insult to God and indicates that a person doubts the perfections of God. To tempt God *explicitly* is always matter for serious sin. An example of this sin is: expressly requesting Christ to show Himself in a consecrated host if He can; or committing a suicidal act and then demanding that God save one's life if He is able. One famous atheist tempted God when he took out his watch and cried out: "If there be a God, I will give Him three minutes in which to strike me dead." When he was not struck down in that time, he proudly stated: "You see, there is no God!"

One *implicitly* tempts God if he does something which by its nature requires an immediate manifestion of His power, wisdom, or some other of His attributes, even though one does not express this intention. To tempt God implicitly in a serious matter is gravely sinful, but in a slight matter, venially sinful. If I am so ill that I am in imminent danger of death and refuse to use the ordinary means of saving myself because I expect God to save me miraculously, I can be guilty of a serious sin. The same is true if I foolishly expose myself to imminent danger of death and expect God to preserve my life. If I am only mildly sick and *rashly* expect God to cure me, I would sin venially, since the matter in such a case is slight. There is nothing wrong, however, in hoping for a miraculous cure (should it be God's will), when one employs the ordinary means of regaining one's health, or in looking for extraordinary help from God after all natural means have failed; in fact, such conduct shows deep, solid faith.

EXAMPLE:

In order to prove that his car can go faster than Fred's, Tony challenges Fred to a race. Fred accepts the challenge, though he knows his tires are very poor and may blow out at any moment. "God will protect me," he says, "because I'm not the one proposing the challenge. Besides, I am the father of three children." So he speeds up to ninety miles per hour.

Fred is tempting God in a very serious matter (his own safety) without any good reason; hence, he is adjudged guilty of serious sin, presupposing sufficient knowledge and realization of the gravity of his conduct.

II. *Sacrilege* is the desecration or disrespectful treatment of any person, place or thing which has been made sacred by a public dedication to God. To violate these objects is an indirect insult to God Himself, since they have been consecrated to Him and so are His own in a special way.

When sacrilege is committed by maltreating sacred persons — that is, clerics, priests, or religious of either sex — excommunication is also incurred. The sin is committed by killing, seriously injuring (laying violent hands upon), or inflicting great indignities on them (such as unjustly imprisoning them, throwing stones at them, spitting on them, etc.). All sins of impurity with such persons (even impure desires for such persons) are also sacrilegious, but no excommunication is incurred.

EXAMPLES:

1. In a "scrub" football game Joe is playing opposite his pastor, Father Nolan. During the game Joe's anger flares, and he deliberately hits and tackles Father Nolan harder than is necessary. He does this repeatedly during the last half of the game. Did he commit sacrilege?

No, because Joe's conduct, playing the game harder than usual, obviously is not meant to be disrespectful and insulting to Father Nolan.

2. Professor Jones, an ex-priest, begins a bitter attack against the Church and its priesthood. Joe and Jim, who are Catholics, immediately get up and tell him in no uncertain terms what they think of his attitude. Then they walk out of class.

Later they worry whether they committed a sacrilege by thus speaking to him. So they ask the Newman Club chaplain. "Of course not," he tells them; "nothing was further from your minds than insulting the consecration and priesthood in him. In fact, you were defending those very things from vicious attack!"

A better answer could not be given.

Sacrilege is committed against *places* by performing any act that is especially repugnant to the sanctity of such places as churches, chapels, or consecrated cemeteries. Included in this category of acts are murder, suicide, a grievously sinful shedding of blood, adultery, etc. Hidden, mortally sinful actions (committed by one person, and privately) would be venially sacrilegious. Private eating in a church without necessity is unbecoming but not sinful.

A very grave sacrilege may be committed *against things* by receiving any of the Sacraments unworthily. As regards lies in confession, however, only those lies told to conceal something which the penitent is *seriously obliged to disclose* would make the confession sacrilegious; other lies told in confession do not make the confession unworthy unless they would be seriously sinful themselves.

We may burn blessed objects when they become useless (objects such as palms, holy pictures, icons, etc.). But to destroy such objects contemptuously would be sacrilegious. We may use blessed candles for studying or general lighting in case the electricity goes off, etc. It is not sinful to throw the bones of blessed food or the shells of blessed eggs into the refuse container.

To quote Scripture for sinful ends (e.g., to seduce someone) is gravely sacrilegious; to quote it in a joke, in such a way that it shows some irreverence, is a venially sinful sacrilege.

Though sinful, to steal money or the personal, private property of priests or religious is not sacrilegious (nor stealing from lay people in church); but stealing money belonging to a church (from vigil-light stands, collection baskets, etc.) would be sacrilegious whose gravity would depend on the size of the sum stolen.

III. *Simony* is the act or the will of buying or selling spiritual things or temporal things annexed to the spiritual, for a temporal price. The word takes its origin, perhaps, from an incident narrated in Acts (Chapter 8). A sorcerer named Simon saw the Apostles performing miracles and bestowing the Holy Spirit by the imposition of the hands. He offered them money for their miraculous powers. St. Peter's scorching answer was brief and to the point: "May your silver be lost forever, and you with it, for thinking that money could buy what God has given for nothing!"

If a person attempts to buy the power of conferring any of the Sacraments or of imparting indulgences, he would be guilty of simony. Needless to add, simony is grievously sinful. It insults God by assuming that God's goodness and mercy can be bought or sold. If such were the case, only the wealthy could enjoy the benefits of His bounty, an absurd thought.

To buy blessed articles (say, a consecrated chalice or an indulgenced Rosary) is neither sinful nor simoniacal if the price is not increased by reason of the blessings attached. But Rosaries, crucifixes and other such articles, when sold, lose the indulgences attached to their use.

How about offering Masses or prayers as stakes in betting? To do so is not sinful, but certainly undesirable, since such practices may, at times, be irreverent or at least seem so.

The stipends offered to have a Mass said are not payment for the Mass, of course, but are given for the support of the priest. The offering of stipends is entirely legitimate and accords with what St. Paul wrote to the early Christians: ". . . The Lord directed that those who preach the gospel should get their living from the gospel" (1 Cor. 9:14).

EXAMPLE:

Mr. Richgiver has a plot in the parish cemetery. When his only cousin, an ex-Catholic and an agnostic, died unrepentant, Mr. Richgiver wanted to give Father Noldin five hundred dollars for a Catholic funeral and burial in consecrated ground. Even after Father Noldin explained that this would be simoniacal, Mr. Richgiver still insisted and offered an even higher sum.

Chapter X

THE SECOND COMMANDMENT

"You shall not utter the name of Yahweh your God to misuse it, for Yahweh will not leave unpunished the man who utters his name to misuse it" (Ex. 20:7).

The Second Commandment forbids us to dishonor God by profaning His name in any way; it also commands us to regard God's name as sacred in our speech as well as in our adjurations, vows and oaths. We object to the disrespectful use of our mother's name or the name of anyone we love; we should do the same for God's name. The Jews of old used to have such reverence for the name of God, Yahweh, that they generally did not pronounce it but used instead another word, *Adonai* ("Lord").

Though the Second Commandment directly refers only to God, it indirectly prohibits all disrespect to persons or things closely connected with God. Just as we honor God by showing honor to His Mother and His saints, so we dishonor *Him* by showing *them* dishonor.

Sins against this Commandment are: (1) irreverently using God's name; (2) cursing; (3) blaspheming; (4) illicit oaths and perjury; and (5) the violation of vows.

IRREVERENT USE OF GOD'S NAME

Using God's name thoughtlessly, without proper reverence, as in expressions of anger, impatience, or surprise, is what is usually meant by "taking God's name in vain." Thus expressions like: "Christ, I'll get him!" "My God, John, don't do that!" or "By God, he'll come home even if I have to drag him there!" are examples of taking God's name in vain, though unfortunately all too frequent in some households.

To use God's name in vain is ordinarily venially sinful; it may be seriously wrong if the anger which causes it is directed against God. To use the names of the saints or of the Mother of God irreverently is also venially sinful. Such irreverent expressions uttered when no one is present are still sinful though the element of scandal is absent.

The use of words such as "Gee" (Jesus) and "Gosh" (God) is sinless because today they have entirely lost their original meaning. Similarly, expressions such as "darn it," "by golly," "ye gods," "the dickens," "the deuce," or "the darned thing," may be reminiscent of certain forms of profanity, but they are not in the least sinful today. Neither is it sinful to use base, coarse expressions referring to the functions of the toilet (and terms closely connected with such) or the name of the devil. Merely to say "Oh, hell!" "What the devil are you doing?" or even "Damn it!" without any particular reference is not unlawful, though inelegant and unbecoming.

Not to be confused with irreverent use of God's name are the pious exclamations which are really intended as a prayer. To use God's name with reverence in everyday occupations is good. Even today in the United States many persons whose parents came from various European nations, often make pious use of sacred names and expressions. Many of the Slav races, for example, literally sprinkle their day with such pious expressions as "For (the love of) God, I will not go there," or "Mother of God, preserve us." True, many such expressions may either be pious, exclamatory prayers, or irreverent expressions, depending on the internal disposition of the individual person. If the person intends them as pious prayers, that is what they are.

What about the person who has the habit of using God's name in vain, scarcely realizing what he is saying? Certainly, if one is truly sorry and trying his best to overcome his habit, yet despite his efforts inadvertently "slips" now and then, he commits no sin. But anyone not trying to correct his habit is considered guilty of venial sin every time he misuses God's name even though he does so without advertence — in other words, thoughtlessly. Why? Because such a person, after becoming aware of his habit and consequently foreseeing these acts, *advertently* decides not to do anything about correcting the habit. Theologians call such a person guilty *in causa* ("in cause"): that is, he does not wish to eliminate the cause of his act.

EXAMPLE:

When in the Army, Tom and Jerry got into the habit of using God's name in vain. Now Tom is sorry about it and is trying hard to overcome the habit; however, despite his efforts, he still "lets go" sometimes without thinking. He commits no sin in this. Jerry, on the other hand, though aware of the habit goes on his merry way without trying to do anything about it. He is considered guilty of venial sin every time he utters the name of God thoughtlessly.

CURSING

Cursing or damning is calling down evil upon oneself or upon any of God's creatures. Not all cursing is sinful; for example, God cursed the serpent in Eden, and Cain for killing his brother Abel. We too can curse or damn the devil as many times as we wish.

But what about cursing as we generally understand the term? Its sinfulness depends on a number of circumstances. To curse animals or objects which have tested our patience or caused us pain is *in itself not a sin*. Thus, if a cow steps on Johnny's toe and he screams out: "Damn you, Bessie!" he is not guilty of any sin of cursing. If anger prompted him to say that, he may be guilty of anger but not of cursing. If he included the name of God in the phrase ("God damn you, Bessie!") he may have committed the venial sin of using God's name in vain but not of cursing. This is true of cursing (1) any animal — be it horse, cat or dog, or (2) any object — be it hammer, baseball bat, or car door.

But to damn or call down spiritual ruin on a human being is sinful: for example, to say to a *person:* "Go to hell!" "Go to the devil!" "God damn you!" Such expressions are ordinarily venially sinful; but if they are said seriously and deliberately, they could be gravely sinful.

One should not confuse cursing with expressions of blasphemy, or with swearing (which is taking an oath), taking God's name in vain, vulgar or obscene speech. Many people mistakenly use the term "swearing" to mean cursing.

EXAMPLE:

After his ace is trumped in a friendly game of cards, Jim let out with, "Damn it, Joe, how do you always manage that?" There is no sin of cursing here, since Jim obviously means nothing by this expression. Neither is there a question of taking God's name in vain, for he does not use it. Hence Jim committed no sin. However, expressions of this sort should be discouraged because it may be only too easy to include God's name in them.

BLASPHEMY

Blasphemy is any speech or gesture that conveys insulting contempt for God; for example, shaking one's fist at the heavens to show contempt for God, or using such expressions as "God is unjust in giving me all these troubles," or "God is unmerciful to let me bear all this sorrow." Julian the Apostate, it is said, always spoke of the Son of God as the Galilean (at that time, a word of insult); at his death, as he lay stricken by a lance, he took a handful of his own blood, threw it toward heaven, and cried out: "Galilean, you have conquered!"

It would also be blasphemous to revile in a *serious* and *contemptuous* way the saints, sacred objects, or priests and nuns in their capacity as sacred persons, for through them God is indirectly reviled. But to criticize or joke about priests' faults *as men* and not as God's representatives is not blasphemous. Criticizing them may be sinful if charity or justice is violated (its gravity must be judged according to the general principles of justice and charity as applied to the act of detraction).

Blasphemy is gravely sinful if at the time of his action the person realizes the meaning of the blasphemous words or gestures and fully intends them as such. Most of the time, however, the person using blasphemous words does so in a sudden, spontaneous burst of anger; in such cases, complete advertence is not present and so neither is grave guilt.

We are permitted to narrate incidents, repeating the blasphemy used by another, provided there is a good reason for doing so. To tell Aunt Susie or Cousin Jake merely out of idle gossip is not a good reason.

OATHS AND PERJURY

An *oath* is a calling upon God to witness the truth of what we are saying. There are times when we not only may take an oath but should do so; for example, if the good of our neighbor or the honor of God requires it. If I am accused of a crime which I did not commit I may swear an oath to confirm the truth of what I say.

In order that an oath be valid (that is, if it is to be an oath at all) two conditions are necessary: (1) the *proper formula,* and (2) the *intention of swearing.*

1. *Proper formulas* for an oath are: "I call upon God to witness," "So help me God," "God is my witness," and other similar expressions. The formula used by a witness in court usually is: "The evidence that I shall give the court and jury, touching the matter in question, shall be the truth, the whole truth, and nothing but the truth, so help me God." There are other formulas which are ambiguous, such as, "God knows," "I speak in the sight of God," or "God sees my conscience." If a person uses such ambiguous formulas with the *clear intention of swearing,* he actually takes an oath. If in doubt whether one actually had such an intention or not, it is presumed that an oath was not taken and so one is not bound by it. No oath is taken by using the following expressions: "In honor and conscience," or "Cross my heart and I hope to die."

2. There must be the intention of swearing (a virtual intention suffices; for instance, in the case of a person having the intention of swearing, who goes to the stand to take the oath but is so nervous and distracted in the act of pronouncing the proper formula that he no longer realizes what he is doing). Without such an intention, even though the person uses the proper formula, no oath is taken. Actually employing the proper formula, without intending to swear (the intention is unknown to the bystanders), is called a feigned oath. To swear such a feigned oath is a venial sin of irreverence if done to confirm a true statement; if done to confirm a lie, it is gravely irreverent toward God; hence, matter for serious sin.

EXAMPLE:

Mr. Veracityam is called as a witness in a lawsuit. He has only one statement to make, that he saw six people at a certain meeting on December 2. When he goes to the stand he is asked to take the customary oath. He pronounces the proper formula, though he does not intend to swear at all. The court quite naturally thinks that he is taking the oath. Then Mr. Veracityam proceeds to tell the court that there were only five people at the meeting in question. Does he commit perjury?

Because his statement is a lie, there is matter here for mortal sin, not of perjury but of grave irreverence toward God. Had his statement been true, a venial sin of irreverence would have been committed.

WHEN TAKING AN OATH IS SINFUL

1. Swearing without sufficient reason is venially sinful. This is about the

same as using God's name in vain. A sufficient reason has to be something more serious than a passing emotional whim; for instance: "So help me God, I really don't want to go the movies tonight."

2. Swearing to a statement which would be sinful for the speaker even without an oath (boasting of one's own sins, for example) would be venially sinful; the same is true of swearing to a detraction (in this latter case, however, it can be seriously sinful if the secret grievous sins of another are disclosed). To promise under oath to do something seriously evil is a matter of grave sin. If the thing promised is only venially sinful, then the oath is venially sinful.

Promises made under oath to perform unlawful actions do not bind. Thus, if a non-Catholic swears never to become a Catholic, the sworn promise entails no obligation in conscience to resist conversion; similarly, a person is not bound if he swears to tell a lie or rob a store. Neither is one obliged to perform something which he swore to do if that thing becomes subsequently useless; for example, if Marge promised under oath to have a Mass said for the recovery of her sick brother and then finds out that her brother is well, she is not bound to make good that promise. The same applies if the person to whom something is promised under oath relinquishes his right to that thing; thus, if Ann promises under oath to support her widowed aunt and her aunt later releases her from this promise, Ann is not obliged to keep the promise. In ordinary cases of promissory oaths one is obliged seriously or venially according to the greatness of the matter promised.

3. The statement to which a person swears must be true, or at any rate one must be convinced of its truth. Perjury (i.e., deliberately swearing to a falsehood) is never permissible and, if done with full deliberation and consent, is gravely sinful, even though it be a matter of a slight lie only. The reason for this: great dishonor is thus shown to God because He is called upon to witness the truth of what is known to be false.

EXAMPLE:

Luke tells a small lie under oath, even though he knows that he is thereby committing perjury. There is matter for grave sin here.

A person *swearing in court* is generally required to have gained the knowledge contained in his statement by personal experience; if he has acquired it otherwise, he should make known the fact as such. It is perjury to use *strict mental reservation* when swearing in a court of law. We are also gravely forbidden to confirm a *broad mental reservation* with an oath if it is prejudicial to those who have a right to know. However, if done to those who have no right to know the truth and if done for a grave reason, then confirming a broad mental reservation with an oath is entirely sinless. If no grave reason exists in such a case, the act is venially sinful.

EXAMPLE:

Earl, living in a Communist country, is questioned by potential informers, purporting to be friends, whether Amelia, a close relative, has tried to escape to a free country. Though Earl knows that Amelia has left the country, he realizes he must use broad mental reservation to protect Amelia's family. So he answers that he has no information about the matter, which could clearly mean, in the circumstances, "no information for you." The potential informers, knowing Earl is a good Catholic, then ask him to swear to this: he does so. Earl is justified in swearing to this broad mental reservation for he has good reason and the inquirers have no right to the facts.

In court Catholics may lawfully and licitly swear on any Bible (Catholic or Protestant) that is given to them at the time. In the spirit of ecumenism, we are considering the Bible here as essentially a book containing the word of God, whatever its version.

OATHS OF ALLEGIANCE

Immigrants who have sworn allegiance to their fatherland and now wish to become citizens of the United States (or any other country) may swear allegiance to the new country of their adoption without violating their former oath. The obligation of fidelity to any nation is always presumed to cease when a person leaves that nation and seeks another country.

In swearing allegiance, immigrants and public officials (the latter by oath of office) make themselves subject to the law of the land and, in the case of public officials, obligate themselves to fulfill their office according to the prescriptions of the law and not to do anything contrary to rightful authority; but this does not mean that they thereby bind themselves under oath to observe every civil law.

If some provisions in the civil laws of one's country contradict divine or ecclesiastical law, the oath taken to observe these civil laws may be made with the proper restrictions (excluding anything against divine or Church law). Because this fact is ordinarily implied and understood, it need not be stated expressly.

VOWS

A *vow* is a voluntary promise made to God to do something possible, good and more pleasing to God than its omission. We must carefully distinguish a simple *resolution* and a *vow*. The person making a vow must not only understand what it involves, but must intend to bind himself under pain of sin to keep this promise. If someone does not have this in mind or has no intention of binding himself under sin, he is not vowing but is merely making a resolution; in other words, he is only giving his word of honor to God. Thus, in confession, we are not making a vow but merely promising God that we will never sin again, gravely at least.

If the matter of the vow is important, it binds under pain of either mortal or venial sin, depending on what one intended when he made the vow; if the matter is slight, it can only bind under a venial obligation regardless of the intention. When the person who vowed had no special intention of obliging himself gravely or venially but still intended to bind himself under sin, he is presumed to have intended to bind himself under pain of serious sin in serious matters (and, of course, only venially in slight matters). If, for instance, I vow to go (from any part of the U.S.) on a pilgrimage to the Shrine of Our Lady of Guadalupe, the matter vowed would be grave. But if, on the other hand, I vowed to say an extra Our Father daily for a week, the matter is slight and, hence, I would sin venially if I neglected this vow.

In case of doubt whether one has made a vow or merely a resolution, that is, if a person doubts whether what he promised was a vow or not, he may assume that he made no vow. A vow must be so *deliberately* and so *consciously* made that the person making it must be fully aware of binding himself under a vow. Likewise, anyone doubting whether or not he has fulfilled his vow is to presume that he has.

A VOW CAN CEASE TO BIND

A vow ceases to bind in the following cases:

1. When cancelled by anyone who has proper authority over the matter of the vow. Hence a husband may annul the vows of his wife. A father has power to annul the private vows of his children who are still minors; the mother may likewise do so if the father does not object. In default of parents, anyone with parental authority may do so. A bishop or privileged confessor can dispense from almost all private vows.

2. When the fulfillment of a vow becomes impossible. Such would be the case, for instance, with someone vowing to donate a large sum of money to the poor but finds that he is unable to give the amount promised. He must, however, donate as much of the sum as he can, for he is obliged to make good that part of the vow which is still possible. On the other hand, we are not bound at all by vows which are "indivisible" (either in themselves or according to the vower's intention), if any part of such vows subsequently becomes impossible to fulfill; for example, if I vowed to make a pilgrimage to Guadalupe in Mexico, but now cannot enter that country, I am not obliged to any part of the pilgrimage (in other words, I am not even bound to go to the border of Mexico).

WHY MAKE VOWS?

Acts performed under vow, being acts of the virtue of religion, are *more meritorious* than the same acts performed without a vow; the bond of religion always unites the soul more closely to God. Human frailty and weakness are also forestalled, since the matter vowed is not left to the indecision of the moment.

We should never be hasty in making vows. In times of distress and trouble people understandably have very sincere intentions and may be quick to make even very serious vows.

A good rule to follow always, as prudent people do, is: pray, think the matter over carefully, and then get the consent of your confessor; this should be an absolute "must" in regard to vows of a serious nature. Every priest knows from his pastoral experience how much spiritual trouble may sometimes be caused by hasty vows; how heavily encumbered a conscience may get by "quickie" vows. But once such vows are taken and become difficult to keep, no one should be afraid to ask the confessor for a dispensation or at least a commutation into some other good work. Never fear — the priest is your friend.

Chapter XI

THE THIRD COMMANDMENT

"Remember the sabbath day and keep it holy. For six days you shall labor and do all your work, but the seventh day is a sabbath for Yahweh your God. You shall do no work that day" (Ex. 20:8-10).

God, after commanding us to adore Him and Him alone, to honor and respect His holy name, prescribes in the Third Commandment the time when we are to worship Him in a particular way. In the Old Law this particular day was Saturday, the seventh day of the week. God wished thereby to remind man that He "rested" on that day after employing six days, as it were (six periods), in creating the universe. And He blessed the seventh day and sanctified it, made it holy (Gn. 2:3). Man, condemned to labor "by the sweat of his brow," needs a rest from his work; also since labor generally distracts his mind from God and draws it to earthly things, God set apart this one day of the week to be especially consecrated to Him — so that man not forget his Creator.

In the New Law the Church, guided by the Holy Spirit and through the power given her by Christ, changed the time of obligation from Saturday (the sabbath) to Sunday. The Apostles themselves were likely the ones to inaugurate this change (cf. Acts 20:7, Col. 2:16), probably at first sanctifying Sunday in addition to Saturday, then by keeping Sunday alone. At any rate, the change had taken place very early in the Church, for the Fathers of the first centuries not infrequently mention the faithful assembled at the Eucharistic Sacrifice and to hear the word of God on the first day of the week.

The Church rightly gives great value to Sunday as the day of common, public worship, celebrating the accomplishment of our faith's principal mysteries. It was on Sunday that the resurrection of Christ occurred, the greatest proof of His divinity and His victory over sin and death; it was on Sunday that the Holy Spirit came down upon the Apostles, communicating the perfection of grace to man.

Two things are necessary for the sanctification of Sunday and holydays of obligation: participation in the Eucharistic Sacrifice and the observance of Sunday rest, that is, abstention from all servile work. The obligation is a serious one.

In the United States there are six such holydays of obligation: Christmas

(December 25), the Circumcision (January 1), the Ascension (forty days after Easter), the Assumption of the Blessed Virgin (August 15), the feast of All Saints (November 1), and the Immaculate Conception (December 8). In Canada only those holydays oblige which are also legal holidays: that is, Christmas (December 25) and the Circumcision (January 1).

Holydays are to be observed by all who are in the particular countries or territories, even though they may only be traveling or visiting there; thus, if a Canadian happens to be visiting in the United States on August 15, he is obliged to hear Mass that day. On the other hand, if an American is visiting Canada on that day, he is not obliged.

In many dioceses of the United States and Canada the obligation of Sunday Mass (and holydays of obligation) may be fulfilled on the previous evening. Since this is not a uniform practice in North America, one must find out for himself whether it applies in the given diocese where one is weekending or visiting.

EXAMPLE:

Mr. and Mrs. Good of Windsor, Ontario, are weekending in Elmira, Michigan (Gaylord diocese) where Saturday evening Mass satisfies the Sunday obligation. They attend Saturday evening Mass at St. Thomas Church there. Next day, Sunday, they spend skiing at Boyne Mountain without attending Mass.
They fulfilled their obligation of Sunday Mass.

The obligation to hear Mass binds all Catholics who have completed the age of seven years and who possess the habitual use of reason. In other words, children who have not attained the use of reason even at the age of ten are exempt from this law; so is a child who has attained it before seven. The mentally deficient of any age who have not attained the use of reason, are also exempt.

EXAMPLE:

Jane, a frail but precocious child of five, definitely equals the reasoning powers of a child of ten. One day a neighbor tells Jane's mother that Jane, since she possesses the use of reason, has the obligation of attending Mass every Sunday. Jane's mother, an educated Catholic, tells her less enlightened neighbor that Jane is not yet bound by this law of the Church. She is correct.

THE SUNDAY MASS OBLIGATION

We know that it is difficult for adults to appreciate the Eucharistic Sacrifice if all we hear about Mass is: "You'd better go or else!" "Deliberately missing Mass on Sunday is a mortal sin," or "You run the risk of hell, if you deliberately miss." Centuries of this type of moral theology and the true meaning of the Eucharistic celebration has slid into the shadows. Mass, for hundreds of years before Vatican II, had become a sort of big secret between the priest and God. And with it some of the true meaning of Sunday has gone too.

True, this method has accomplished something: it has kept many people dutifully plodding into the churches on Sunday ("They go just because they fear hell"); and this cannot be minimized, but it has turned some away too. For others it has turned the joy and love of praising God into a gladless fulfillment of "their obligation." Even with the meaningful liturgical reforms of recent years, the mental outlook has not changed much among the masses of faithful.

The obligation is there. It always was. But not the reasons behind the obligation. The obligation to be present at Sunday Mass which appears so formalistic and mechanical to us now was something that was burned into the Christian conscience in the centuries between Nero and Diocletian, during the period of the Roman persecutions. There was no Church law, nor is there now, which said that Christians had to attend Sunday Mass in face of torture and death! It was not the precept of "Sunday Mass or else" which explains why men, women and children willingly ran the risk of arrest, imprisonment and death every week of their lives to be at the Eucharistic Sacrifice. They did it because they appreciated what the Eucharistic Sacrifice was and what their part in it was; and because they were convinced of the absolute necessity to take their own part in the self-oblation of Christ, a necessity which to them was even more binding than the instinct of self-preservation. This conviction was based on the whole doctrine of redemption and on the last command of Jesus to His own Apostles at the Last Supper. It was based on the will of Christ who intends by His sacrificial-atoning death to draw all men unto Himself and in a most special way the members of His body, the Church.

They appreciated how the Eucharistic celebration was the very heart of the Church's life and they willingly faced hatred, calumny, slander and the hor-rifying threats of torture and death to take their part in it. As members of Christ's body, the Church, each was convinced he had to take his own part in the fulfillment of the will of God who in an unbloody way offered Himself anew every Sunday for the redemption of mankind. To affirm one's belief without proving it every week by cautiously treading one's way through the empty streets in the predawn to the corporate act of worship, the Eucharist, was merely empty talk, pointless and fruitless. If one were a Christian, one sim-ply took such risks in spite of the constant threat to freedom, to life for himself and his family. And they died by the thousands.

The Eucharistic Sacrifice is the greatest act of divine love that mankind has been privileged to witness, an act uniquely divine, which mortal mind can never adequately grasp because the boundless love prompting it can never be understood completely. Mortal genius could not even imagine the fact before it happened. But the early Christians understood this better than we do, just as they understood better the mysterious, intimate union of God with His people in forming one mystical body. And they better appreciated than we the need of that whole body, and each of its parts, to participate each in his own way, in the self-oblation of Christ. This, and their reciprocating love for God were the compelling force, not mere bare precept, behind their braving life and limb to take part in the Sunday Eucharistic Sacrifice. Nothing else can explain it; noth-ing else will explain it.

Still, the People of God have never entirely lost this sense of compelling urgency though it had become blurred and clouded through centuries of rig-oristic legalism. They have, after all, offered the Eucharistic Sacrifice, without precept, in every conceivable human circumstance, for every conceivable human need, from birth to death and after it — at great events and small, in sickness and in health, in sorrow and in joy, in famine and in opulence. Be-sides, the holy common People of God by the tens of thousands have partici-pated in the weekday Sacrifice, day by day and month by month through the successive centuries, faithfully, unfailingly, across all the parishes of Christen-dom. Why have they done this? Because they loved God and felt the urgency to take part, prompted by that love.

For those who truly love God there is literally no need of a precept oblig-ing them to Sunday Mass. They would keep on coming and taking their part in the self-oblation of Christ regardless. In truth they possess the gladsome free-dom of the children of God. But the weaker brethren who have to be "forced," compelled by precept, will remain slaves. For them and for the scrupulous, though perhaps in a lesser degree, we must delineate the gravity of the obliga-tion and speak of certain conditions which must be fulfilled: (1) *proper inten-tion;* (2) *bodily or corporal presence;* (3) attendance at a *whole or complete Mass;* (4) *sufficient attention.*

HOW THE MASS OF OBLIGATION MUST BE HEARD

1. By *proper intention* here is meant the intention of hearing Mass; the in-tention of fulfilling one's Sunday obligation is not necessary. Therefore, when-ever anyone, forgetting what day it is, hears a Mass purely out of devotion on a holyday (or Sunday), and then later remembers that it is a holyday (or Sun-day), he is not obliged to attend another Mass. Moreover, the intention of hearing Mass need not be made explicitly; as long as a person goes to church for Mass as do other Catholics, he has this intention.

2. By *bodily or corporal presence* is meant being physically there so as to be reckoned among the attendants at the divine service and so as to be able to follow the Mass at least in its principal parts. Hence a person satisfies his Sun-day obligation by being actually inside the church, even though because of overcrowding or some other reason he cannot see the priest; the same is true of one who is in the sacristy (even with the door closed), provided he can follow in general what is going on at the altar (for example, by the singing, the responses, or even by the rising and kneeling of the congregation). But what of one out-side the church? He is considered bodily present if he can reasonably be regard-ed as part of the congregation, say, within fifty yards. Such would be the case of one in a group extended outside a crowded church, or even in a house quite near the church, if he can see the priest or servers at the altar.

The Sunday Mass obligation cannot be satisfied by hearing Mass over the radio or television (we would not be bodily present at such a Mass); however, it is an act of worship on the part of those listening or viewing, if they reverently follow such a Mass via the radio or TV and unite their minds and hearts with it.

3. *Attendance at a whole or complete Mass.* Naturally, to fulfill the obliga-

tion of Sunday Mass (whenever we say "Sunday Mass" we also mean that of the holydays of obligation), we must attend a *complete* Mass and not just a part of one. This means we must be present from the beginning of Mass to the end. Missing a notable part (on account of either the amount or dignity) of a Mass of obligation voluntarily and without sufficient reason does not satisfy the obligation. (To cite the older moralists, here are some examples: missing everything preceding the Gospel together with what follows the Communion of the priest; missing everything from the end of the Preface to the beginning of the Consecration; finally, missing everything between the Consecration and the Lord's Prayer. Anyone missing the Consecration does not fulfill the obligation; however, if one is present at all the other parts except, for a necessary reason, the Consecration, it may be presumed that the Church would not oblige him to attend another Mass. To miss less than the above-mentioned parts voluntarily would constitute slight matter and therefore would be venially sinful. If a person misses an important part of the Mass [the omission of which would cause his obligation not to be fulfilled] he must make up for it by attending, in another Mass, the portion missed. We must, however, always be present at the Consecration and Communion of the same Mass.)

4. *Sufficient Attention.* Also, to fulfill our obligation of Sunday Mass, we must have at least that degree of attention which would make us aware of the progress of the Mass in its principal parts, as well as abstaining from any actions which of their nature are incompatible with this attention. Such incompatible, irreverent actions are deep and sound sleep (not just nodding occasionally), writing, reading a novel or newspaper and other similar actions. If we engage in such actions during a notable part of the Mass, we do not satisfy our obligation of attending Mass.

What if one yields and yields fully to willful distractions during the whole Mass? Must he attend another Mass? No, he is not obliged to hear another Mass; for he has, strictly speaking, fulfilled his Mass obligation, though he is guilty of venial sin on the score of willful distractions.

The following actions are compatible with sufficient attention and so may be done during Mass: playing the organ, singing in the choir, acting as usher, taking up the collection, and going to confession (though not an ideal time for confessing).

MUST WE GO TO THE MASS OF OUR OWN RITE?

We fulfill our Mass obligation if we attend Mass celebrated in any Rite of the Catholic Church; thus, if on some Sunday a person of the Latin Rite wishes to go to a Melkite or Ukrainian Catholic Church, where Mass is celebrated in the Byzantine Rite, he may do so. In fact, all of us should occasionally attend the Eucharistic Liturgy in the various other Rites — to become acquainted with the real catholicity and universality of the Church. We do not need any kind of permission to receive Communion at Masses celebrated according to Rites other than our own. In most of the Eastern-Rite churches the faithful receive Holy Communion under both species (under the forms of bread and wine). The bread used is leavened.

We may fulfill our Sunday Mass obligation by attending Mass celebrated in the open air. We may do so also in any Catholic public or semipublic oratory, in the chapels of hospitals, colleges, prisons, religious communities, seminaries, etc.

REASONS WHICH MAY EXCUSE FROM SUNDAY MASS

According to the mind of the Church, any moderately grave reason or inconvenience can and does excuse one from the obligation of attending Sunday Mass. Thus, anything causing considerable hardship or harm either to oneself or to another is sufficient to excuse. The following are therefore considered excused (hence, no permission is needed from the pastor) because of the moderately grave inconvenience involved:

1. The sick or convalescents; those who have to remain at home to care for the sick, for children, etc.; pregnant women (in the first or last months of pregnancy) who cannot endure the air in the church; rescue workers in time of fire or flood.

2. Women or children who would incur the grave displeasure of their husbands or parents by attending Mass.

3. Those who would be obliged to travel for more than an hour, one way, to church. Also those who would have to walk for that length of time; a somewhat less distant walk would excuse one in inclement weather or on account of personal frailty. If travel distance would constitute a moderately grave inconvenience because of the expense incurred in taking the car, trolley, bus, or train to Sunday Mass.

4. People hindered by the duties of their state; for example, watchmen, cooks, policemen on duty, firemen, and so forth.

5. Workingmen who would deprive themselves of reasonably necessary sleep if they went to Mass. Also those who cannot give up their work without relatively grave loss.

6. Unmarried women who are pregnant may also remain at home if by doing so they can avoid disgrace.

7. Those lacking decent clothing to whom attendance at Mass would necessarily be associated with great embarrassment.

A person cannot excuse himself from Sunday Mass on the score that he has committed one or many grave sins; such a person is still bound by the obligation of Sunday Mass.

EXAMPLES:

1. *Mr. and Mrs. Jones have three small children. Because only one Mass is celebrated in their parish church (the only church within a twenty-mile radius), either Mr. Jones or Mrs. Jones always has to stay home to care for the children. Hence each has to miss Mass every other Sunday.*

That is an entirely sinless arrangement. However, if there were two Masses celebrated in their church on Sundays, then each should attend one of these Masses.

2. The Garcias, a Mexican family of migratory workers, do not attend Mass on Sundays while "on the road" because they would be too embarrassed to go in the poor clothes they have with them. They are justified.

3. Mr. Neverlate arrives at the last Mass on Sunday just before the Consecration. He could not get his car started; otherwise, he would not have been late.

Is he guilty of sin? No.

MISSING MASS ON ACCOUNT OF TRIPS

A person may miss Mass once or twice for the sake of necessary recreation, such as a pleasure trip if he has no other opportunity during the year, or if it is the last opportunity he will ever have for a certain outing; in these cases, the motive for going on the trip should never be just to escape the obligation of going to Mass.

One may, for some good reason and not just to evade the obligation, set out on a trip, say, on Saturday afternoon, even though he realizes very well that he will be miles away from a Catholic church on Sunday. Thus, if I want to pay a weekend visit to relatives living in some churchless section of the state, I would be justified because of my valid reason.

EXAMPLE:

Ted is out camping for two weeks with several of his non-Catholic friends. He misses Mass on the two Sundays when they are out in the woods, because it would take him a good hour and a half to walk to the nearest church and he has no car. He did not sin.

Sometimes a person doubts whether his reasons are sufficient enough to warrant exemption from the obligation of Sunday Mass; in cases of doubt, one should seek a dispensation from the pastor. Hence anyone who wishes to absent himself from Sunday Mass for some reason he feels may not be grave enough of itself to excuse from this obligation, may ask for a dispensation from his pastor. Every pastor has the power of granting this dispensation in individual cases for just cause. In our era of telephones, it is generally not difficult to get in touch with the pastor at short notice and ask for the dispensation in doubtful circumstances. If possible, ask rather than stay away from Mass with a troubled conscience.

SERVILE WORK FORBIDDEN ON SUNDAY

In the sanctification of Sunday, emphasis must always be placed on the matter of worship, not on the "rest" or abstention from servile work. Startling as it may seem the early Church did not forbid certain kinds of servile work on Sunday. If we can sum up its attitude, it was something like this: the faithful must keep themselves free on Sunday to listen to the word of God, to participate in the Eucharistic Liturgy and to pray. Only later, in times of decadent theology, did preachers begin to teach the casuistry and rigid legalism of servile work and in a sense reverted to the very distorted rigidity that the Lord condemned in the Pharisees. In turn, the true meaning of Sunday began the long slide into gloom. In a sense this distorted meaning of Sunday and its rigidity is still with us. We mention all this merely to make one point: that we are entitled to interpret the Church's law on servile work in a broad light, that is, a person may give himself the benefit of a doubt whether some action constitutes servile work or not. "The sabbath was made for man, not man for the sabbath" (Mk. 2:27).

To begin with, perhaps it would be best to state exactly what the Church's law is on the matter (to which we are still bound): on holydays of obligation and Sundays one "must abstain from servile work and from judicial proceedings . . . from public markets, fairs, and other public buying and selling" (Canon 1248). The law is clear but, since it does not define the meaning of the various terms, its application is baffling, even to experts — so don't feel bad if you can't decide whether you can throw those dirty sweatshirts into the automatic washer, or if it's all right to run to the drugstore to pick up that bottle of after-shave, or phone Sears' bargain basement and order that cute little hat!

At any rate, we shall try our best to unravel some of the confusion with tried and traditional efforts and trust your forgiveness if we may sound like some ecclesiastical Perry Mason.

By servile work is meant (as the terms *servile, servant* or *slave* suggest) that work which people who can afford it usually have done by hired help; in other words, that work which requires principally bodily rather than mental activity. We cannot always look at the nature of the work itself; in all cases we must also take into consideration common opinion regarding it — how people generally look upon it. We should remember, however, that servile work is servile work even though we do it for someone else *gratis,* or even for recreation.

Some examples of normally unnecessary servile work (and therefore forbidden on Sundays) are: plowing, digging, sowing, harvesting, cutting logs, loading trucks, building, heavy laundering, tailoring, plastering, ironing, whitewashing, painting (not the artistic type), work in factories, mines, etc.

The obligation of abstaining from unnecessary servile work is grave. Reliable theologians hold that unnecessarily doing heavy work (such as digging, loading trucks manually, etc.) for more than two and a half hours, or light servile work (such as painting a fence, etc.) for about three hours is a serious violation of the Church's law; also there is no difference whether the work is done all at one time or for shorter intervals adding up to the above amounts on any given Sunday. Doing such work for lesser periods is not a serious violation.

WHAT IS PERMITTED ON SUNDAY?

1. The recreations of walking, riding, driving, rowing, even though these be very fatiguing.

2. Liberal and artistic works, such as studying, teaching, drawing, architectural designing, painting pictures, playing music, delicate sculpturing, em-

broidering, crocheting, taking photographs, typing and writing. These works are lawful even if they are done for remuneration.

3. Necessary housework such as cooking, washing dishes, making beds and sweeping. But not canning, ironing, etc.

4. Naturally, one may wash himself, take a bath, brush his clothes, shine his shoes, etc.

5. To do light home sewing or mending, to clean or oil a bicycle and other brief tasks. Even though these be totally unnecessary, they are lawful because of their insignificance.

6. To "putter around" the garden or lawn; watering the grass or trimming plants is also permitted. These, however, could be servile, if they entail much work.

7. It is perfectly all right to play games such as football, baseball, golf, tennis, basketball, hockey, etc., for recreation; this also holds true for fishing and hunting.

Perhaps the following considerations may also be helpful: Does the work impede the sanctification of Sunday? Is the labor performed for unnecessary gain? Even when not done for gain, is it commonly considered not exercise or recreation but manual labor? If the answer to any of these is affirmative, then the work should be considered servile. Of course, in doubt, the easiest solution would be to phone the pastor and get a dispensation, if he can be reached.

WHAT EXCUSES FROM SUNDAY REST?

Necessity always excuses one from the prohibition of servile labor; that is, if considerable harm or loss would otherwise result either to oneself or to another. Also if anyone would be seriously inconvenienced because of not doing some certain work on a Sunday or holyday of obligation, he would be excused from the prohibition of servile work. Thus, if there is no time or opportunity for mending clothes on weekdays, one may do so on Sundays. For the same reason, working people may tend their little gardens on Sunday. If a storm is threatening, farmers may gather fruit, harvest their grain, hay, etc. Mechanics may sharpen and repair the tools which farmers and others need on Monday. If, let us say, a salesman has little spare time during the week and his automobile has to be in a good condition for business trips, he may repair it on Sunday. Of course, any necessary work is allowed in case of fire, flood, etc. We may perform works of charity for those in need — works such as taking care of the sick, burying the dead, sewing for persons in dire need.

Necessity and public utility also excuse: hence the following are permitted to work on Sundays — policemen, firemen, soldiers, switchboard operators, railroad employees, druggists, chauffeurs, cooks, butlers, newspaper boys, those who work in restaurants, gas stations and the like.

EXAMPLES:

1. After hearing a forecast of heavy rains, Farmer Jones and his family work feverishly all Sunday afternoon to harvest the last of their oats. They are completely justified, for there is an obvious necessity here, not just an excuse.

2. Lois and Anne are waitresses at the new Nibble Inn in the suburbs of Boyne City. Either one or the other has to work there on Sundays. Lois volunteers to take over every Sunday and thus give Anne, who is married, a chance to be at home with her family. Lois commits no sin in working every Sunday because the reason of public utility is sufficient to excuse her; furthermore, she performs an act of charity in volunteering to work on those Sundays when it would be Anne's turn to work.

For any good reason, we may ask for a dispensation from our pastor to do servile work on Sunday or a holyday. Hence, if anyone feels uneasy or doubtful whether he has a grave enough reason to be excused from the prohibition of Sunday labor, he should seek a dispensation.

EXAMPLES:

1. Jim, an apprentice printer, is given permission to use the office equipment on Sunday, the only time the machines are not in use, to set in type and print a short history of the armored division to which he belonged in Vietnam. He knows that printing is servile work and that this work will take about ten hours. He asks his pastor for a dispensation and receives permission to do the work.

2. June and Alice want to give a surprise birthday party Sunday evening for their younger sister. In order that it may be a memorable occasion, they would like the whole house decorated. But conscientious Alice gets doubts about the "servile work" involved in the extensive decorating. They can't possibly put them up Saturday night, for then it wouldn't be much of a surprise. What should they do? Phone their pastor for a dispensation!

Judicial proceedings are forbidden on Sundays, that is, the business of a courtroom ordinarily done on weekdays. Such proceedings would be: passing judgment, acting as witness, pleading cases, summoning the defendant or witness, requiring the oath, carrying out the sentence and the like.

Consulting a lawyer on Sunday is not forbidden. Nor are judges or lawyers prohibited from doing legal work privately, such as holding private consultations, getting their cases ready for trials by preparing briefs, etc.

CIVIL OR COMMERCIAL OCCUPATIONS

Civil occupations such as marketing, public buying and selling, public auctions, fairs, trading, or shopping in stores are also forbidden on Sundays and holydays of obligation. Some of these activities, however, are justified by local custom — for example, the "market days" in Central and South America; the buying and selling of necessary groceries in some regions during certain hours. Private persons are not forbidden to confer or to agree on the purchase or sale of cattle, houses, lands, etc., on Sundays or holydays.

Chapter XII

THE FOURTH COMMANDMENT

"Honor your father and your mother so that you may have a long life in the land that Yahweh your God has given to you" (Ex. 20:12).

Not unreasonably those who cooperate in bringing other persons into existence at least to a certain degree represent God to their offspring. By God's authority and in His name, they have given the very highest of gifts, the gift of life, to these new beings. Eve, the first mother, acknowledged this when Cain, her first child, was born. She said: "I have acquired a man with the help of Yahweh" (Gn. 4:1). Related to the duties of children toward their parents are the obligation that children have toward anyone participating in parental authority in any way.

The Fourth Commandment is also concerned with the obligations of parents toward their children, and superiors toward their subjects. This is as reasonable as it is clear from the natural law, which dictates that those bringing offspring into the world should help this new life reach maturity. To expect parents to take proper care of their children until these are ready to leave the family hearth is as natural as expecting birds and animals to feed and protect their young.

THE DUTIES OF CHILDREN

The duty of honoring parents, as imposed by the Fourth Commandment, implies three things which children must do: (I) love, (II) reverence, and (III) obey their parents.

I. The Love Owed to Parents

Certainly parents are entitled to love from their children. From the moment of their child's birth they lavish on it loving and anxious care. Then follow the years of heroic effort, work, sleepless nights, worry and unending solicitude for the child's spiritual and material upbringing, much of which entails great personal sacrifices for the parents. These considerations aside, the Fourth Commandment should prompt children to love their parents — with internal love as well as with external affection, a duty lasting until their parents' eyes are closed in death.

It is easy to return love for love and happy, indeed, the child brought up in tenderness and love. But the child who has felt unwanted, uncared for, and unloved will find it difficult to truly love his parents. Even so, such children must try, they really must, to love their parents; God would not have it otherwise. For such only supernatural motivation will be perhaps the only thing that will move them to awaken or keep alive a strong love for their parents. Fortunately, God provides that.

In giving the Decalogue, God told us, "I show kindness to thousands of those who love me and keep my commandments." But in giving the Fourth Commandment, He attached an additional reward, the only Commandment to which He did, as if to make it easier to observe it in difficult circumstances: when God said, "Honor your father and your mother," He added, "so that you may have a long life in the land that Yahweh your God has given to you" (Ex. 20:12). He repeats this promise in Sirach (3:6): "Long life comes to him who honors his father." Or, as St. Paul puts it to the Ephesians (6:1-3): "Children, be obedient to your parents in the Lord — that is your duty. The first commandment that has a promise attached to it is: *Honor your father and mother,* and the promise is: *and you will prosper and have a long life in the land.*" Words well worth mulling over.

That's not all. In Sirach (3:3-6), God holds out more for those who honor their parents: "Whoever respects his father is atoning for his sins, he who honors his mother is like someone amassing a fortune. Whoever respects his father will be happy with children of his own, he shall be heard on the day when he prays." That's God's promise to those honoring their parents: atonement for sins, happiness with one's own children and the assurance of being heard when praying! Promises worth thinking about!

Decisive proof of filial love, like any other love, is shown by deeds, great and small. Interior love will show itself through words of understanding, through acts of kindness and affection, little gifts on special occasions, doing favors gladly, making them happy at family celebrations, trying to be with them in times of sorrow, writing to them faithfully when far away. Most of all, however, our love must be proved in helping them in emergencies and in their old age. Here is what God says about it: "My son, support your father in his old age, do not grieve him during his life. Even if his mind should fail, show him sympathy, do not despise him in your health and strength; for kindness to a father shall not be forgotten but will serve as reparation for your sins. In the days of your affliction it will be remembered of you, like frost in sunshine, your sins will melt away" (Sir. 3:12-15).

On the other hand, for those who fail to live up to their duty of filial love, God has these words: "The man who deserts his father is no better than a blasphemer, and whoever angers his mother is accursed of the Lord" (Sir. 3:16-18).

To really hate one's parents or to wish them serious evil is a matter for grave sin. Sometimes a child, in a burst of anger, will say he hates his parents; generally the child does not really mean it and says it without reflection. In this as well as in all other serious matters, we must first look to the deliberation (remember, grave guilt is incurred only with sufficient reflection and full consent besides serious matter).

Keeping this in mind, adult sons and daughters sin seriously against love due to parents:

(1) If they refuse to help their parents when they need food, clothing, shelter, etc., especially in their old age. Unjustly withholding grave amounts of their pensions, social security payments, or other sources of sustenance is a serious violation not only of charity but also against justice.

(2) If they fail to call a priest for them when they are in danger of death. This includes the false sense of kindness in deceiving them about their critical condition (danger of death). After all, they are responsible that their parents are not prepared for death and may die without the last sacraments.

(3) If they speak ill of them or if they directly insult them by scolding, etc. Refusal to speak to parents, or even to greet them, never visiting them, rarely or never writing to them, can also be grave sins if one knows that such conduct grievously pains them.

(4) If they unjustly cause them serious sorrow, hatred and worry.

(5) If they stir up serious quarrels and enmity over the just provisions of the last will and testament, and this even after the death of their parents. Concern over their decent burial is also a serious duty of every child.

II. The Reverence Due to Parents

We must reverence our parents in our hearts as well as in our external conduct and words. The obligation holds good even if the parents are objects of public disgrace or are leading openly sinful lives; even in such cases they are still the parents and so their children must regard them as such.

There is matter for grave sin against filial reverence by unjustly striking, threatening, contemning, disdaining, despising, insulting or ridiculing one's parents by word or deed; also by being ashamed of them or by refusing to recognize them in public because of their humble state, poor clothes, lack of culture or education, etc. There is no question of sin, however, where this shame is completely spontaneous on the part of the children and does not involve the will. If offspring, despite this spontaneous feeling of shame for their parents, act in the same way they would act if there were no shame, their conduct is blameless.

It is not sinful to try restraining one's parents, even by physical force (but there must be no internal contempt), for some good reason — when they lose the use of their reason from insanity, old age or intoxication. Similarly, a person who has the obligation of supporting parents in need may have good reason for not wanting them near (e.g., because of some crime they have committed).

III. Obedience Due to Parents

Children, as long as they are under parental authority, must obey their parents in all that is not sinful. Naturally, the parents have a right to exact this obedience from their progeny, since they are held responsible for them before God.

As long as the child lives under the authority of the parents he must obey their legitimate commands. The obligation ends when the child either ceases to be a minor (civil law usually regards the person's minority as ending on his twenty-first birthday), or when he gets married, enters religious life, or otherwise legitimately takes an independent place in the world. But even if a person is over twenty-one and still resides with his parents in their home, he must obey them in everything pertaining to domestic order and discipline. Hence, if such a person is told by his father or mother that on date nights he must be home by twelve o'clock, he must obey.

We know, parents do not understand. They probably thought the same way about their parents too. But if truth be told, the young people probably understand their parents even less. One thing is certain, though, without the young person's willingness to sit down and talk over the differences with his parents, without curbing his tendency towards snap judgments about parental motivation dealing with him, and without driving away resentful thoughts about his parents, there is no hope of bettering one's relationship with parents or of avoiding many family quarrels. Parents generally are surprisingly reasonable. Try it.

Parents, however, may not command anything that is obviously sinful. If they do so, the children have no obligation to obey in this matter. In fact, they have an obligation *not* to obey in such a case; for example, if Steve's father tells him to steal a tire from a gas station, Steve must not obey his father's command. In cases where parents command their children to do something forbidden merely by certain laws of the Church, the children may obey with a clear conscience (in these instances, the given Church law would cease to bind because its observance would entail a moderately grave inconvenience; whether or not the parent is justified does not enter into the morality of the child's act). Thus if a father tells his seventeen-year-old son to dig a ditch for a sewer on Sunday (unnecessary servile work), the son may do so.

SINFULNESS OF DISOBEDIENCE

In matters of great importance parents have the right to command their children under pain of mortal or venial sin according to the gravity of the matter. The sinfulness of disobedience will then be grievous or slight, accordingly. We may add that perhaps most commands (even regarding serious matters) oblige only under pain of venial sin. Parents may also choose not to bind under any sin at all. If the parents merely give a counsel, or make a request without any intention of asserting their parental authority (i.e., without binding under pain of sin), the children do not sin by not responding, just so they maintain an attitude of fitting respect for their parents; for example, if mother tells her fifteen-year-old son, Johnny, to use a fork instead of a spoon with which to eat the dessert, Johnny will not sin if he still prefers to eat with a spoon.

If, in matters of grave importance, a mother or father gives an order very seriously and earnestly, it is presumed that the parent wishes to command under pain of serious sin. Thus, if Joseph's father strictly forbids him to "chum" around with a certain group of disreputable men because of the great spiritual danger involved, Joseph is bound under pain of grievous sin to obey that prohibition. In such instances the parents do not have to intend explicitly to bind under pain of sin or even to demand obedience explicitly; the right to obedience was given to them by God and the extent of the binding force upon the child is determined by how much the parents want to be obeyed.

In educational matters the obligation of obedience lasts until the child becomes of age; minors may not, therefore, undertake certain work or enlist in any branch of the armed forces against the will of their parents. Though little realized, perhaps, but children can sin gravely if they are grossly careless and neglectful of their own academic and vocational formation, thereby causing their parents great anxiety, worry and waste of money.

CHOICE OF VOCATION

In the choice of vocation children do not have to obey their parents; in this they are entirely free. Parents do not have the right to oblige their children to adopt a particular state of life. Naturally children should consult their parents about a matter of such lifelong importance. Parents have practical experience and no amount of sophistication can beat that. Their advice should never be lightly disregarded. Still, if the children have some grave reason for not letting their parents know about their choice, they may get married or enter religious life with a clear conscience. In such cases, however, prudence would direct them to consult their confessor or some other qualified counselor.

If the children do not follow the sensible advice of their parents in regard to marriage, they would generally commit venial sin.

OBEDIENCE TO OLDER BROTHERS AND SISTERS

The authority which older children have over the younger ones in the temporary absence of the parents is usually understood to pertain to peace, safety and good order within the family circle.

EXAMPLES:

1. Mr. and Mrs. Ellis are going out for the afternoon; they tell their eldest daughter, May, who is twelve, that she has authority over Tony and Grace, her brother and sister (aged nine and ten), in all things pertaining to their safety and proper conduct. They likewise admonish the younger children to obey their sister.

The younger children go out to play. A short while later, May checks on them and finds Tony and Grace playing in the street. Knowing this is a dangerous place for small children, she commands them to get off the street. They refuse, even when May reminds them that their parents intended her to have such authority over them.

There is at least matter for venial sin here on part of the two younger children.

2. Billy, left in charge of his younger brother Benny, demands that Benny stand in a corner and salute him twenty times. He tells him it's a sin not to obey.

Benny, being intelligent and well-instructed, tells his brother that this type of command has nothing to do with the obedience his parents expect of him. He refuses to obey.

There is no sin here, of course, in Benny's refusal to obey the unreasonable command. But there is on the part of Billy an abuse of authority. No wonder a child, in his evening prayers, can come out with: "Dear God, I wish you could please get my brother to stop driving me crazy. Your friend, Benny, age 5½!"

THE PARENTS' DUTIES

A fundamental duty of parents toward their children is love and affection. Every heart craves love and affection, but the tender hearts of young children especially yearn to be loved. Concerning this special need of children for love, modern psychology and psychiatry have only reiterated in more sophisticated terms what the Church has taught for nineteen centuries. If the parents have this love — most parents do, since this is a natural instinct — they will tend to maintain a reasonable control over their children; they will be neither too indulgent by giving in to every whim, nor will they be too strict, too excessively domineering. Parents offend against this obligation of love if they show favoritism to one or the other child above the rest. Young hearts are particularly sensitive in detecting favoritism.

PARENTS MUST SUPPLY CHILDREN'S NEEDS

Parents must take care to provide for the physical well-being of their children; that is, they must provide them with the proper food, clothing, education and other necessities for the health of both mind and body. The obligation begins even before birth; they must avoid anything that is injurious to the unborn child, anything which might impair the development of the life in the mother's womb. If parents cannot provide, despite their best efforts, the necessities (clothing, food, shelter and health) for their minor children, they must dismiss all false sense of pride and honor and ask for help from others; they must seek it before the children suffer an irreparable loss — this includes going to the social welfare agencies. The obligation to provide food, clothing and housing will last until the child is old enough to take care of himself.

Parents also have the very serious obligation of seeing to it that their children receive every help they need for saving their souls. This includes having the child baptized without delay after birth, making provisions for his reception of the sacraments of Penance, Holy Eucharist and Confirmation at the proper times. Another obligation parents have is to provide for the religious instruction of their children, for, "Anyone who does not look after his own relations, especially if they are living with him, has rejected the faith and is worse than an unbeliever" (1 Tm. 5:8). Parents must also keep a watchful eye on the habits of their children, correcting the bad and encouraging the good; they must take care that their children are kept away from bad companions, immoral magazines and books, and evil amusement places. To do this effectively, they must take time to know their children's friends and places of entertainment. In a word, they must take care that their children live up to their true faith in all that they do.

All this presupposes the good example of the parents themselves. Words, bare rules and restrictions will avail nothing without example. Their deeds always outshout their words. Whatever the parents are and stand for serve as the basis for the growing child's value system. Their authority should always be a responsible one, always helping the children to distinguish between right and wrong, between virtue and vice. Their reprimands should be without rancor, without bitterness; otherwise, their children will not grow to responsible maturity. Parents' contradicting one another, or countermanding each other's orders is highly detrimental towards the growth of children's responsible maturity; so is a distorted system of values in which stealing rates the same kind of reprimand that a dented lampshade does. Sociological studies indicate that inconsistency of discipline in the home is an important factor in contributing to the delinquency of children. Difference of opinion between parents should be discussed, calmly and quietly in private.

Parental attitudes can be equally harmful, especially the attitude of "youth needs to be watched constantly" and the treatment of their teen-agers as children, their young men and women as teen-agers. Two harmful reactions are likely: either a slavish obedience to the parents or explosive rebellion. The one robs the child of his unique personality development (the "mama's boy" or daddy's "little girl") rendering him or her inadequate to the challenge of productive living; the other results in the parents' inability to reach their children — sometimes for years.

EDUCATION OF THE CHILD

Parents, in choosing a school, must always realize that an education is worthless, and less than that, if it does not further their child's spiritual interests. They must, if possible, send their children to Catholic schools. Church law (Canon 1374) is clear about the point. Even the natural law itself forbids parents to send their children to schools, including colleges and universities, if these are dangerous to faith or morals.

The consequences of completely secular education are deplorable. At its completion the young Christian is lamentably deficient not only in knowledge of his faith but often also in character training. It takes a good theologian to refute the many false doctrines presented in such subtle ways as only some "liberal" professors know how to employ. What chance has a boy or girl with mere high school training in religion to stand up against a professor of intimidating prestige who teaches that religion is an outgrowth of man's primitive fears, that it is interesting merely as a phase of man's evolution? Or in a class of modern psychology where the professor "disproves" the existence of individual souls and, hence, "proves" the redundancy of salvation? He may claim that Jesus was one of the greatest religious teachers in history but on a level not much higher than Mithras or Mohammed. False views regarding fundamental realities of life such as marriage, social relations and love are clothed in such subtle plausibility by some instructors that the student easily finds himself accepting them as authentic.

Other professors are gentlemanly enough not to attack religion outright, but their summary dismissal of many important religious and moral truths will often lead the student to conclude that religious knowledge has little if any relevance to modern life. Students brought up in Christian homes where both mother and father taught the supreme importance of religion by word and example, find to their amazement at secular universities that the things they were taught back home do not matter here. If one goes to church, fine. If not, fine, too. It doesn't matter either way. Religion? Interesting as a phase in the development of the human race perhaps, but not as a way of life. Theology is all right but not worth the time for any serious study. After all, what great scholars of today bother to study theology?

In the end, if argument from minds rated as top-notch in the country's esteem does not lead the Christian from practicing his faith, then the atmosphere — created by treating both religion and Christ as unimportant — too often will.

All this, of course, does not mean that all who go to secular universities will lose their faith. Many do not; in fact, many become more strongly faithful to God and Church. Because others are inimical to religion and God, they are aggressively on God's side, they give the fullest loyalty to the Newman Club or to some other good organization on their totally secular campus. They show doggedness in studying their own faith and its practices. Such, fortunately, do exist on the secular campuses — and may explain the fact that some of the greatest Catholic leaders, clerical and lay, have come from secular universities. But, unfortunately, they are the exception, not the rule in such institutions.

As we have said before, the natural law itself forbids Christians to attend schools, on any level, if these are dangerous to faith or morals. Where the danger is proximate, it is a matter of grave sin.

The principle is clear but, practically speaking, the application of it is difficult and complicated. Which schools and universities (by name) are in such a class? As regards elementary and high schools, it used to be simple: the bishop of one's diocese decided. It was he who determined under what circumstances and with what precautions against the danger of perversion attendance at non-Catholic schools in his diocese was permitted. Usually a given bishop enforced the Church law more rigidly wherever facilities made attendance at Catholic schools possible and not excessively difficult; he applied the law more leniently wherever attendance at Catholic schools was difficult or impossible (generally because of lack of facilities). Today it's no longer that simple.

Of late, some Catholic schools, it seems, have allowed "novel doctrine" to be taught in their religion courses; as a result, many parents are deeply disturbed about the orthodoxy of such teaching, so much so that many parents, in conscience, have taken their children out of such schools. Some of the "novelty" being taught may only be legitimate updating in conformance with Vatican II, but some of it is not, *definitely not,* Catholic doctrine. Circumstances vary in different parts of the country, in different parts of the same city even, from parish to parish, from school to school.

In some places legitimate reform is taking place, quietly and happily for all concerned. In other places there is abuse, with near and outright heresy being taught — prompting one archbishop to warn the Catholic parents of his archdiocese that indeed they have an obligation in conscience to pull their children out of some Catholic schools where error was being taught and their efforts to correct the abuses were in vain! Such abuses regarding moral doctrine in fact, prompted the writing of this book, so that parents may have solid moral guidance to give their children.

The sheer complexity of the problem precludes any blanket solution regarding all Catholic schools. Even bishops, despite their best efforts, cannot prevent some error from seeping into the schools much less into each classroom. What is a parent to do?

We can only reiterate that in those schools where efforts at redress have proven vain, parents (by natural law) have the strict obligation of rendering the danger of perversion remote by sufficient safeguards. This means in some instances, perhaps, proper religious instruction and training in the home will be enough to counteract the errors taught at school. If this is not effective, if all else fails, the only proper safeguard may indeed be to take the child out of that particular Catholic school and transfer him to a secular one. Part of the problem is precisely that the child thinks that everything taught in a Catholic school is legitimate Catholic doctrine, whereas in a secular school *he knows* not everything taught there is correct, not in accord with Catholic teaching. Hence it is much easier to counteract error taught in the latter.

MUTUAL OBLIGATIONS OF HUSBAND AND WIFE

Through St. Paul, God speaks of His own love for His Church, that is, for the People of God redeemed by His own death, to describe the love which ought to be found in married life. It was love that drew the Son of God to sacrifice Himself on Golgotha. This is indeed an incomparable vision of what married life should be: a life of self-sacrificing love. Sacrifice and love are merely two aspects of the same reality: one cannot exist without the other. They are, in fact, the key to a totally wonderful, secure, happy and blissful married life. Much of the happiness or misery, many of the successes or failures, of joys or sorrows in wedded life are directly proportionate to this mutual love and sacrifice.

Sacrifice is difficult but not always unpleasant. Only love can make the difference, only love can make it a joy. What is repellent becomes attracting if done for a person one loves. If charity covers a multitude of sins — and it does — mutual love will also cover a multitude of human failings in a husband and wife; certainly it will pour the soothing balm of compassion and understanding over what could have been many a deadly wound in their marital bliss.

"Give way to one another in obedience to Christ. Wives should regard their husbands as they regard the Lord, since as Christ is head of the Church and saves the whole body, so is a husband the head of his wife; and as the Church submits to Christ, so should wives to their husbands, in everything" (Eph. 5:21-25). The husband is the head of the family; his wife and children are subject to him in everything that has to do with family life and domestic order; hence, his word must be the final decision in all cases of doubt or dispute involving domestic matters.

But marriage does not give him the right to be a despot; his wife is not a servant or slave, but a companion, a spouse. Perhaps this very thing made Paul cry out with the immense intensity of his God-given conviction that husbands ought to love their wives as their own bodies, to love as Christ loves His Church, the members of His Mystical Body. A husband who loves his wife like that will make his important decisions by consulting his wife's opinions, by discussing the issues with her. In any case, he must administer his property wisely so that he will be able to support his wife and children.

The duties of the wife are chiefly those arising from her position as the husband's loving helpmate. She is bound to obey her husband's reasonable commands and she must respect his authority. She would sin if she neglected her domestic duties, or if against her husband's will she spent from the common fund larger sums than those usually spent by women of her social position. The wife may manage the household independently of her husband either by mutual consent or if he takes no interest in household affairs, or if for some other reason he is incapable of doing his duty in this regard. In face of each other's faults, especially irate temper, peace and harmony in the home rest in gentleness and patience, in forebearance and sometimes silence — all of which are rooted in love. The Scriptures give some solid advice to both: "A mild answer turns away wrath, sharp words stir up anger" (Prov. 15:1). Amen!

Salvation will come to the wife, St. Paul says, through her husband for Christ did no less for His Church; he expects that the same salvation will come to her husband through her, his wife. Hence, husband and wife must help each other to observe marital fidelity and grant the marriage right when one of the partners seriously requests it (and provided there is no just cause for refusing it). They have an obligation to live together. Not to do so against the other's wish would be matter for grave sin unless there was an important reason to excuse it. It is permissible for the husband to be absent for a long time, even against the will of his wife, for a very important reason (e.g., the welfare of the community, care of important family affairs, the nature of his job, and the like). If the wife requests that she go with him, he must take her if this can easily be arranged. For short periods of time he may absent himself without a serious reason and even if it be against her will. The wife, however, cannot leave her husband against his will; for he is the head of the family; nevertheless, if grave harm would otherwise threaten her, she may do so.

The choice of residence belongs to the husband, except in the following cases:

1. If he had settled upon a certain place of residence when he and his wife were marrying and no valid reason has since come up to change this agreement.

2. If he should desire to change the place of residence for any purpose or reason that is immoral.

3. If the wife could not follow her husband without serious physical or moral harm.

4. Finally, if the husband has the wanderlust and the wife did not know it before marriage.

The wife may *request* a change of domicile if the present location of the couple is seriously harmful to her either morally or physically.

EXAMPLES:

1. Anne and Ralph get married just before he is inducted into the Army. After his basic training, Ralph is stationed at Fort Knox and is told that he will be there a year at least. He begs Anne to come and live with him near camp, as this can easily be arranged. She refuses on the grounds that she would be very lonely there. Is that excuse enough? No, she would still have a grave obligation to go if he insists, at least in this instance.

If, however, Ralph were to be stationed at Fort Knox for only a few — say four — months, Anne's obligation would not be so great, since there would be a proportionately valid reason (the serious inconvenience of moving for a short period of time) for declining her husband's request.

2. The newly wedded Angie and Angus have a quarrel over her new hat. She storms out of the house and goes to her mother's. Despite her mother's insistence, she refuses to go back to her husband. Finally, after three weeks, she relents and is reunited with her husband. She did a very serious thing (staying away from her husband for three weeks against his will); there is matter here for grave sin on her part.

DUTIES OF EMPLOYERS AND EMPLOYEES TOWARD EACH OTHER

Because both employer and employee have certain rights, it follows that each has certain duties corresponding to the other's rights. Charity in addition to justice should underlie their mutual conduct toward each other.

The employer has the duty of treating his employees as fellow human beings, not as slaves or machines. To fulfill this duty the employer must not merely refrain from abusive language to them — this is important, but paying the employee a living wage and making working conditions safe is much more important. The gravity of sin is in direct proportion to the seriousness of his willful failure to provide such.

Neither may the employer overtax the worker's strength. Since young men and girls are weaker and cannot stand as much strain as other seasoned workers, employers must be particularly careful in this regard when heavy work is to be done. The employer must also regard the spiritual welfare of his employees by giving them sufficient time for attending to their religious duties when these impinge on working time. Moreover, he must do all he can to clear the immediate surroundings of evil influences such as easy access to gambling, narcotics and lewd women.

EXAMPLE:

Mr. Jones, construction foreman of a big mining company, tells one of the workers to ride on top of a precariously balanced load of sulphuric acid. Because there is no union here to protect him and since he needs the job badly, the worker gets on the load despite the grave danger to life and limb. Here the foreman has seriously violated the law of justice and charity toward the worker.

On the other hand, the worker has the obligation of showing his employer due respect in word and action; he may not ridicule him or show contempt for him; he must obey his reasonable commands pertaining to the job; finally, he must do his work conscientiously by neither wasting company time nor inflicting needless damage.

EXAMPLE:

Unlike other shops, the shop where Clem is employed does not have an agreement with the union to give ten minutes off before quitting time for washing up. But Clem and many other workers have been taking ten minutes off for several months now; the foreman simply ignores the fact. Clem wonders now whether he is sinning against justice in doing this.

It would seem that Clem may, without sin, continue to take ten minutes off until he or anyone else is told not to do this by the management; the reason is that if the management seriously wanted the practice discontinued, it would soon put an end to it.

Trade unions generally have done a good job in effecting labor reforms to protect the rights of workingmen. Before the unions were established, employers and management had a great advantage over labor: they were able to use high-pressure methods to achieve their ends and then could afford to hire competent advisers and lawyers to safeguard their dubious practices and outright injustices.

Unions, however, must not forget the obligation to respect the just claims and rights of employers; moreover, they cannot effect or risk anything which would be unjustly prejudicial to the employer or to the general public. Union officials are directly responsible, union members indirectly. The morality of collective union injustices is judged according to the principles outlined regarding the cooperation of public officials in enacting legislation opposed to faith or morals, while the individual union member's responsibility is the same as that of the citizen voting for a party or candidate representing anti-Christian or immoral principles.

CHILDREN'S DUTIES TOWARD PARENTAL REPRESENTATIVES

Those taking the place of parents, whether temporarily or permanently, share the parents' rights to reverence, love and obedience. Such would be the case, for instance, with nurses, governesses, older brothers and sisters and others appointed to care for a growing child. As a general rule, though, absolute authority over the child is not conceded to such persons by the parents, and so they would not be able to impose a precept, command, or prohibition binding the child under pain of serious sin. The same holds true for the child's teachers at school. In a boarding school, however, where the child lives night and day, the head of the school may impose commands or prohibitions under *serious obligation* provided such precepts are deemed necessary for the proper education of the child; the parents are presumed in these circumstances to wish the head of the school to have the necessary authority.

EXAMPLE:

Jerry's teacher, Miss Harpo, who is prone to dismiss the methods of modern pedagogy as so much nonsense, tells him to stand in the corner because he has pulled Louise's hair. Jerry stubbornly refuses to obey. Then she pushes Jerry into the corner, but Jerry defiantly goes back to his desk. Jerry's disobedience was venially sinful.

DUTIES TOWARD ECCLESIASTICAL AUTHORITY

All of us must honor and respect our guides in spiritual matters. For Catholics this means the bishops and priests of the Church. In establishing His Church, Christ gave the apostles the power to teach, to sanctify and to rule its members; furthermore, He empowered them to pass on this authority to their rightful successors: the chief shepherd of the Church, the Pope, and the other bishops. All Catholics *owe obedience* to them, the living line of apostolic succession, for they have the right to define and interpret the natural law and the divine positive law. Proper reverence is also due to priests because they cooperate with the bishops in the care of souls. Christ's words, "Anyone who listens to you listens to me; anyone who rejects you rejects me, and those who reject me reject the one who sent me" (Lk. 10:16), are as truly applicable to His representatives today as they were to the Apostles themselves. This is the Church in its juridical structure.

The other part of the Church is the whole People of God: the Church in its entire membership. Under impetus of the Second Vatican Council more and more lay people appreciate the importance of their role in the Church's mission. Their zeal and activity proves it. Still, not all the People of God have yet understood their rightful role or, worse, labor under a misconception of it. Deterred perhaps by the baneful abuses of some individuals, clerical and lay — purportedly acting under the aegis of Vatican II reforms — they have sickened of everything connected with post-conciliar reforms. But that is all the more reason why they should become better informed of what Vatican II actually proposed. This can be done only by carefully studying the conciliar documents themselves, firsthand. By doing this, responsible lay people will be able to accomplish two great things: (1) they will appreciate their own part in the Church, and (2) they will be able effectively to counter the abuses, the pseudo-reforms or revolts masquerading under Vatican II reforms. We should all be encouraged by the lessons of history: through the centuries, wherever heretical inroads into the Church were stopped effectively, it was the laity that did it!

OBEDIENCE TO OUR HOLY FATHER, THE POPE

The Pope, as the successor of St. Peter and the Vicar of Christ on earth, possesses the primacy of universal jurisdiction in the Church; with this power he has the right as well as the duty to direct the members of the Church, both clergy and laity. Because of his duty to preserve the purity of Catholic doctrine and to clarify doubts endangering faith or morals, God has guaranteed the Pope freedom from error when making solemn pronouncements; that is, when he speaks *ex cathedra* to the universal Church on matters concerning faith (e.g., the dogma of the Assumption), or morals. These *ex cathedra* teachings must be accepted by every Catholic. In them the Pope is using his supreme apostolic authority. This type of pronouncement is extremely rare.

Most of the time the Pope teaches without speaking infallibly, as for example, in his encyclicals; this is called his ordinary teaching authority. Catholics should never dismiss this type of teaching lightly either — in deference to his authority as Pope and head of the Church.

EXAMPLE:

Tony has just read the encyclical Humanae Vitae of Pope Paul VI. He and his wife are discussing the binding power of the teachings in an encyclical. Tony insists that it would not be sinful for Catholics to respectfully disagree with one or the other of the statements in the document; for example, some of the reasoning or argumentation behind certain statements. "Look, Jane, I love and honor the Holy Father but my mind is not convinced of his fear that a man, 'growing used to the employment of anti-conceptive practices, may finally lose respect for the woman . . . and may come to the point of considering her as a mere instrument of selfish enjoyment, and no longer as his respected and beloved companion' (Humanae Vitae, n. 17). To my mind, this is just not so in real life. We know many couples who practiced artificial contraception for a long time and the husband still respects his wife." "But, darling," his wife argues, "a good Catholic would commit a sin of disobedience if he does not accept every statement of an encyclical."

There is no question of disobedience or disrespect for the person of the Holy Father in failing to be convinced by this particular statement. Not every sentence in an encyclical has to be literally accepted. Refusing to accept the main moral issues of this encyclical, or any encyclical, however, is a matter of disobedience. Again, this is not to say that there may not be legitimate shades of interpretation sometimes.

DUTIES OF CITIZENS

Citizens are obliged to love their country and their fellow citizens. In an age of protests and civic revolt many have lost sight of this basic obligation. This means *living in harmony with fellow citizens* and promoting common, humanitarian goals, never by violent protests or, worse, by revolutionary activity. When Christ said, "Render unto Caesar what is Caesar's," He meant just that. Heavens, there were enough social abuses and inequality in His time! And there were enough false Messiahs in His day who were preaching violent overthrow of government and violently advocating social reforms. Where did they end up? Dead, that's where, and they took thousands of people with them. Any chance of successfully accomplishing their purpose went to the grave with them.

Christ died because He wanted to die for us, not because He preached violence. His way, the peaceful way of effecting reforms, succeeded and the world's greatest armies could do nothing for hundreds of years against it.

A citizen cannot prejudice the common good in favor of some particular class or clique. Usually advocators of violence and violent protests are doing just that. A truly Christian citizen shows respect, loyalty and obedience to lawfully constituted civic authority. And never forget it.

This does not mean that Christian citizens should be unconcerned with the problems of community and country; on the contrary, they should always be the "salt of the earth" in social, economic and cultural endeavor on national and local levels. The ever-increasing influence of government on all levels of human life affects everyone, for better or for worse, and demands ever-increasing involvement on the part of the Christian — but peaceful involvement, within the establishment. Through organized pressure and votes, enlightened Christian citizens can and must put honorable and capable men into key government positions, both in political, elected officialdom and in the civil service. This is effective involvement, civically responsible involvement and Christ's kind of involvement.

MILITARY CONSCRIPTION

Every country has a right to defend itself as best it can against unjust aggression and so it may use any lawful means of resisting. At such times military conscription may be necessary. If such is the case, citizens are bound in conscience to answer the call, and to defend their country, if need be, at the cost of their lives, even if the legislator does not believe in supernatural sanction and looks upon all laws as merely penal.

Volunteers for military service are obliged in strict justice to keep their contract by rendering the services required.

OBEDIENCE TO TAX LEGISLATION

Echoing the words of Christ, St. Paul pointedly directs: ". . . You must pay taxes, since all government officials are God's officers. They serve God by collecting taxes. Pay every government official what he has a right to ask . . . whether it be direct tax, or indirect, fear or honor" (Rom. 13:6-7).

Every citizen, out of legal justice, should certainly bear his fair share of the burden of his country's expenses in maintaining the common good, peace and security. Citizens should especially be conscientious in fulfilling this obligation during times of national depression and emergencies such as war or imminent danger of the same.

To what precise extent, outside such special periods of urgent need, tax legislation also binds *in conscience* is a disputed point. We may follow any authoritative view in settling our conscience. Lying, however, is never permissible in this regard and, moreover, if apprehended for tax evasion, a person is bound in conscience to accept the penalty imposed.

Chapter XIII

THE FIFTH COMMANDMENT

"You shall not kill" (Ex. 20:13).

Human life does not belong to man, so he has no right to destroy or injure it. If a friend lets us use his truck for the summer's work, naturally he expects us to take care of it while it is in our hands; he certainly assumes that we will not deliberately wreck it. The summer's work done, natural reason tells us that we must return it to him in a condition which bespeaks our gratitude for his kindness and generosity.

Reason likewise tells us that we are not free to abuse God's gifts of soul and body; we must take care of them for as long a time as He lets us keep them. If we use them as though they were our own, we are usurping the rights of God. God gave us the Fifth Commandment to remind us of this.

The Fifth Commandment forbids, in the first place, suicide and all unjust killing of our fellowmen; in the second place, it forbids all unjustified mutilation, wounding, violence, quarreling and every other act which prepares the way for unjust killing. Because death can result from neglecting health, the preservation of health is also imposed in this Commandment.

SUICIDE

To kill oneself directly and by one's own authority is gravely sinful. A person is also forbidden to do anything from which death may follow accidentally, if he has suicidal intentions in doing it. Suicide is a horrible aberration, even according to nature, for it is contrary to the deepest instinct of nature, the instinct of self-preservation. God is the exclusive master of life; He alone has the right to dispose of life. Anyone destroying his own life is doing what is not his to do, what only God may do. The Lord said, "It is I who deal death and life" (Dt. 32:39). The sin of voluntary suicide is especially odious because of the unique danger in which it places the soul: since the chance to repent would seem to be cut off by the very act.

Unless there is evidence of either last-moment repentance (if there was a moment left) or lack of full responsibility, the Church will generally refuse ecclesiastical burial to a suicide. By this the Church is in no way passing judgment on the unfortunate person's state of conscience. That rests with God and only God can judge. Certainly we cannot. By her refusal of church burial, the Church wishes to impress on us all the horror of self-destruction, that suicide is the very worst road for escaping the trials of life no matter what the desperation — that it settles nothing except possibly our own eternal self-destruction. We can only hope that most suicides, as seems to be the case, are committed when the mind is temporarily deranged, when the person did not know what he was doing.

EXAMPLE:

While honeymooning at a lodge in the Rockies, Helen and Roy quarrel violently. Desperately, she rushes into the car and careens down the twisting, narrow mountain roads. "I don't care what happens to me now," she whispers to herself, "if I get killed, that'll make him miserable for the rest of his life."

To expose one's life to such grave danger needlessly is seriously sinful. It may be that Helen, under grave emotional stress, does not fully realize the gravity of her act; hence, her guilt is lessened accordingly. It is difficult to judge in such cases.

INDIRECT KILLING OF ONESELF

In considering suicide above, we were concerned with the *direct* killing of oneself, with death desired either as *an end in itself* or as *a means of obtaining something else.* A person would desire death as an end in itself if he wanted to kill himself simply in order to die or if he yearned for death as synonymous with total oblivion. On the other hand, he would desire death as *a means to an end* if he wanted to obtain something else but knows that the only way he can get it is by dying. For example: Tarnof shoots himself in order to escape the torture which he cannot otherwise evade. Another example: Magnolia is trapped in a burning building; just before the flames reach her, she shoots herself with a shotgun which happens to be in the room with her. The killings in both of these examples, because they are a *direct* willing of death, are absolutely forbidden by the natural law as reiterated by the Fifth Commandment.

The case, however, is entirely different if, in order to escape the flames, Magnolia jumps from a window even though it is forty stories from the ground. Here she does not directly intend her death; for she really wants to remain alive if she can after jumping. She foresees that she probably will not escape alive if she jumps, yet if she does die, she has only permitted her destruction. Her objective is merely to escape the flames, and death as a result of the jump would not be an essential factor in effecting such escape; even if by some stroke of fortune she were not to die as the result of the fall, her objective would still have been accomplished. This is an example of the "double-effect principle" which we discussed earlier. There was also a proportionate reason for going through with the action. Other examples of this "indirect suicide" would be: a woman leaping from a window to avoid being seized and violated by a libertine; in wartime, the blowing up of an enemy fortification, an ammunition dump, a ship or some other such objective in view, even though the person foresees that his own life will be lost in the act. Should it happen sometime that the brakes of an automobile fail and the car begins dashing downhill, one may steer it aside — even at the risk of running over someone — in order to prevent its going over an embankment.

THE DESIRE TO DIE

One may desire to die for a *reasonable cause and with resignation to God's will.* To be spared some extraordinarily great temporal misfortune, such as an exceedingly prolonged and painful illness, would be a reasonable cause, as would the desire of the Beatific Vision or union with God; but it would be grievously sinful seriously to desire death in order to escape the *ordinary* hardships of life.

EXAMPLE:

Mrs. Brown has been ill with arthritis for fifteen years, eight of which she spent flat on her back in bed. Now the pain is so excruciating that she has no desire to live any longer. "Please pray that God will let me die soon," she tells her family, "so that I won't have to suffer so much."

There is nothing wrong in her desire for death, for she has reasonable cause and her resignation to God's will is clearly shown by her words.

MUTILATION

Mutilation is an excision, cutting, or other action by which the use of a member or an organic function of the body is either wholly or partially destroyed or suppressed. Examples of mutilation are amputation of an arm or foot, the cutting out of tongue or eye, and the removal of the uterus, ovaries, etc.

Mutilation is lawful only when necessary to preserve the health of the whole body or to maintain a reasonable state of well-being, that is, necessary removal of organs or members which threaten one's life or health. Otherwise, mutilation is gravely sinful. To remove unnecessarily a part of the body having an unimportant function (e.g., the ear lobes) is venially sinful.

Misinterpreting Christ's warning on sin, some believed He advised mutilating the body to keep from offending God with that particular member: "If your hand or your foot should cause you to sin, cut it off and throw it away: it is better for you to enter into life crippled or lame, than to have two hands or two feet and be thrown into eternal fire" (Mt. 18:8-9). In this passage, it is true, the Master used a strong figure of speech to impress on us the necessity of avoiding the occasions of sin; but He certainly did not intend His words to be taken literally.

To perform surgery for removal of organs or of members which threaten another's life is not only lawful but an act of mercy; also it is lawful for us to have such operations performed on ourselves. In extreme cases individuals may amputate their own members if this is necessary to save their lives. For example, in the Korean War when a ship was hit by several bombs, Sailor X's legs were pinned between twisted steel. He succeeded in extricating one leg, but the other was hopelessly caught between two huge steel beams. The order to abandon ship was given. In the confusion everyone forgot about him. In desperation he seized an ax which happened to be near, hacked off his own leg, then crawled to the nearest lifeboat. His action was perfectly lawful.

Plastic surgery is a form of mutilation. To undergo plastic surgery for unworthy motives, the late Pius XII stated, is not lawful; but where a justifying reason exists it is permissible.

EXAMPLE:

Lily's parents decide that Lily should undergo plastic surgery, because her face, deformed from birth, is the cause of many cruel jokes and sordid witticisms both at school and on the playground.
This reason justified the contemplated operation.

STERILIZATION

Another form of mutilation is *sterilization*. Sterilization consists in rendering the generative organs incapable of begetting or bearing children. Whether done by surgical operation, intravenous injections, or X-ray, sterilization to prevent offspring is always gravely sinful.

If an operation necessary for procuring the health of the body inescapably involves sterilization, the person may undergo such an operation; for instance, Mrs. While has cancer of the uterus and in the opinion of the doctor this organ must be removed in order to arrest the growing infection. Mrs. While may licitly undergo the operation. The resulting sterilization is an unsought and indirect consequence of a necessary measure.

There are two other kinds of sterilization: *punitive* and *eugenic*. Discussing the morality of these two types in a work such as this is impractical. But we can say that *eugenic* sterilization is absolutely forbidden under any circumstances. As to *punitive* sterilization, some theologians hold it is not wrong in principle if imposed in such a way as to constitute a true punishment. Modern penology does not incline to this form of punishment anyway.

PROPER CARE OF THE BODY

We must use at least the ordinary means for preserving life and health. Under ordinary means we understand "ordinary" food, clothing, housing and physical recreation; likewise, remedies such as medicine, rest cures, and other helps that are not beyond the means of the sick person. Engaging a physician is also an ordinary means. Naturally, if it is a question of some slight sickness which can be cured by ordinary home first aid, we need not call a doctor. If I refuse to use ordinary care in preserving my life, I am virtually committing suicide.

In modern society, medical science, various health organizations, social services, the legislation and disbursements of governments have wiped out or at least held in check the most dangerous contagious diseases and plagues. This is possible only through the cooperation of the person and community. Civil legislation and personal cooperation in these matters which affect the health of the people in general strictly bind in conscience; for example, required vaccinations for various diseases, hygienic measures for the prevention of communicable disease, pure food and drug regulation, etc., are ordinary measures for preserving the health of everyone, and hence, are morally binding. The seriousness of personal guilt in disregarding such preventive measures depends on the gravity of possible danger to oneself and to the community at large. If the danger is great, the possible moral guilt is great accordingly. The same may be said for the senseless conformity to fashion if it is harmful to health, e.g., the wearing of inadequate clothing in severe winter weather (the wearing of mini-skirts can be sinful on two counts: danger to one's health and immodesty).

Are we obliged to use extraordinary means to keep alive? No, as a rule, we are not obliged to do so. God does not exact from us what is beyond the ordinary power and strength of men in general. Today an operation for appendicitis is usually considered an ordinary means; hence such an operation would generally be obligatory for anyone whose life was thus threatened. How about a person suffering, say, from gangrene in a vital organ or limb? Would he be obliged to have it amputated? Ordinarily, such a person has the right to choose between the risk of dying and the prospect of living without that member. If one could purchase a sure cure for his disease, say, at the cost of several thousand dollars, he would not be obliged to do so. People, even if wealthy, are not obliged to go to far-distant places or health resorts for a cure; nor need they summon the best-known physicians, even though they would otherwise die. No one is gravely obliged to undergo a major surgical operation except a person who is necessary to his family or to his country — and this, only if the success of the operation is almost certainly assured.

EXAMPLE:

Mr. O'Reilly, a father of twelve children and their sole support, will certainly die if he doesn't have an extremely painful operation; the doctors tell him that he has three out of four chances for complete recovery if he submits to surgery. He is gravely obliged to undergo the operation because of his family's need for him.

SHORTENING ONE'S LIFE

It is sinful to intend shortening one's life or to actually shorten it without a proportionate reason. The gravity of moral guilt depends on the extent of injury done or intended: to shorten one's life notably would be gravely sinful; to shorten it slightly would be venially sinful. If I can readily get other jobs but, sick of living, I take up an extremely unhealthy occupation in order to shorten my life, I am guilty of sin.

On the other hand, it is not forbidden, for a legitimate and proportionate reason, to undertake work which is of its nature dangerous and which, even if foreseen, will either shorten one's life or injure one's health. A person may not, however, directly intend this effect; the conditions necessary for the principle of double effect must be verified. Accordingly, the following and others in similar occupations would be considered to have a proportionate reason for their work, even though dangerous and may shorten their lives: workers in paint factories, steel mills, smelteries, brass foundries, glass-manufacturing plants, chemical plants and sulphur mines (managers and owners in such plants are obliged in conscience to establish and make use of safety measures and devices for the best possible protection of their workers); steeplejacks, doctors, nurses and clergymen who minister to those suffering from contagious diseases.

We do a great act of charity if we expose our lives to danger in attempting to save someone, say, a drowning person, or in trying to rescue a person trapped by flames. We are not obliged to perform such acts of heroism but in doing them for love of God and neighbor we can gain heaven itself.

IMMODERATION IN EATING AND DRINKING

Immoderate indulgence in food or drink (other than alcoholic) is venially sinful even though the person foresees he will thereby shorten his life to some extent. Eating too much, even to the extent of feeling decidedly uncomfortable, is a venial sin. Scrupulous people usually do well to consider themselves not guilty in this matter; once they begin to worry about it, they will feel odd and uncomfortable after every meal, not because of overindulgence. but because of a dyspeptic condition brought on or at least fostered by scrupulosity.

Even if a person eats until he vomits, he is guilty of venial sin; however, such excess cannot be excused from serious guilt if he occasions great scandal or if he seriously harms his health thereby — and foresees it and willfully does it.

To take alcoholic liquors with *moderation* involves no sin. It becomes sinful only when excessive or immoderate. Normally, the gravity of sinfulness depends on how much this excess is known to affect the individual. Each must then follow these principles in regard to drinking:

1. It is gravely sinful if one foresees that this drink or this amount of drink will result in *complete loss of reason.* By *complete loss of reason* here is meant that the person reaches such a state that he can no longer distinguish between right and wrong. Other ways of determining *complete loss of reason* are the following: (a) the loss of one's senses; (b) if, after the drunkenness has passed, the person cannot remember what he said or did while under the influence of drink; or finally, (c) if one does something which he never would have done when sober (by no means is this to be taken in the sense of feeling unusually prankish and gay, or just being hilariously daring in singing songs, etc.).

EXAMPLE:

Dale knows from repeated experience in the past that this glass of mixed

drinks will be enough to "knock him cold" (unconscious). Yet, because he wants to celebrate a great event and be "one of the gang," he downs it as if it were tea and passes out. There is matter for grave sin here.

A sufficient reason for depriving oneself of the use of reason temporarily would be to take the drink as an antidote for blood poisoning or for some other equally serious reason. Merely to drive away the blues is not an adequate reason.

It is gravely sinful to make another person completely drunk (by trickery, etc.), unless there is sufficient excuse, as for example, to prevent him from committing a serious crime (this latter is an application of the principle of double effect).

EXAMPLE:

Knowing that Gerald Baldie loses all use of reason after just two shots of whiskey, one of his pals "spikes up" his soup with half a glass of that drink. All seem to think it screamingly funny.

There was matter here for grave sin on the part of Gerald's pal.

2. It is a venial sin if one has reason to believe that this drink or this amount of drink will result only in a partial loss of the use of reason; that is, when one foresees that it will neither deprive him of the loss of his senses nor of the power to distinguish right from wrong. Thus, if the individual knows that a certain amount of this drink will cause him some dizziness and only a partial loss of reason (but he still will know what he is doing and will be able to judge right from wrong), it would be venially sinful for him to take it.

EXAMPLES:

1. Connie knows that if she takes a glass of wine she will have a dreadful headache, but in no sense will she be even partially drunk. Since she does not want to offend her hostess, she takes the wine and graciously drinks it.

She does not sin in the least.

2. Robert is out drinking with his friends at the club. After his third highball, he knows that he has had enough. Still, at the insistence of his friends, he takes another, though he knows that he will become partially drunk.

His guilt is venial.

We should remember that at times we have an obligation of charity to abstain from drinking in the presence of a person who would *surely* go to excess as result of our example. If, for instance, I am going out with a friend who has great weakness in the matter of drink, I would do well not to indulge in alcoholic beverages — to make it easier for my friend to avoid drunkenness.

Driving while somewhat under the influence of drink, may involve sinfulness; its gravity depends on the danger to which such a driver is exposing not only himself but others.

Sobriety is a virtue which causes one to control his appetite for alcoholic drink. All of us should have this virtue. The tragic effects of alcoholism are well known and we need not belabor the point here. For most alcoholics there is but one remedy: total abstinence. How this is achieved, of course, is a different matter. Of all methods of treatment, the work of Alcoholics Anonymous, combined with sympathetic spiritual direction, seems to be the most effective to date.

USE OF NARCOTICS AND HALLUCINATORY DRUGS

In general, the morality of taking narcotics and hallucinatory drugs (heroin, opium, LSD, etc.) is judged in the same way as the use of alcoholic drink. All that was said about intoxicating drink applies to narcotics and hallucinatory drugs, except that the latter are much more dangerous to health and life. Such risk must always be considered in evaluating the seriousness of the sin. Many minds have literally been ruined and have never returned to normal after hallucinatory drugs had been taken; many suicides have occurred under their influence. The evils of drug addiction can scarcely be exaggerated — no sin however grave, no crime however hideous, is impossible to the addict trying to satisfy his craving. Perhaps no other addiction is more difficult to overcome.

To use narcotics in small quantities and this very infrequently for calming the nerves, for insomnia, etc., may be justified but foolish when so many good medical remedies are available. But even such limited use becomes gravely sinful if it produces an habitual craving for the narcotic.

EXAMPLE:

While at a college party, LSD is being handed out freely. Jerry is undecided. "Look, man, blow your mind just this once," urges a friend; "I've taken a trip dozens of times, and it hasn't hurt me." Jerry knows that if he takes the two sugar cubes, soaked with LSD, he will go "completely under." After an hour, he relents and takes them. Next day he is none the worse for his experience.
There was matter here for grave sin.

MURDER

Murder is the unjust, direct killing of an innocent person. Murder is never permitted to anyone, not even the State. Only God has the supreme, exclusive ownership over human lives.

Those who in any way assist others in committing murder, whether by giving advice, by offering a bribe, or by intentionally providing the instruments of the crime, share in the guilt of that murder. The perjurer who by his false swearing causes the conviction and death sentence of an innocent person is also guilty of murder!

Manslaughter differs from murder in that it is the unintentional killing of a person and is done without malice but usually due to negligence. The gravity of the sin of manslaughter depends on the circumstances, on the amount of negligence, carelessness, etc.

God is the only one who can allow men to take the lives of other men. In some circumstances, He does permit this; if some other higher right conflicts with the individual's right to life, the lesser right always gives way to the greater. This happens in the case of capital punishment, war, etc. Some types of killing are really murder but hide under refined names, such as, *mercy killing, feticide* and *abortion*.

MERCY KILLING

Mercy killing, also known as euthanasia ("easy death"), is the act of painlessly putting to death persons suffering from an incurable disease, in order to end their misery. Usually, this is done only when the victim himself requests it.

Public sympathy in the twentieth century tends to defend euthanasia or mercy killing; this seems to be the result of a highly developed sensitiveness to the sufferings of others which our civilization has cultivated. Now, in itself, sensitiveness to the suffering of our fellow human beings is a good thing and should lead us to do all we can to relieve that suffering in a legitimate way. This, indeed, is very, very Christian. But to let this beautiful sentiment get out of control by trying to relieve suffering by unlawful means, as in mercy killing, is a different story — it is as ugly as it is immoral!

Cases of euthanasia have been appearing with increasing frequency during the last several decades; some states have even attempted to make it legal! Juries in some instances have refused to convict the mercy killer. But this is a matter of morality, not of sentiment. It makes little difference what sentimentalists contend, euthanasia has been, is, and always will be a grave crime, and should be called by its proper name: mercy murder and mercy suicide.

The basic reason why mercy killing is wrong is one we have already stated: God and God alone has the exclusive ownership of human life, and so He and He alone has the right to decide when this life shall end. In mercy killing, the killer assumes or rather usurps this right over life by destroying it, and hence the criminal act committed is either murder or suicide. This is just another example of the immoral idea of the end justifying the means.

Even from a purely natural point of view, many good reasons can be given against the practice of euthanasia. It would greatly lessen confidence in doctors. Any gravely ill patient — and it could be you — would wonder uneasily whether his physician considered his case incurable or one that involved too much prolonged suffering, and so might administer drugs to kill him. What of cases in which keeping the patient alive is completely economically unfeasible, involving great expense to relatives, to insurance companies, to the State — especially if the cured patient will not be able to contribute much to society anyway (e.g., an elderly person)? This alone is reason enough to undermine confidence in doctors completely. What of the heavily insured person or a person of great wealth, whose relatives would profit handsomely if he were put out of the way? A patient like that would hardly trust any doctor! Indeed, if doctors were licensed to deal out death, a few unscrupulous ones could always be found for hire to send anyone gently and quietly to permanent sleep. No fuss, no bother. It would be euthanasia in literal truth, "easy death." Need we say more?

EXAMPLES OF GRAVELY SINFUL EUTHANASIA:

1. Dr. X discovered that the baby he had delivered was hopelessly crippled and would probably die within five years anyway. So, in order to spare the parents the burden of caring for it, he let it catch cold and die.
2. Mrs. X is hopelessly ill, and her son knows that long suffering lies ahead of her. Several times each day he gives her triple doses of the pain-killer left by the doctor; he knows it will weaken her heart. As a result, she dies of heart failure at the end of the week.

FETICIDE

Feticide, the direct killing of the fetus (or the infant) in the mother's womb, is never allowed because it is likely murder. When an innocent person is killed, unjustly and directly, it is always murder; in feticide the living fetus (another name for an unborn person) is directly murdered. Even though the purpose may be noble, and even if otherwise both mother and child would die (hardly possible in this day of medical wonders), we are never allowed to destroy the living child. Both mother and child have a right to life, and neither has a better right than the other; hence, directly to kill the one in order to save the other is a violation of that sacred right founded in the natural law. Forbidden, therefore, are all forms of feticide, craniotomy, decapitation, embryotomy, and evisceration of a living fetus or of a fetus that is probably alive. In most instances today help may be rendered in difficult cases of parturition by Caesarean section or similar lawful operations.

ABORTION

The expulsion of the immature human fetus from the womb of the mother is called *abortion.* By "immature" here is meant one which is not viable, that is, not able to live outside the womb. It is not abortion if for good reason the birth of a viable fetus is hastened.

Directly to procure an abortion is always gravely sinful — because it is likely murder. The earliest witnesses of Christian tradition treat this truly pagan practice with horror. Because there is an element of doubt whether the fertilized ovum from its very onset is a living being possessed of an immortal soul does not give anyone the right to directly abort it, just as the element of doubt does not give the right to a hunter to pull the trigger at what may be a human person or an animal. No matter what praiseworthy motive prompts direct abortion, it is not justified. Thus, even if it means saving the mother's life or the good name of an unmarried, criminally assaulted girl, it would be gravely sinful to procure an abortion directly. Likewise, anything that is done *with the intention of effecting an abortion* is gravely sinful, even though abortion may not actually follow.

EXAMPLES:

1. Mildred has been keeping company with Wilfred for three months and has indulged in unlawful relations with him. Now she is pregnant. She tells Wilfred and he urges her to have an abortion. In desperation she consents. (The penalty of excommunication is incurred for abortion that actually takes place, both for those guilty of it or those cooperating positively in it.)

2. Gladys, who is pregnant, dances wildly in order that an abortion result. There is matter here for grave sin even though the desired effect does not ensue. In this case, if the abortion does not follow, no excommunication is incurred.

A mortally ill mother may lawfully take medicine to restore her health even though an abortion will ensue provided that there is *no other remedy* and that the restoration of health does not result from the abortion itself but *from the medicine taken*. Likewise, lawful is the removal of a dangerously diseased uterus even though the enclosed nonviable fetus is removed with it — provided, of course, that the removal of the uterus is the only means that will save the mother's life. As careful analysis shows, this is not the same as direct abortion, though the effect for the fetus is the same (such cases are justified by the principle of double effect). The four conditions are fulfilled: thus (1) the action (removal of the uterus) is good, for it is the removing of an infected part of the body; (2) the good effect (saving the mother's life) is not produced by means of the evil effect (*death* of the fetus); (3) there is a sufficient reason (saving the mother's life) for permitting the evil effect to happen; (4) the evil effect is not intended in itself but is merely permitted to happen, for it necessarily accompanies the good effect. These same conditions are verified in the case of the medicine, provided health is not restored by means of the abortion but by the medicinal remedy. In cases of ectopic gestation (extrauterine pregnancy) the four conditions above also apply.

PREMATURE DELIVERY

Premature delivery may be induced for any proportionately good reason when the child is viable. One must always delay such a delivery until it is morally certain that the child can live outside the mother's womb, if this can be done without great danger to the mother's life. If the mother's condition is gravely dangerous, one may proceed to premature delivery as soon as it is probable that the child is viable.

EXAMPLE:

After eight months of pregnancy, Mrs. Good's condition is critical; it is like-

ly that she will die if the child is left in the womb. The doctor proceeds to induce a premature delivery. His action is lawful, since a child, eight months after conception, is viable.

CAPITAL PUNISHMENT

We know from the Scriptures and from the evidence of entire Christian tradition that God has given to the State the right to take the life of those who by their evil conduct have forfeited their claim to life: "If a man strikes down any human being, he must die" (Lv. 24:16; cf. also Gn. 9:6, Nm. 35:16ff., 31ff.). But the State cannot indiscriminately and arbitrarily use this power of life and death over its citizens; the State exists to protect the rights of its citizens, not to take them away. Therefore, this power must be exercised so as not to invade the individual citizen's rights; that is, a person can be punished by death only if this is necessary to protect others against his criminal violence and injustice and if no lesser punishment avails.

The accused must normally have ample opportunity of pleading his case: the crime committed by the accused must be such that is legally deserving of capital punishment and guilt for such a crime must be established beyond doubt. In other words, such a punishment may be inflicted only by public authority of the State and by the due process of law. Any other course is nothing but private revenge. Lynching and mob violence, therefore, are immoral: for (1) those who engage in lynching or mob violence do so on their own authority (they ignore the right to life which a criminal has until properly constituted authority, by due process of the law, judges that he has indeed committed a crime grave enough to forfeit his right to life); and because (2) of the great danger (this is a matter of experience) that a mob thirsting for blood will kill someone innocent of the crime. It is difficult enough, at times, even for reasonable and careful public authority not to make such a mistake after examining the evidence with unemotional thoroughness. An angry mob, acting in the passion of the moment, is never secure in making a right judgment.

Any person joining a mob which purposes to lynch, kill or wound a man, whether that man is actually guilty or merely suspected, gravely violates the Fifth Commandment.

Only in urgent necessity and when given permission to do so by their superiors may policemen, guards and others with similar authority, shoot on sight (that is, without warning or without giving a command to halt) a criminal condemned to death who is trying to escape from their custody. The same holds true for shooting a public enemy who, beyond doubt, is guilty of a crime punishable by death. Sentinels, guards, etc., may shoot at one who refuses to obey when they give the challenge to halt, provided, of course, that they were given orders to shoot and that they try insofar as possible *merely to wound and not to kill.* Federal officers, border patrolmen, police, etc., may act in a similar manner toward smugglers who attempt to flee in spite of the orders to halt. Naturally, they are allowed to protect themselves against bandits and others, even to the extent of mortally wounding the assailant if this is necessary for self-defense.

DEFENSE AGAINST UNJUST AGGRESSORS

Everyone has a right to life and everyone has the right to defend himself against unjust aggression, even to the extent of killing the assailant if necessary. An assailant who threatens to take my life or to rob me of something valuable, either spiritual or material, is called an unjust aggressor.

In unjust aggression there is a clash of two rights; the aggressor's right to his own life and my right to life (or valuable goods). Not that the assailant's right to life is subservient to mine. It isn't; the rights are equal. But I may defend and protect my own life and property, even to the extent of killing the one unjustly attacking me. The principle involved here is that of the twofold or double effect. The primary purpose of my act is defense of my life; the harm, even the death of the assailant, is a secondary effect. Even if his death did not follow, my purpose would have been accomplished (if he were rendered unconscious only, etc.). The same is true in cases of aggression by the insane or intoxicated. I retain my right of self-defense.

Naturally, I may not go to the extreme of killing an assailant if the circumstances do not warrant it; for example, I would never be justified in killing a man just to prevent him from taking my set of golf clubs or just because I *imagine* that he is going to attack me.

In order to use force licitly against an aggressor, the following conditions must all be verified:

(1) The attack must be *actual or immediately imminent;* that is, it must be practically present and such that it cannot be evaded, e.g., the assailant reaches for his knife or revolver or sets his dog on me. To kill before the attack is actually imminent is wrong because of the grave danger of using this force against a purely imaginary attack. Nor is it permissible to kill after the attack is over, for then the act would no longer be self-defense, but revenge. Consequently, a woman may not kill the man who has ravished her. For the same reason it is unlawful to vindicate one's honor by killing the person at whose hands one has already suffered injury. The matter is entirely different, however, in the case of a thief escaping with a large sum of money, etc.

(2) The attack must be *unjust.* Thus a thief who is justly fired upon by the protector may not fire back on the excuse of saving his own life. Similarly, as my right to protect myself is based upon my right to life, I may use, in self-defense, proportionate force against an insane or intoxicated person.

(3) The force used *must not exceed what is necessary to ensure* self-protection; it is to be proportionate to the loss threatened. If the assailant can be rendered harmless by being wounded, then killing him would be unlawful; and wounding the assailant would not be lawful if disarming him or summoning help would be sufficient. Because of excitement and the need for instantaneous action, the person attacked seldom sins gravely by exceeding the bounds of a blameless defense.

(4) Common sense tells us that we cannot *kill unless the goods to be defended are of great value.* Defense of the following is considered of great enough importance to allow killing: one's life, chastity, temporal goods of great value in themselves or of grave moment to the owner because of his poverty or need;

and defense against grave mutilation. Naturally, killing is not allowed if the stolen goods can later be surely recovered by the police, etc. In defending temporal possessions of small value, the aggressor may be killed only when he attacks the life of the owner.

Whatever one may do for his own self-defense or to protect his own rights, that he may also do for the defense of others.

The practical question may be asked: How can one think of these conditions when confronted with such a great danger? Besides, there is usually no time to think. Really, the conditions are such basic common sense that usually a person automatically acts in accordance with them. A normal person generally would not think of killing anyone making off with his tennis racket! Obviously, in serious doubt whether killing the attacker is the sole means of defense, the innocent person can rest assured that he may always settle the doubt in his own favor.

But are we obliged to defend ourselves if this can be done only by killing the aggressor? No, generally speaking; we have no obligation to do so, for we are bound only to use ordinary means to preserve our life, and the use of violence is regarded as an extraordinary means. Sometimes, however, charity may impose an obligation to defend oneself; this would be the case, for example, if my life were necessary for the family or common good or if I considered myself in state of serious sin (since death would imply the loss of my soul). There may also be a duty of charity to protect others (wife, children, parents, etc.) against unjust attack. If anyone, even a complete stranger, is in danger of death (from violence, etc.) we must, out of charity, go to his assistance even at the cost of grave inconvenience to ourselves; this is a serious obligation too often and too easily forgotten in our impersonal urban society. Policemen are obliged to defend others against unjust aggressors by reason of their office; this, then, is for them an obligation of justice besides one of charity.

EXAMPLES:

1. *The Green and the Blue families have been enemies for years. Two months ago in a fight, Bertrand Green took a broken beer bottle and horribly disfigured Harry Blue's face. Last week Harry waited for Bertrand on a dark street and attacked him with a knife; Bertrand also managed to pull his knife and a fearful fight ensued. Finally, Harry had Bertrand down and pleading for his life. Then Harry didn't know what to do — to let him go would only be courting more trouble, he thought; so he calmly and deliberately stabbed Bertrand through the heart. "I did it in self-defense," he pleads to the police.*

Harry committed murder, for conditions number 1 and number 3 were not verified.

2. *In Vietnam Bugsy and Obarianyk, Americans, capture two Viet Cong soldiers while out on patrol. Though the Viet Cong are disarmed, Bugsy believes that it will be difficult to bring the prisoners back to their fire-base and begs Obarianyk, his superior in rank, to shoot them instead. "No, Bugsy," Obarianyk counters, "that would be murder, not self-defense. It would be wrong to shoot them unless they try to attack us or to escape, or something of*

that sort. If they try anything funny, of course, don't be afraid to shoot." The two men then bring the prisoners in.

Obarianyk is right; it is not lawful to kill prisoners of war who have surrendered unless they commit serious offenses after capture. This is the application of the law of self-defense.

3. Harry and Kay, a young married couple, awaken to the sound of screams. Harry rushes to the window and sees a man stabbing a young woman on the sidewalk. Lights go on in other houses down the street. Harry wants to rush out and help, but his wife pleads with him: "Listen, Harry, don't be a hero; don't get involved, you might get killed." Harry then wants to call the police. But again his wife deters him: "Honey, don't get involved; you'd have to testify in court and miss a lot of work on account of it; besides, there are other neighbors who will phone the police." So Harry does nothing to help. Neither, apparently, do any of his neighbors. The girl is found next morning, dead. This is based on an actual case.

There is matter for serious sin here on the part of everyone hearing the screams; at the very minimum, help should have been summoned by phoning the police, calling on a few neighbors and going out en masse to disarm the attacker (the man would probably have run away then).

DUELING

A *duel,* a prearranged fight between two persons who have agreed to use deadly weapons, rarely occurs in our society; so there is no need to discuss its morality here. Dueling takes on the malice of both suicide and murder and is grievously sinful for both contestants accordingly.

WAR

Most of us are more than just acquainted with the horrors of war — not only with the vast destruction wrought by modern war but also with the dreadful moral and spiritual evils involved. So we need not describe war; most of it is so horrifying that it cannot ever be adequately described. Still war, terrible as it is, may be justified even today.

In some instances we as individuals are allowed to defend ourselves against unjust aggressors or to prosecute our rights with force, if there is no higher authority that will protect them. The same is true of nations, but to a greatly intensified degree; the right to wage war is based on the necessity of national self-defense. In fact, a nation has an obligation to defend itself (because of the people's vital dependence on it and their right to a decent life in accordance with their dignity as human beings). Certain conditions, however, must exist before war can be waged and justified.

1. There must be a violation of the nation's right, either actual or imminent; for example, unjust attack on its military installations, cities, supply lines, etc. The nation attacked must not have given just cause for the attack for, if it had, the attacking power would not be guilty of an injustice.

2. War must be undertaken only as the final resort, the last, extreme

measure in the political order; in other words, only after every peaceful effort to settle the contention has been attempted and failed. This includes such measures as embargoes, diplomatic arbitration and the like.

3. There must be solid reasons to believe that greater evils will befall the nation if it abstains from war than if it fights. Even a wronged nation is not justified in defending itself by engaging in war if it foresees that war would result in greater harm than good to its own interests. If a particular nation were to plunge its people into war with no hope of victory or of righting the situation, the war would be considered unjust, unless, of course, that nation was in a position to call to its aid other and more powerful forces.

What a country can do for itself in thwarting aggressors, it may also do for another, weaker nation, especially if bound by treaties and agreements.

As private citizens we must consider these conditions earnestly, because they will be the basis for forming our conscience regarding our obligations when our country is at war; everything will depend on the justness of the war.

The following are the obligations of citizens as regards a just war:

1. A citizen must help his country if it is involved in a just war; if the war is not just, then he may not help. Anyone may volunteer for service in a war which is certainly just. A volunteer (unless he will be drafted anyway), since he freely chooses to fight, must investigate in order *to make certain* whether or not the country is involved in a just war.

Both conscripts and the soldiers already enlisted before the declaration of war may, in doubt, presume that their country is in the right and so may fight with a clear conscience.

2. The conscientious objector is obliged to follow his sincere convictions in this matter. However, he is not excused from rendering noncombatant assistance (e.g., medical corps, ambulance service, etc.) to his country.

EXAMPLE:

Willard, a good Catholic and an excellent citizen, in all sincerity could not justify his answering the call to arms by his country during the war in Vietnam. Despite endless discussions he still could not square his conscience with the situation.

He was not only free but obliged to follow his conscience in this matter.

MORAL CONDUCT IN WAR

In the U.S. and Canadian military forces, problems of conscience (what is allowed, what is not allowed in the individual's conduct in war) may easily be solved by adherence to the respective military codes (with all their attendant minutiae) drawn up for its personnel. But one moral fact may not be clear: carpet or saturation bombing of entire cities and areas. Vatican II explicitly states: "Any act of war aimed indiscriminately at the destruction of entire cities or extensive areas along with their populations is a crime against God and man himself. It merits unequivocal and unhesitating condemnation" (*The Church in the Modern World,* Chapter I, 80).

ANGER

Anger is an outburst of resentful emotion connected with a strong desire for revenge. An angry person wishes to inflict harm on another as a punishment. There is a distinction to be made between *sinful anger* and sinless anger, usually called *just anger;* the former is an immoderate desire for vengeance, while the latter is a moderated desire for vengeance prompted by some good motive such as honor of God, zeal for justice, etc. If I hear an atheist blaspheming God on a street corner and I become angry because I do not want to hear insults heaped upon the Savior I love, my anger is just. But even just anger is sometimes difficult to moderate and may easily become unholy.

How can I tell whether my anger is moderate or immoderate? Certainly, if any one of the following is true, then my anger is immoderate: (a) if I wish an innocent person to be punished; (b) if I wish the guilty to be punished more than they deserve; (c) if I wish to punish in an unlawful manner; (d) if I wish to punish merely out of personal spite.

EXAMPLE:

After twice telling her two sons to keep off the newly waxed dining-room floor, Mrs. Benning finds them tramping over it again. She flushes with anger and resolutely administers the customary punishment — "five stripes" with her husband's razor strop.

Mrs. Benning's anger, we believe, was sinless; for she punished the guilty in a moderate and entirely lawful manner. If she had done it out of personal spite, a thing most mothers would not be guilty of, she would have sinned venially at most.

THE GRAVITY OF SINFUL ANGER

As an immoderate outburst of emotion, anger is a venial sin; however, it may become gravely sinful if, for example, a person would deliberately fly into such a rage that he can be considered to have lost his reason; or if he foresees he will fall into grave sins of blasphemy, cursing and the like (deliberate anger with these foreseen results would in such a case be considered a proximate occasion of grievous sin). Anger can also be mortally sinful if it is so felt or expressed as to offend charity and justice seriously. Even in serious matter, of course, without full consent and realization, there is no grave guilt.

HATRED

Hatred is a *voluntary* and bitter detestation of a person or a thing. For a clearer understanding of hatred and its sinfulness we shall classify it as (1) personal hatred, and (2) hatred of a quality.

1. *Personal hatred* is a detestation of another in which we wish him evil *as* evil. If I detest Mr. X to such an extent that I wish him total blindness, I want this tragedy to befall him solely because of its evil effects.

Personal hatred may be either gravely sinful (if the evil wished another is grave) or venially sinful (if the evil wished another is slight).

EXAMPLES:

1. While walking down the road, Martin sees Luke, his mortal enemy, driving blindly through the rain. As Luke nears the railroad tracks a train is coming toward him at full speed. Martin hates Luke so violently that he hopes the train will hit him.

Grave matter is present here, but sufficient deliberation necessary for serious sin is very likely absent, keeping in mind the "spur of the moment" situation.

2. Mrs. Comely finds it difficult to like Mrs. Beauty. When they meet on the street on Saturday, the hideous desire of wanting Mrs. Beauty to be struck with leprosy comes into Mrs. Comely's mind. As soon as she is aware of this sinful desire, she banishes it and politely smiles at Mrs. Beauty.

She committed no sin whatever, since this desire was entirely involuntary; in fact, Mrs. Comely definitely performed an act of virtue in overcoming the temptation.

2. *Hatred of a quality or action* is the aversion with which we regard another because of habits or deeds that are detestable to us or threaten us with harm.

Hatred of a quality may be good or evil depending on what is the object of the hatred.

a. If the object at which my hatred is directed is some evil quality or action or habit in another and does not touch the person himself, then my hatred is not sinful. This is the "hatred of the sin but not of the sinner" which the Gospels teach.

For example, I regard Mr. Trotter with aversion because of his known habit of gambling funds needed for his family's support. My attitude towards him would be friendlier if he corrected this grave fault. To cite another instance, Jane Doe has come to hate in her husband his constant detraction of her relatives, with whom he cannot get along. This is not a sin for Jane if she does not let this hatred of her husband's "quality" of detraction erupt into a general hatred of him as a person. However, she must be forgiving and sincerely try to ease the strain between her husband and her relatives.

EXAMPLE:

I regard Mrs. Pill with aversion because of her open affair with a married man. I wish her no harm and only desire that she may mend her ways before she ruins her life or that of the man. There is no sin in my feelings about her.

"Hatred of a quality" is also the natural aversion which some people have for others of a "certain type" — they just can't put their finger on what makes them dislike these people but they simply do not like them. Naturally, we should try to correct our attitude by making a special effort to notice all the good qualities of such people; also by going out of our way to be pleasant to them. There is much virtue in thus trying to control our likes and dislikes.

b. If the object at which my hatred is directed is some virtue in another, my hatred is sinful; for example, if I hate my next-door neighbor solely because of his solid piety (not to be confused with the irksome, saccharine type of pseudo-piety).

RACIAL PREJUDICE

Hatred and discrimination against anyone because of race, color, or creed is judged according to the same moral principles which apply to hatred, except that the evil wrought may be far greater than that done through acts of simple hatred. An unkind word or act will do more harm, will "hurt" more, if done to our brother of another race, color or religion and, therefore, is much more serious than the same unkindness in ordinary circumstances. The reasons for this are not merely psychological on the part of the racial minority or religion; indeed, these may be at the "breaking point" of accumulated acts of unkindness and prejudice. What may not be a serious breach of charity between members of the same race can easily become grievous when done to members of another race or creed. Many times, justice is also violated. We cannot overlook all this in judging the morality of such actions. Furthermore, racial prejudice and discrimination are especially insidious because they are often difficult to recognize and admit even to oneself.

The bishops of the United States termed race relations as the main moral problem of our times. Although the Fathers of Vatican II obviously tried to follow Pope John's directive not to engage in condemnations, they found racial and religious discrimination too disturbing not to condemn: "The Church repudiates [reprobat, commonly understood to mean 'condemns' for all practical purposes] as foreign to the mind of Christ, any discrimination against men or harassment of them because of their race, color, condition of life, or religion" (Declaration on the Relationship of the Church to Non-Christian Religions, Number 5).

Another passage from the same document is worthy of lengthy meditation by every Christian: "We cannot in truthfulness call upon that God who is the Father of all if we refuse to act in a brotherly way toward certain men, created though they be in God's image. A man's relationship with God the Father and his relationship with his brother men are so linked together that Scripture says: 'He who does not love does not know God' (Jn. 4:8).

"The ground is therefore removed from every theory or practice which leads to a distinction between men or peoples in the matter of human dignity and the rights which flow from it."

ENVY

Envy is the sadness that one feels at the good another has or can have, as if that good constituted an affront or a lessening of one's own good. Often envy is accompanied by the desire of seeing the person deprived of the particular good which offends the envying one.

Envy has its origin in pride, which can bear neither a superior nor a rival. When we consider ourselves superior to anyone who was or is on our own level, we are prone to sadness on seeing the other succeeding more than we. Envy is not the mere sadness we may feel in seeing some good quality in another and regretting that we are not endowed with the same. In this case we are sad because we do not have such a good quality and not simply *because another* has it. This is almost similar to emulation, a good sentiment which urges us to imitate, to equal and, if possible, to surpass the good qualities and virtues of others, but always by lawful means.

Neither is it envy to be depressed because another, by reason of his possession (e.g., a particular office), is in a position to harm us; nor is it envy to feel sad because another has something that he does not deserve. Finally, it is *hatred and not envy* to begrudge our neighbor his possessions, not because these are looked upon as a diminution of our own good, but simply because we do not want him to prosper.

SINFULNESS OF ENVY

If the good envied is great and momentous, then sufficient matter for grave sin is present. The greater or more valuable the good that is the object of envy, the greater is the sin. But this is true only when these envious impulses are fully and deliberately consented to and when the envious person deliberately wishes another to be without the good. Often these impulses are just emotional, or, at most, feelings in which there is little reflection, deliberation and consent; hence, such would be venially sinful.

EXAMPLE:

Mrs. Mat has a new hat. Her neighbor, Mrs. Pinch, looks at it longingly and regrets that she can't afford a new one. As the two walk down the street together, Mrs. Pinch secretly wishes that the strong wind would blow the hat into the street, where it would be run over by the heavy traffic.
Mrs. Pinch's guilt would be venial.

SCANDAL

The Fifth Commandment not only forbids us to injure or destroy the life of the body, but also implicitly forbids us to inflict harm on the soul of another. This is done chiefly by giving *scandal*. Giving scandal consists in performing some act (or saying something) which either is evil or has the appearance of evil and which therefore is the occasion of sin for another. To be scandalous it is sufficient that our words or acts *may* induce another to sin, not that the sin of another actually follow. Hence if a person realizes that he is giving scandal, he is held accountable for it, even though in that particular case his scandalous words or actions do not actually incite another to sin.

EXAMPLE:

Several high-school boys are working on the road-repair crew. Working in the same crew is Mr. Gorbeduck, who proceeds to tell some very foul stories. He does not care whether his words will incite the boys to sin or not. His action is scandalous, regardless of whether any of the boys will actually sin because of his talk.

A person does not give scandal if he knows that the witnesses of his wrongdoing are either so depraved or so virtuous that no influence is exerted on them. Such would be the case if, say, Pat blasphemes in the presence of Jim who curses habitually and would do so independently of the bad example; or if, on the other hand, Pat curses in the presence of a priest or some other good person who would not at all be moved thereby to commit the same sin.

DETERMINING GUILT IN SCANDAL

The sin of scandal is grave or venial according to the nature of the sin to which another is knowingly incited. If I scandalize another so that he is incited to venial sin, my guilt is venial; if I scandalize him so that he is incited to commit a grave sin, my guilt accordingly is seriously sinful (presupposing full realization and consent).

Only a venial sin of scandal is committed, however, if the other person sins gravely mostly because of his own personal depravity and only partly on account of some scandalous triviality which he uses as an excuse or opportunity to sin. Such, for example, would be the sin (venial sin of scandal) of girls who by their slightly immodest dress give some depraved young men an occasion to sin against chastity (the girls would sin gravely, however, if they directly and very deliberately intended by these means to lure these young men into sin).

This brings us to an important distinction which must be made between the two kinds of scandal: namely, *direct* and *indirect* scandal.

1. *Direct* scandal is that done with the intention or desire of leading another into sin. If, for example, John, knowing that Miss Z cannot help but overhear, indulges in impure conversation with some of his friends with the intention of thereby alluring Miss Z into sin with him, John is guilty of *direct* scandal. A person guilty of *direct* scandal is guilty of a twofold sin, a sin against charity, and a sin against whatever particular virtue the scandal is directed.

2. *Indirect* scandal is that in which the other's sin is foreseen but not at all wished. An example of this would be the case in which, say, Mrs. Drew stays home on three Sunday mornings taking care of her sick child though she realizes well that, as a result, certain gossipers of the parish will sin by rash judgment and will even miss Mass themselves on the pretext that "if saintly Mrs. Drew can stay away from Sunday Mass so many times, so can I miss once." Needless to say, Mrs. Drew commits no fault in doing what she does. Indirect scandal is not wrong provided there is a proportionate reason for permitting the foreseen scandal to result and provided that the action itself is not bad (it must be good or at least indifferent). In the preceding example, Mrs. Drew cer-

tainly had a proportionate reason for her action, and the action itself (taking care of her sick child) was certainly a good act. For the same reason, it is lawful for parents or employers to leave money lying about in order to test the honesty of their children or employees.

Conversely, indirect scandal is illicit if the action itself is bad (e.g., stealing, lying, etc.) or if there is no proportionate reason for performing it. For example, Ruth, an extremely attractive girl, knows for sure she is the object of a certain dissipated man's immoral desires. One lunch hour Ruth saw him eating in a certain restaurant and though she could easily have gone into the restaurant across the street, she went to eat in the one where the young man was. In this case, Ruth's scandal-giving (indirect) was illicit because of her insufficient reason. Ruth would have been entirely justified in her action if eating in a different restaurant would have caused her proportionate inconvenience.

It is considered a great hardship, say, if a girl might never use a certain street because she has strong reasons to think that someone living there sins gravely at the sight of her; to choose another street once in a while would only be a slight inconvenience. The rule in such a case is that she would be justified in habitually using that convenient street; but once in a while she should choose another way home. Similar situations naturally would call for similar actions.

In considering scandal-giving, we need not be scrupulous about the matter; scrupulosity is to be avoided in this as in other things. There may always be some persons around who, because of malice or downright hypocrisy, will find in the innocent actions of others occasion to sin. These are the pharisaically scandalized. Thus, if a person "scandalizes" (to rash judgment) some puritanical old busybody by drinking a bottle of beer at lunch hour, he need pay no attention at all to this "scandal." Even though a person foresees that his good or indifferent actions will be an occasion for someone to be pharisaically scandalized, he may always go ahead with a clear conscience.

EXAMPLE:

Judge Aaron knows that his next-door neighbor is scandalized (and may commit a sin of rash judgment) when he drives Gladys, his cook, to her mother's every Friday evening. At ten o'clock he always drives her back. "Why should I take my wife along on these wearisome trips?" he says; "she would be bored to death."

Judge Aaron does no wrong in thus "scandalizing" that neighbor.

There are others who are easily scandalized because they are weak. They are the ones who find an incentive to evil in someone else's good or indifferent acts because of their own feeble moral character. Circumstances must determine the extent to which we are obliged in charity to avoid indirectly inciting such persons. If we have a proportionate reason for performing a good or an indifferent act which would scandalize the weak, we may go ahead and do it; otherwise, we may not. Parents may licitly discuss among themselves topics which would definitely scandalize the young. In charity they must refrain from such conversations in the presence of youngsters unless they have good reason for doing otherwise.

EXAMPLE:

William knows that his friend Thomas has a weakness for drink; if he starts, he always ends by getting thoroughly intoxicated. So out of charity, William never stops at a bar when Thomas is with him, precisely because he realizes that under the circumstances charity obliges him not to give Thomas an easy excuse for drinking.

On the other hand, in order to avert scandal we are never allowed to do anything which is wrong in itself. Hence we may not deny our faith in order to avoid giving another an occasion to ridicule it; nor may we tell a lie to prevent an outburst of anger in another. But we may, without fault, refrain from fulfilling a positive precept (even a grave one) that is not necessary for salvation, in order to avoid giving serious scandal to the weak. Thus, a wife in a mixed marriage may forego church support (donations) when this would occasion a series of blasphemies on the part of her husband or cause quarrels, etc.

REPARATION FOR SINFUL SCANDAL

Ordinarily, a person repairs sufficiently for his sinful scandalous actions by the good example of refraining from such bad actions in the future; also by following the directions given by one's confessor regarding this matter.

Chapter XIV

THE SIXTH AND
NINTH COMMANDMENTS

"You shall not commit adultery" (Ex. 20:14).
  "You shall not covet your neighbor's wife" (Ex. 20:17).

SECTION ONE

In His love, God wants mankind to share His own divine perfections in some way; so He shares His work of creation with His people. He calls them to partnership with Him in the creative formation of His people. He implanted in men and women the wonderfully sacred power of procreating other human beings. They are to generate the body and He, to create the immortal soul. God could have willed otherwise; He could have reserved to Himself the work of directly forming each separate human being, as He had formed the first man and woman. Had this been the case there would be no reason for sex and its accompanying characteristics.

But God established the present order of things. He established a system of reproduction that requires the cooperation of human parents — and for great numbers of people this is a very real means of gaining heaven. God has the child come into the world weak, helpless and in need of parental care for his continued existence; He has the child develop and mature slowly, constantly needing parental solicitude for his physical, mental and moral training. All this is God's plan for human sex, human reproduction and for the human development of the child.

Moreover, God has given to each individual not only the faculty of generation itself but also a certain vital urge for placing the acts belonging to this generative faculty, acts which are conducive to the reproduction of the species. This urge is of tremendous importance; the sacrifices entailed in bringing children into the world and rearing them are so difficult and so long-lasting that

The author expresses his deep gratitude to Reverend Gerald Kelly, S.J., and to the Queen's work, St. Louis, Mo., Father Kelly's publishers, for graciously permitting him to use extensive excerpts from Father Kelly's Modern Youth and Chastity (St. Louis, Mo., 1944) in this first section of the chapter. Although the author has added many passages and changed others in an attempt to simplify the matter in question, he wishes to make acknowledgment of the material as substantially the work of Father Kelly.

the species would be in grave danger of extinction without this vital stimulus. That, in brief, is the reason for the powerful impulse called the sex urge, inclining a man and a woman toward that union which is necessary for procreating children. This also explains the natural attraction of the male and female for each other. God, who made human nature and knows it perfectly, knew too that in order to keep men and women working along with Him in His designs, He had to give them sufficiently powerful and satisfying inducements for undertaking the great sacrifices involved in the rearing of children and that is the reason why He made love so flaming, the urge so powerful, the pleasure connected with the act of generation so sweet. There are other powerful inducements to help, but these are the primary ones.

Aside from the teachings of Sacred Scripture and the Church, reason itself clearly tells us that one may yield to the promptings of the sex urge only in the married state. It is only in this (the married) state that the natural purpose of sex is accomplished. This natural purpose is actually threefold: *biological, psychological and social.*

BIOLOGICAL PURPOSE

From the *biological* point of view, sexual activity is essentially reproductive or generative; it has for its object the reproduction of new life. This terminology is not coined by the Church; it is found in any scientific textbook. When a man uses his generative faculty, the processes set in motion are those which naturally culminate in the expulsion of the male germ cell; the female processes are intended solely as an aid to the reception of the male germ cell. This is the biological activity of procreation and it is the one prerequisite for the production of new life which the parents voluntarily contribute. This is the most basic purpose of the generative activity. The fact that new life sometimes results and sometimes not depends on other circumstances, not on the act placed by the parents.

PSYCHOLOGICAL PURPOSE

From the *psychological* point of view the use of the generative faculty in a human being is not intended as a merely animal act but as the culmination and really concrete expression of a deep love. Before marriage, there is a buildup of friendship brought about not only by a platonic kind of love but by a real and personal sex attraction. According to the plan of nature, two hearts are blended into a single desire for total and perfect consecration to each other. At marriage this consecration is solemnly made in a contract; and after that it is sealed by the conjugal act. If and when this order is followed, sexual intercourse achieves its true *psychological* purpose; it is an act of love which is utterly self-giving, not for a mere hour or a day but for life.

SOCIAL PURPOSE

Finally, a great *social* purpose is served by conjugal intercourse. Since the actual physical union, aside from the biological purpose of procreation, is to increase and perpetuate that mutual love of husband and wife of which it is so expressive, it serves the very important purpose of providing for the proper rearing of children. We know that children are not like brute animals. They come into the world weak and helpless, totally unable to care for themselves, and they remain more or less in this condition for a long period of time. It is easy to see that their minds need careful development; their characters need firm but loving training. They have a deep, natural craving for mother-love and father-love. God made them so; He willed that the mutual and lasting love of the parents should be not merely for their own happiness and well-being, but also for the sake of their children. Thus we can readily see that the purpose of marriage (and hence of marital intercourse) is not only the procreation of children, but is also directed toward the education of the children, that is, toward their full and proper human development. Herein lies the foundation stone of true family life and therefore the foundation stone of truly progressive human society. This is what we call the *social* purpose of the generative faculty.

THREEFOLD PURPOSE OF SEX DEFEATED

Plain common sense or reason will tell us that all generative activity exercised outside the marriage state defeats one or more of the above-mentioned natural purposes and is therefore morally wrong. Moreover, since these purposes are of such great importance, any act which goes contrary to them is seriously wrong.

The social purpose of generative activity is violated by *fornication.* Since only the married can provide for the proper education or rearing of the child (as explained above), the *social* purpose of sexual intercourse demands that it be limited to those who are united by the lasting bond of marriage. Fornication is also contrary to the *psychological* purpose of generative activity. The individuals perform an act which implies a complete, mutual self-giving, yet they offer no real guarantee of permanent fidelity. Only the marriage contract itself contains this guarantee. It does not require profound thought to see that since fornication is wrong, then *adultery* is an even greater sin; not only does it contain all the sinfulness of fornication but it also is a violation of the marriage contract.

By seeking venereal pleasure from the solitary use of the generative faculty, be it through external acts (masturbation, touches, etc.), or stimulating thoughts, one defeats even the *biological* purpose of the faculty. The generative processes are set in motion in such a way that they cannot result in procreation. Such acts are therefore wrong. The same is true of sodomy (impure acts with persons of the same sex), of contraception, or any manner of artificial birth control. All these acts defeat the most basic purpose of the generative faculty, *procreation;* that is why they are called *unnatural.* Since these are even physically unnatural, such acts are wrong also for married people.

Just as fornication is wrong, so also it is wrong for people outside the married state to indulge in such natural preliminaries to the sexual union as passionate and intimate embracing or kissing. The mere intention of not proceeding further does not remove such actions from the realm of grievous sin. The reason is that this type of sexual activity has the definite natural purpose of immediately preparing for union and of arousing the desire for union; the right to such acts belongs only to those who have a right to the complete act, that is, to the lawfully married.

This is just a sketch of the argument from reason. But it does show us the natural law, a law which obliges all persons under all circumstances. Both the Sixth and the Ninth Commandments, like all the other Commandments, only reiterate and emphasize what is forbidden by the natural law. The Sixth Commandment forbids all *actions* which are opposed to the orderly propagation of the human race, that is, every *external* sin against chastity — while the Ninth Commandment forbids all *internal* sins — that is, all unchaste thoughts and desires.

NO EASY ANSWERS

As every priest knows, the Sixth and the Ninth Commandments occasion more questions than any other of the Commandments, not because these are considered more important than the rest but because the sexual instinct or urge is ever present and strongly assertive. In the rectory, in the confessional or wherever else the priest may be, if there is time and opportunity, the priest will be asked such questions as: "When is kissing a sin?" "Is conversation about sex sinful?" "Is it a sin for me to go to an X-rated movie?" etc. The stream of questions seems endless. Fine, that is very good, and they should be asked. The priest is happy to be of help at all times. The only thing that worries him on this score is that he will not be able to make himself sufficiently clear, since such questions cannot be adequately answered without taking into consideration a large number of factors. The questioners, naturally, ask the questions with a hope of brief and definite answers, without even dreaming of the numerous matters that have to be considered: the circumstances and facts which will make the same action mortally sinful in one instance, and venially sinful in another, and not sinful at all in still another case. The fact is that such questions are among the most difficult to deal with adequately. The priest only hopes that he can convey his answer clearly.

We hope we can do it in treating of the matter of chastity and the principles which must be applied for settling one's conscience in its regard. To be practical, the answers must necessarily be as brief as possible but always without sacrificing their clearness.

VENEREAL PLEASURE

Venereal pleasure can be defined sufficiently as the particular pleasure which is felt in the organs of generation when these organs are noticeably aroused by some sexual stimuli such as touches, sights, words, thoughts, imaginations and the like. It is also sometimes called sexual pleasure. Outside the marriage state (with its rights and privileges) it is mortally sinful to yield to this kind of pleasure — that is, to desire it or to enjoy it and consent to it fully.

Venereal pleasure is aroused by actions which are either *directly* or *indirectly venereal.*

DIRECTLY VENEREAL ACTIONS

By *directly venereal actions* we mean those actions which of their nature have the one and only direct effect of procuring venereal pleasure. Such acts are: sexual intercourse or its natural preliminaries; intimate, passionate kissing and embracing; acts of self-abuse (masturbation); sexual intimacies with one of the same sex. Outside marriage, *all directly venereal actions are grave sins of impurity because they are against the law of God,* again, presupposing full realization and consent. No matter what "good motive" one has for indulging in such acts, the acts are always wrong when deliberately performed; no good intention can ever make them right. For example, an unmarried girl cannot participate in passionate kissing or embracing even though otherwise she will "lose her man" or have to lead a very lonely life. Nothing can make these acts sinless when they are deliberate.

To guide penitents, the following is a brief explanation of the foregoing actions:

I. *Fornication* is voluntary sexual intercourse between an unmarried man and an unmarried woman. If it takes place with a person engaged to someone else, the fact of the engagement need not be mentioned in confession. Those thoughts, words, touches, and looks as well as kisses and embraces *which lead up to it or immediately follow it* need not also be mentioned in confession because morally they constitute only one sin with the sin of fornication. (Obviously, if fornication does not take place, then they must be confessed as separate sins.)

II. *Adultery* is sexual intercourse between a man and woman, one or both of whom are married to others. A grave sin against chastity, adultery has the additional grave malice of being a violation against justice: the violation of the conjugal rights of the married partner of the one who has sinned. Hence adultery must always be confessed as *adultery* and not simply as fornication. If both of the sinning parties are married, the fact must also be mentioned in confession, for then there is a twofold injustice. This is true even if the wronged husband or wife openly favors the sin or gives his or her consent to the guilty partner.

III. *Incest* is sexual intercourse between persons so closely related by ties of blood or marriage that they are forbidden by the Church to marry. The malice is twofold: the offense against purity and the violation of an existing relationship.

IV. *Self-abuse* (masturbation or pollution) sometimes incorrectly called onanism, is an act of arousing venereal pleasure in oneself by some form of self-stimulation.

V. *Sodomy* is a sin of impurity committed between two persons of the same sex, or between two persons of the opposite sex who indulge in unnatural acts.

A word here about complete and incomplete sins against chastity. Even if the forbidden act is not consummated, it still partakes of the malice of the consummated sin; hence, if the usual conditions for grave sin are present, the violation of chastity is gravely sinful.

It is important, too, to understand that when we say that the preceding acts are always grave sins, we mean that there is always *serious matter* for mortal sin (however brief the action). But, as said before, *full consent* of the will and *sufficient reflection* or *realization,* must also be had in conjunction with *serious matter* before a person is guilty of grave sin. If such an action were performed through ignorance of the evil involved, or without forethought, or when one was half-awake, then there may be little or no guilt on the part of the doer.

EXAMPLE:

Before going to a Catholic high school, Robert did not know that solitary acts of impurity were sinful. As soon as he suspected that they were wrong, he refrained from performing more of such acts; at confession the following Saturday he asked the priest about them and found that not only were such acts sinful but seriously so if fully deliberate.

Of course, Robert did not sin by such acts up to the time he found out about their sinfulness, because nobody can sin without knowing it; hence he is not positively obliged to confess these acts. However, all such subsequent acts (after he found out that they are gravely sinful), must be judged according to the principles mentioned previously.

INDIRECTLY VENEREAL ACTIONS

There can be any number of actions, situations, or circumstances — and there *are* almost countless numbers of them — which tend to, and frequently do excite sexual passion, but which also serve a purpose entirely distinct from the stimulation of venereal pleasure. The following are a few which may arouse venereal pleasure to a greater or lesser degree: study about sex (such as is necessary for knowledge of medicine, physiology, morals, etc.); kissing, caressing, dancing; reading books, magazines, etc.; attending films which touch on sex and plays which have "off-color" or suggestive parts; unguarded looks or glances; conversations about sex, etc.

Now each of these has for its primary object a purpose which is entirely separate from venereal pleasure, but often enough venereal pleasure results from these actions as a sort of by-product. Thus medical students and seminarians study about sex because the information is useful or necessary for their profession; others do so in preparation for their own future life. Dancing and movies, though they contain suggestive parts, provide recreation for the mind. Moderate kissing and caressing serve as a sign of one's affection for another. And so on. These actions will affect different people in different ways; some may not be affected at all.

There are the facts. The question is: "May *I* do such things without violating chastity?" This question everyone must answer either *before he begins* such *indirectly* venereal actions (if he knows beforehand that his passions will be aroused by such actions), or *while doing such things* (if he *becomes conscious* that the action is sexually stimulating for him).

In deciding whether such actions may be *begun* or *continued* without sin for me or at least without serious sin, I must know whether I will violate any of the following three principles: (1) *the intention must not be impure;* (2) *there must not be a proximate danger of consenting to the venereal pleasure aroused or of performing a directly venereal action by thus exposing myself;* (3) *there must be a relatively sufficient reason for performing these actions* (it would ordinarily be a venial sin not to fulfill this last condition if the first and second conditions are fulfilled).

Now to see what we mean by these principles. We must remember that these actions are sinless only if *none* of the three principles are violated.

1. *The intention must not be impure.* We can easily see that if one does any of these indirectly venereal actions in order to arouse his passions (so that he can enjoy the venereal pleasure) or in order to prepare the way for some directly venereal act — say, fornication, adultery, etc. — his act is against chastity. Any of these indirectly venereal actions may be externally quite modest, but they are turned into really impure acts by the intention. Say, Joseph kisses a girl in order to arouse venereal pleasure within himself; his act would be made impure by his intention, even though the kissing is done in a quite modest and decent way. And so for other things: looking at pictures, reading books, attending movies, etc. If one's intention in doing such things is to arouse or to further venereal passion, they are serious violations of chastity and so are gravely sinful (again, if done with full realization and consent). This is true whether the action is begun or continued for that evil purpose.

2. *There must not be a proximate danger either of consenting to the venereal pleasure aroused or of committing a directly venereal action by thus exposing oneself.* When a situation involves the *proximate danger* of sin, we speak of it as a proximate (that is, near) occasion of sin. One would do well to go back and carefully review the section of the book treating *proximate occasions* of sin. But to make the matter clear by applying the principles given there to our present discussion, we shall begin by giving some examples. Say, Bill kisses his girl friend. When he kisses her his intention is not impure, nor does the kiss exceed the limits of modesty externally, though it does arouse some incomplete venereal pleasure. So far, then, his intention is good and the action is not a directly venereal one. But what if he knows that this apparently chaste action of kissing generally leads him to go too far — say, to try to commit some directly venereal action (fornication, for instance), or that he generally gives in to the venereal pleasure that is aroused in him?

Or to take another example: Susie reads a magazine, not a really bad magazine but one which does have in it a few parts that are suggestive and sexually stimulating for her. Let us suppose that she does not read for that purpose — that she merely wants some recreation or some information (to "keep posted on the times"). Thus, she is not sinning as far as her intention is concerned, and she is not doing something that is a directly venereal action. But what if she knows that such reading generally makes her waver in her good intention and that she generally consents to the venereal pleasure which is thus aroused?

We see from the examples that these actions, though not wrong in themselves, involve a proximate danger (near occasion) of sin for both Bill and Susie. Everyone is bound under pain of mortal sin to avoid performing such indirectly venereal actions if he is *practically certain* that the actions either will cause him to *yield* to venereal pleasure or will lead him to some sin of impurity. Ordinarily, then, we may say that we are obliged under pain of serious sin to avoid such occasions. If, however, the occasion cannot be avoided, as may happen in certain rare instances, then we must find some means that will fortify us against the danger; in other words, we must make the danger more remote so that we are less likely to fall. Expert counsel is usually required in such cases.

Another kind of danger, as we know, is *remote* occasion of sin, which is a situation in which one generally does not lose self-control; that is, it seldom or never proves to be a source of sin to that person. For instance, let us say that Susie's sister reads the same type of magazines that Susie does, knowing that she is scarcely ever disturbed by the "off-color" passages contained in them and knowing that she never actually gives in to any sin as a result of reading them. Such reading is a *remote* danger to Susie's sister. Consequently she is not bound to avoid this reading, for we are not obliged to avoid remote occasions of sin.

Now, as everyone knows, there lies a wide zone between the two extremes (proximate and remote); this might be termed *intermediate* danger. For instance, Jane, Susie's friend, also reads such magazines. She cannot say that they are a proximate occasion of sin for her, nor can she say simply that the danger of sin is thoroughly remote. She cannot say that she *generally* loses control of herself and sins, but neither can she say that she really *seldom* sins as the result of such reading. In other words, her margin is somewhere in between the two dangers — it is rather intermediate. She sometimes but not generally falls into sin as a result of such reading. To expose oneself to *intermediate danger without any reason* is venially sinful. If there is a proportionate reason, there is no sin.

Before we leave this principle of proximate danger, we shall make a few remarks on some things which generally are to be considered as proximate occasions for almost everyone. Everyone must take it for granted that he is quite normal in this regard unless he is sure that he is an exception. There are some who would not be incited to sin as would the average person (e.g., a very virtuous person or one much accustomed to the various circumstances that will be referred to in this paragraph, etc.). For example, the modern burlesque show is planned along such sexually stimulating lines that it is a proximate occasion for almost anyone. So are movies condemned because of excessive sex; almost nude adults of the opposite sex or pictures of the same; really obscene literature; night clubs and hotels with lewd floor shows, etc.

EXAMPLE:

Having nothing to do, Frank and John go to a burlesque theater, even though they know that this constitutes a proximate danger to serious sins of impurity.

There is matter for serious sin here.

3. *There must be a relatively proportionate (sufficient) reason for performing indirectly venereal actions in order that their performance may be entirely justified — that is, not even venially sinful.* We have seen that if one performs an indirectly venereal action he avoids committing a grave sin provided he has no impure intention and the action is not a willful, proximate danger as regards either consenting to the venereal pleasure aroused or consenting to some other sin of impurity. Now, if these two conditions are fulfilled and we have a proportionate reason for performing these indirectly venereal actions, there is no sin involved at all. But if we do not have a proportionate reason for performing such actions, then we would be guilty of a *venial* sin of negligence or insincerity.

Such "proportionate" reasons are very numerous and vary in value. A university student who must read a modern novel that contains some suggestive passages certainly has better reason for reading it than a person who reads the same book merely for recreation or relaxation. A student of physiology has a better reason for reading a physiological textbook than a person who is interested in physiology merely as a hobby or who is just curious to know the contents of the book. Now, the rule to follow is this: *The greater the danger and risk involved in performing such indirectly venereal actions* (e.g., reading, dancing, etc.) *the better the reason should be for doing such things.* In other words, if an indirectly venereal action is to be perfectly justifiable — that is, not even venially sinful — we must have a relatively sufficient reason for doing it.

For those to whom such actions are only a remote danger of sin, any reason such as relaxation, recreation and general information will suffice. Thus normal recreation is a sufficient reason (and, hence, excuses even from venial sin) for doing things which result in slight stimulation, such as is noticed by some people when they dance, or glance at slightly suggestive scenes in movies, magazines, pictures, etc. Those for whom these actions present a danger approaching closer to the proximate occasion — that is, an "intermediate" danger — need a better reason in order not to sin venially (e.g., reasons such as acquiring useful information for one's profession, or any useful or necessary purpose connected with one's occupation, job, etc.). The acquisition of knowledge that will be useful or necessary for their future work permits medical students, nurses, instructors and theological students to study matter which may at times be strongly stimulating. The necessity of a medical-physical examination (whether it be required for a job, the military, or simply a health check-up) permits the intimate actions that are necessarily involved in such an examination.

EXAMPLE:

Ken, a young medical student, nearly always gives in to venereal pleasure in one of the classes taught by an atheistic professor who has no regard for chastity. Now Ken is gravely concerned to know whether he is seriously obliged to absent himself from this important class.

At this point it is obvious that this particular class is a proximate occasion of serious sin for Ken; hence he must find the means to remedy the situation. Ken does not necessarily have to discontinue those classes, but he must make the occasion less proximate — that is, either remote or "intermediate." He can do this by more frequent prayer, mortification and, most of all, by receiving the Sacraments of Penance and Holy Eucharist more often.

Such, in general, are proportionate reasons. But what of people who are overly sensitive to indirect sexual stimuli — that is, those who are either "bothered" by things which ordinarily do not disturb other people or are greatly troubled by things which are only slightly disturbing to others? Such hypersensitive people may act as the others do in such matters, provided that their intention is good. Sometimes it is even advisable that they should make a special point of doing such otherwise normal things, so that they may overcome this extreme sensitivity. But cases differ. For others it is better to be more careful. All persons hypersensitive in this regard need sound personal direction from their confessor.

In conclusion we may say that any time our actions (the indirectly venereal) are reasonable, they are entirely sinless; we may think or act and ignore the sexual stimulation which will result as their by-product.

Keeping in mind the principles enunciated, we may say that the following examples do not provide sufficient reason and so would be *venially* sinful: curious and imprudent looks; lingering on dangerous thoughts through *idle curiosity;* and other similar actions.

Throughout this discussion we have not referred to those cases in which there is fundamental lack of sincerity. We are expected to avoid laxity on the one hand and scrupulosity on the other. "But," says Father Gerald Kelly, S.J., "it does happen at times that people merely deceive themselves in the matter of impurity. They want venereal pleasure, but they do not like to admit it, even to themselves. Hence they read strongly stimulting things, dwell on stimulating thoughts, always with a certain pretense that they have some other motive. In reality they violate the second principle [listed as our first — there must not be an impure intention], but rationalize themselves out of guilt, at least serious guilt. It is often difficult to judge these cases, as mental quirks develop easily in one who is not sincerely devoted to chastity."

IMPURE THOUGHTS AND DESIRES

So far we have been dealing mostly with principles applying to actions which are or can become sinful, such as are forbidden by the Sixth Commandment. Now we shall summarize the principles as they apply to the Ninth Commandment, that is, to thoughts and desires.

Thoughts which are commonly called "impure" are those which improperly concern themselves with things or actions associated with the procreative process. They are "mental pictures" of these things. Now, everyone should know that any thought of this kind which is not willful cannot be sinful, or, at any rate, mortally so. (We must always keep in mind that for us to be guilty of mortal sin, not only *must the matter be serious* — in this case the matter *is* serious — but also we must *fully realize* that we are doing something mortally sinful and then *fully consent* to it; all these elements are required for a mortal sin.) Our imagination is rather rebellious at times, and no matter what we try to do about it, it often retains disturbing images. This is only natural; we have no absolute control over that imagination of ours, and so should never worry about a matter like this. In fact, worry only intensifies such disturbing images.

EXAMPLE:

Betty is horrified at the filthy and obscene thoughts that frequently come into her mind. She tries her best to drive them away but they persist in coming back. There is no sin on Betty's part. The fact is that in driving away such thoughts she is really practicing and strengthening the virtue of chastity.

Another thing we should understand clearly is that not even all *willful* thinking about sex and matters pertaining to it is sinful. We have learned that there are some kinds of external actions (the directly venereal, such as intercourse) which are never permissible to unmarried people, and some (sodomy, adultery, etc.) that may never be done by anyone, married or unmarried, but there is no action that may not be thought about. For example, in studying or reading this chapter, one has necessarily thought about many impure actions. The mere thinking about them did not make them sinful.

Then when are thoughts about sex sinful? The answer is that whenever we dwell pleasurably on something that is sinful for us in our state of life and whenever we do any of the following (with full realization and consent), our guilt is considered grave.

1. When we *willfully and deliberately* entertain any thought *in order to stimulate or promote venereal pleasure;* this violates principle number 1 — impure intention — concerning indirectly venereal actions. The malice of this sin is the same as that of the forbidden pleasure which is thought about.

2. When we *willfully* and *deliberately* keep in our minds thoughts which involve proximate danger either ot performing an impure action or of approving such an action, or of consenting to venereal pleasure; this violates principle number 2 in regard to indirectly venereal actions.

EXAMPLE:

Dale takes up the study of biology. When he comes to the part on human reproduction, he knows from experience that if he dwells on this kind of matter for any length of time he will be so moved that he will end either in consenting to venereal pleasure or in committing solitary acts of impurity. Therefore, dwelling on such matter, though licit in itself, is a proximate occasion of grave sin for Dale; hence he is gravely obliged to avoid the occasion altogether or else to make it more remote.

3. Whenever we think about sinful actions with *willful approval* of what is sinful. This is generally done in either of the following three ways:

a. If we think about any sinful act (fornication, self-abuse, sodomy, adultery) with the willful desire or intention of committing it. Here we give approval of the sin. This is what is meant by "impure desires." The malice of the sin varies with the object of the evil desire (e.g., self-abuse, fornication, adultery, etc.). This object of the impure desire is always to be mentioned in confession; for instance, "I consented to the impure desire of committing fornication," and then one must mention the number of times one has consented to such a desire. Whenever one accuses himself of impure desires in confession, he need not mention the corresponding impure thoughts which accompanied such desires; for desires, of their very nature, always include impure thoughts. But since it is possible for one to give in to impure thoughts only, without desiring or intending to commit any impure act, it would not be sufficient for the validity of confession (unless one did not know of this) to accuse oneself merely of impure thoughts if he also yielded to impure desires. Evil desires include the thoughts, but thoughts do not include desires.

EXAMPLE:

Joe gives in to the desire of sinning with his fiancée, but when he takes her out that evening he is deterred from any wrong action by the fact that she becomes angry over an imagined slight and asks to be taken home at once.

Up to the point of consent to the desire, this desire was merely a temptation. But when Joe gave in to the desire, his explicit intention was to commit a sin in the future. Such intentions are called "impure desires" (their willfulness being understood); but more correctly they should be called impure and willful desires. In confession Joe must accuse himself of intending or willfully desiring fornication and not merely of entertaining impure thoughts.

b. It is also mortally sinful if, having once committed some act of impurity (e.g., fornication or self-abuse), one now thinks about that act and willfully rejoices over the fact that he has committed it. For example, if John has once committed the sin of fornication and now thinks about the act and is *deliberately* joyful over the fact that he did it, he is willfully approving what he did. The malice of the sin is the same as that of the sinful act over which one rejoices, and so in confession one must mention not only the retrospective enjoyment but also the sinful act itself.

c. It is mortally sinful to think about a sinful action and willfully to delight in imagining himself performing the act (here one has no intention of really performing the external act and he is not approving anything which he may have done in the past). For instance, Bill thinks about the sin of fornication and willfully takes pleasure in imagining himself performing the act; he really does not intend to commit the sin even if opportunity presents itself; he has strong motives which would impel him not to do so. Here again, when confessing, one must mention the act which he imagined himself performing. The malice of this sin of deliberate delectation is about the same as the action itself; it is of the same species.

In the above-mentioned cases, we have always used the words *willful ap-*

proval in order to stress the fact that these thoughts, desires or this joyfulness become sinful only when one *willfully consents* to them *after he has realized their presence in his mind.* There will often be the involuntary sense of approval or desire which one will feel when he thinks of the various sexual acts, because such things are naturally attractive to the lower appetites. But this is not sinful because it is not an act of the will; it is merely the natural urge. The sin comes in only when our will consents to enjoy the pleasure thus produced in us. In other words, after realizing that the pleasure is there and that it will be gravely sinful to consent to that pleasure, we then deliberately decide to give in and enjoy it. It is then that mortal sin is committed.

Another point: as explained earlier, in the aforementioned cases of approval, the sin committed is the willful approval of an act which would be sinful for that person to perform. Now, if anyone approves of an act which he may legitimately perform and enjoy, then such approval would not be sinful. This would be the case, for example, with married people; since they have the right to the marital act and all that leads up to it, they are perfectly justified not only in thinking about such acts, but also in desiring and rejoicing over them before and afterwards. However, even married people may find that if they dwell on such thoughts and desires for any length of time, they may thus expose themselves to the danger of committing the sin of self-abuse, for such thoughts may become very stimulating.

MORE APPLICATIONS OF THE PRINCIPLES

Although we have already given many particular cases to which the principles apply and in which the principles themselves are illustrated, we shall now treat certain types of cases which seem to be the most baffling to the average person — that is, as far as the application of the principles is concerned. At any rate, these cases seem to occasion most of the questions in regard to the Sixth and Ninth Commandments.

INDECENT LOOKS AND SIGHTS

Certainly to look at a human body is not in itself sinful; this is one of the indirectly venereal actions which we have spoken about. The sinfulness involved, when there is any, must then come from some other quarter, either from the motive or from the occasion of sin which it presents. Obviously, if a person indulges in such looks in order to enjoy the venereal pleasure aroused therefrom, he is committing a serious sin (always presupposing full deliberation, realization and consent); this would also be the case if such looks are known to be a proximate occasion of sin for the particular person. As we have pointed out already, the sight of an unclothed adult of the opposite sex would be for the normal individual a proximate occasion of mortal sin, and in general one would be seriously obliged to avoid looking at such a sight. This, however, is not prohibited in all circumstances, since such looks may at times be necessary and good. It is permissible to look at an unclothed person of the opposite sex when there is sufficient reason to justify risking such a danger (e.g., a physician examining or operating on a patient) but the obligation not to will, or not to consent to any venereal pleasure that might arise, still remains. To look at a nude adult of the opposite sex merely out of curiosity and briefly would only constitute matter for venial sin, since such a glance would ordinarily not present a proximate danger of serious sin.

This is only the application of the principles that were given above in regard to indirectly venereal actions. These same principles apply to all other such sights, including pictures of the nude, if these are really clear, attractive and lifelike. Ancient art does not usually present severe temptations by its representation of the nude.

ART AND MORALITY

When we say that ancient art does not usually present severe temptations by its representation of the nude, we mean that (aside from exceptional cases) the ordinary person's passions generally would be affected not at all or only slightly. On the other hand, certain exponents of so-called modern art, which term comprises several different schools, as realism, humanism, etc., do very definitely, strongly and deliberately arouse the passions of the ordinary person.

What some of these modern artists seek from art the Greeks sought from something quite different — from wine and from the various debasing forms of sensual excess, but never from art. For them art was the portrayal of the beautiful whose effect was a purification of the mind, the senses and passions. When the Greek sculptor made a statue of a nude discus thrower, the spotlight, as it were, was thrown on the beauty and perfection of the whole muscular body with all its supple grace and power. If he made a bust of a woman, it was the aesthetic nobleness of her countenance, its lines, and the exquisite charm of her expression which mirrored the delicate beauty of both her body and soul. In his work the Greek tended to rescue man from the tyranny of the gross, the material, the brutal, and to lift him to higher planes of thought and emotion; in a word, to purification.

When certain modern artists represent the nude in sculpture or painting, they tend to the exact opposite. Consciously or unconsciously, they accentuate — and we say this frankly — sex and sex appeal, the material and the sensuous; they depict sheer animality.

We do not, of course, wish to imply that the purpose of all modern art is to arouse sexual passion. While there are certain undeniable grossnesses in modern art, it must be said that one very strong purpose of these schools — carried out in a most valid way by the better exponents — is to portray the vitality and often the beauty inherent in common, material and yes, sometimes ugly things. This is a spontaneous reflection of a certain phase of human development. But it can indeed be subject to abuse.

Fundamentally, all depends on the attitude with which the artist goes about painting his picture: whether his mind and heart are pure enough and strong enough not to stoop to sensuality and sexual depravity.

No artist has the right to degrade. The artist and his work are not excused from the laws of morality. The artist's action is a deliberate or human act (that is, he knowingly and freely performs it, and hence he is responsible for it). If his work is such that men cannot use it without committing grave sin, then the artist is himself guilty of serious sin because he is offering them a proximate occasion of mortal sin.

The theory "art for art's sake" is an evident fallacy: everything that a man does should be for his highest interest, conducive to his ultimate end, which is eternal beatitude. Art must always be a means to this end. It should always be "art for man's sake"; if it is not, then it ceases to be a good, for there is no good opposed to God the ultimate Good of human life. Art has no rights against God, and if it is opposed to Him, it ceases to be art.

What we have said concerning art is true of all artistic creation, be it literature, drama, the dance, or other forms. The excuse so often offered for the veritable deluge of objectionable novels and movies that is flooding the world, is that they represent real life; that this is life as it is found in the world. It is actual, in the sense that it does occur, but it is certainly not the norm or true form of life, but rather its pathology, like cancerous growths of the body; it depicts a moral deformity as repulsive as leprosy or cancer. It is hardly the subject matter for artistic creation. Painters usually do not set their easels before a manure heap or a sewer, and then proceed to depict faithfully that which is offensive to the senses; so what excuse is there for writers and motion-picture producers to descend into the moral sewers which unfortunately do run under life?

There is a definite need to protect man, with his morally crippled nature, from these deliberately concocted enticements to sexual and other immoralities; hence the need of censorship, against those who deliberately exploit the most humiliating weakness of mankind. That is the job of the various censoring bodies, be they national or merely municipal. If a production does not show correct attitudes toward the principles of morality, they must give it the rating that warns viewers of the dangers inherent in it, since attending it would constitute a proximate occasion of mortal sin for the average man and woman, for you and for me. One need not be an early Victorian or a Puritan to see that.

If some productions are objectionable in part, it means that some people will not be so gravely affected by them as to be severely tempted; but, on the other hand, there are others who may be tempted (at least by the parts which are objectionable or which are opposed to morality).

How is a person to judge in his own case the morality of looking at works of art or of movies which are objectionable in part? Merely by applying the principles which were given for indirectly venereal actions. Hence I can continue to look without mortal sin: (1) if I do not have an impure intention, or (2) if such sights do not constitute a proximate danger of consenting to the venereal pleasure aroused or of performing a directly venereal action by thus exposing myself.

EXAMPLES:

1. Terry is looking at a popular photographic magazine which contains some pictures of the near nude. These do arouse Terry's passions to some extent, but he is quite sure that they will not cause him to consent to the venereal pleasure aroused, nor will they lead him to commit any impure act. In the absence of an impure intention on Terry's part, it is venially sinful for Terry to continue looking at those pictures. Furthermore, such an occasion can easily become proximate.

2. Betty is enjoying a book on Greco-Roman sculpture. Though many of the pictures are of the nude or near nude, they do not bother her very much; furthermore, she has no impure intention but merely wants to know more about the artistic and to enjoy it. She does not sin in the least by looking at the book.

Her brother, however, finds that these same pictures do affect him to the extent, indeed, that he is "just about certain" that if he keeps on looking at them he will consent to venereal pleasure. He is, therefore, seriously obliged to discontinue looking at the book.

Afterwards, Betty gives the book to her friend Richard. Richard deliberately uses the book solely to arouse and enjoy sexual pleasure. In having this deliberate intention, Richard is considered to sin gravely, even though the intended result is perhaps not effected.

As we have said before, veil and fan dancing, striptease performances and the like are considered as presenting a proximate occasion of serious sin to the ordinary man; hence all must avoid them under pain of mortal sin. The same is true of the stage shows and floor shows in certain night clubs and hotels where dancers and performers wear less than the essentials of trunks and brassieres. Some scanty clothing may be worn in these performances, but the lack of a decent minimum of apparel, together with the provocative movements and gyrations of the dancers and actresses and the influence of evocative, sensuous music, combine to arouse and stimulate venereal pleasure; hence it is a proximate occasion for sin for most men.

EXAMPLE:

Will has never seen a striptease performance. A couple of his neopagan college chums try to persuade him to go to a certain night club where there are such "hot performances."
Will is obliged under pain of mortal sin not to go there.

KISSING AND EMBRACING

Kissing and embracing as we ordinarily understand them are marks of affection. It is difficult to give any definite rules on what would be sinful and what sinless because of the different ways in which these things can be done and of the different reactions that are experienced by people on account of their temperament, virtue, etc. Some cases, of course, are clear.

Kissing and embracing can be such that they do not ordinarily arouse any venereal pleasure. Such would be the case with kissing and embracing between parents and their children, even though this kissing and embracing may be prolonged and repeated. Strong affections are felt in such kissing, but there is normally no stimulation of venereal pleasure. There is no sin here.

EXAMPLE:

Edward, on coming back from Vietnam, is so overcome with love at the sight of his aunt, his only living relative, that he falls on her neck and kisses her for two whole minutes. Naturally there is no sign of venereal pleasure, though it seems to him that he is almost bursting with emotion.
There is absolutely no sin in this.

Then there is what we may call *non-passionate* kissing and embracing between men and women, friends or lovers. This is the kind in which only slight venereal pleasure or no such pleasure is aroused. This would be classed as a remote danger of sin, for it can easily be controlled; consequently, in itself it would not be sinful. Many times this type of kissing and embracing is just another way of saying, "I like you" instead of "I love you" or "Thank you," or, again, merely a way of saying "Good night" to a girl.

Kissing and embracing done in a modest and moderate manner by two people eligible for marriage and genuinely in love, in order to manifest their love for each other, is not sinful, even should passion unintentionally be aroused — provided, of course, that this kissing and embracing have not proved to be a proximate occasion of serious sin for one or both parties; that is, if the persons know from experience that this kissing generally does not lead one or the other to consent to something seriously sinful. If there is a remote or "intermediate" danger to serious sin (as previously explained concerning proximate, "intermediate" and remote dangers of sin), one is not bound under pain of *mortal* sin to avoid it; though it would be venially sinful to expose oneself thus.

On the other hand, when kissing and embracing are ardent and prolonged for some time, they are generally accompanied by strong passion and so present a grave danger of consenting to venereal pleasure. When this is the case, such kissing and embracing are seriously wrong. These acts are then styled *passionate*. So-called tongue-kissing (or soul-kissing) is also usually mortally sinful for the same reason.

EXAMPLE:

Michael and Mary, both unmarried, are very much in love and show it by kissing and embracing at times. Now Michael knows that such kissing as they do approaches the immoderate: his passions are aroused despite the best intentions. Generally — that is to say more often than not — he overcomes the temptation to consent to the sexual pleasure thus aroused; therefore he believes that he is not gravely bound to avoid such kissing.
He is correct, but he would sin venially by thus exposing himself. He must also make sure that this is not a proximate occasion of serious sin for Mary.

Kissing "for the thrill" in the sense of experiencing the general "good feeling" produced by non-venereal excitement over the act is not sinful. Here there is no question of any reaction in the genital organs but only an increase of pulse and respiration and, to some extent, a feeling of exhilaration. However, even this may prove a danger in some cases.

Kissing out of a spirit of mischief or forcing a kiss on a girl who resists would hardly be a question of sin against the virtue of chastity.

It is not sinful to hold a girl's hand, to stroke her hair, to pat her on the shoulder and the like, because venereal pleasure would not ordinarily be aroused. If it does happen to be aroused, it must be judged according to the principles already enumerated (the intention and the danger of sin involved).

Those in love should remember that dangerous kissing and embracing are not at all necessary in order to show or express the love each feels for the other. The tone of voice, the little courtesies the two show each other, their loving consideration for one another, their facial reactions to the deep love that they are experiencing, in a word, everything they do, can be turned into an evident indication of their genuine affection.

READING

First of all, reading is almost the same as thinking, and its morality is solved on the same principles. However, it may often be more dangerous than mere thinking because reading offers new and novel food for thought, sometimes very attractively phrased.

Secondly, certain kinds of reading is forbidden by the Church and such matters may not be read without permission. Regarding the Sixth Commandment, this includes: (a) books or articles that attack the Catholic teaching on chastity; (b) books or articles that are professedly obscene.

The phrase "professedly obscene" in reference to literature (and floor shows) is not to be taken here in the rather wide and vague sense which it is frequently given but in its real and technical sense. Such things are judged as obscene in the real sense of the word if both of the following elements are verified: (1) their theme or their general content is of an impure or sexually exciting nature; and (2) their manner of presentation is such as to throw attractive emphasis on that impure or sexually exciting element. For example, adultery is a sin of impurity; now, when a book or play not only centers on adultery but portrays it in an attractive manner, in such a way as to make it on the whole pleasing and appealing to you, such a book is obscene. This includes the pseudoscientific trash which is really nothing more than a sugar-coated allurement to vice and perversion. Books or articles that attack the Catholic teaching on chastity are those that defend artificial contraception, free love, premarital sex, divorce with remarriage, etc.

In forbidding this type of reading the Church is simply applying the divine command to safeguard Christ's moral teaching and to protect her members against grave moral dangers. Reading such materials without permission is seriously sinful, even for the individual who feels that he would not be harmed by them. If for some good reason one must read such a book, he must obtain permission from his bishop. The bishop will judge whether one's reason for reading such books is sufficient or not and will insist on proper safeguards.

Reading works, other than the categories included in the Church's prohibition, may still involve sin. Father Gerald Kelly puts across the matter briefly, yet thoroughly and clearly, in his *Modern Youth and Chastity:*

"Here again we find certain *clear cases of mortal sin:* (a) if one reads about sinful things and *approves* them; (b) if one reads even good things (e.g., a physiology book) for the purpose of exciting venereal passion; (c) if the reading involves the proximate danger of harboring seriously sinful thoughts or desires, or of one's doing something seriously sinful or of consenting to venereal pleasure.

"Also, there are some clear cases in which *no sin is involved.* Those who have a serious reason for reading (e.g., doctors, nurses, spiritual directors, young people about to be married who need some instruction regarding the physical side of marriage) do not sin, even though they should be strongly excited, provided they control their wills. Even mere entertainment justifies one in ignoring occasional slight motions of passion caused perhaps by a few suggestive pictures or passages in books or magazines that are otherwise decent.

"But mere entertainment is not usually a complete justification for reading things that one finds strongly stimulating, even in an otherwise decent book or magazine. There is no reasonable proportion between mere amusement and strong temptation; hence negligence manifested by delaying over such passages would be venially sinful. In fact, if one indulges in this kind of 'amusement' repeatedly, especially if he forms the habit of curiously going back over stimulating scenes, he might have reason to suspect the sincerity of his motive. At the minimum, a habit of this kind is very dangerous."

EXAMPLES:

1. Joe is reading a book by Steinbeck. Some passages of extreme realism cause him rather notable but not severe movements of the flesh; they also arouse some involuntary carnal desires. Joe, however, is able to ignore these and is reasonably sure that he will not consent to anything sinful.

At most Joe could be guilty of venial sin, for there is neither a sinful intention on his part, nor do these passages constitute a proximate occasion of mortal sin for him (we presuppose that he also does not approve of the sinful conduct about which he is reading). If any of these three circumstances, i.e., impure intention, proximate occasion of mortal sin, and the willful approval of sinful conduct, were true of Joe, he would then be sinning mortally.

2. Caledonia is reading a biography of King Henry VIII. Her kind heart is full of sympathy for him and she understands how his passions could lead him to those depths of immorality. Now she is worried as to whether this was approval on her part of his immoral conduct and, therefore, whether she is guilty of mortal sin.

In the first place, we repeat that no one can ever commit a mortal sin without knowing it; hence she certainly did not sin seriously. Furthermore, having a heart full of sympathy and understanding is something quite different from approval of someone's conduct. The hearts of many saints overflowed with sympathy and understanding for, say, prostitutes; but, as we know, they certainly never approved of such women's evil conduct. The fact is that the

Divine Master acted in the very same way toward the woman taken in adultery; and, of course, His kind heart went out with this same understanding, sympathy and kindness toward Magdalene, who had not merely one but seven devils! So Caledonia need no longer worry.

CONVERSATION

Everyone, of course, should know the difference between *vulgar* and *impure* or *obscene* language. *Vulgar* language is the use of coarse expressions such as "damn," "hell," or words and phrases referring to the functions of the toilet — all of which are unbecoming in Catholics and in polite society, but which generally are not sinful in the least. *Obscene* or *impure* language is talk about sex and sex life. By talk here we mean taking part in a conversation which usually tends to arouse venereal pleasure in the hearer. Being one of the indirectly venereal actions, such talk is judged according to the same principles governing all other indirectly venereal actions.

We know that there is serious sin: (a) when the motive of one or both of the parties is impure (e.g., seeking to induce the other to sin or to arouse venereal pleasure); (b) when the conversation is such that there is a proximate danger of consenting either to venereal pleasure or to some other serious sin against chastity — this would nearly always be the case if the conversation were strongly obscene and protracted and were between members of the opposite sex. Obviously, if the conversation is equivalent to a method of mutual stimulation, it is matter for serious sin. Since conversation is somewhat like *thinking* in that it is an external expression of one's thoughts, there is matter for grave sin if one were to give external expression to his impure thoughts, that is, to sinful desires, boasting about sins committed, or giving approval to the sins committed by others.

Among adults of the same sex whose age has lessened their susceptibility to matters of the Sixth Commandment, conversation about sex (conversation which could easily arouse venereal pleasure in listeners of a mixed group or in a group where youngsters are present) is often only a venial sin. However, if youngsters are around, the serious sin of scandal may easily result. Although sex is talked about much more freely today than formerly, some of this talk is too free; but it is difficult simply to give mechanical rules for such situations. Each has to judge the danger for himself.

Of course it is permissible to engage in serious conversation about sex if there is sufficient reason to do so and suitable precautions are taken.

EXAMPLES:

1. The men in William's department are thoroughly calloused to conversation about sex because so much of it has been batted around there every day. Hence William feels that he is not sinning by taking part in such conversation.

Provided that his intention is not impure, it would still be venially sinful for him to engage in such conversation, for it is evident that there is always some danger of arousing the passions of someone present.

2. Nineteen-year-old Thomas was bothered about a few things pertaining to sex. As his father was dead and he needed someone whom he knew to be good and whose judgment he could trust, he turned to his middle-aged boss. The matters they spoke about were very intimate, yet both knew that they were permitted to discuss such delicate problems frankly and sincerely because there was sufficient reason. They were right.

HOW ABOUT 'HUMOROUS STORIES'?

This is another problem difficult to gauge. Jokes and "funny" stories about sex are generally to be discouraged; it would be ideal to dismiss them with, "Better not tell them"; but this would not answer the question of their sinfulness.

In the first place, we must remark that these stories are at least supposed to be humorous, not obscene; the entertainment value of such stories is derived from the combination of humor and the natural interest which people usually have in regard to matters of sex.

In general, the sinfulness of telling such stories is to be judged by the principles applying to other indirectly venereal actions — that is, the motive cannot be impure, and the danger of consenting to serious sin or venereal pleasure must not be proximate. There are many people who tell these stories without being bothered by them and the thought of sin does not enter their minds; yet they must be careful lest they give scandal. If they know that their audience will not be bothered by such stories either, there would hardly be a question of scandal. Thus stories of this type would quite likely do little if any harm in a group of adults of the same sex. There would be more danger in a mixed group of adults. If adolescents are present in such a group, there would generally be grave danger that these stories might sooner or later prove to be a source of serious temptations for these young, impressionable minds; hence, in such circumstances, serious scandal could easily be given. There are exceptions, of course.

We simply cannot give any definite rule for young people in regard to the sinfulness of telling such stories among themselves, because the resulting reactions are so varied with each group. What is almost harmless for one group is sheer poison for another. One would have to know the group in order to gauge the danger, and even then it is difficult to be certain.

EXAMPLE:

After a round of golf, Mr. Baxter joins a group of colleagues, all of whom are middle-aged men. They are telling jokes, not a few of which are risqué. Just to be one of the gang, he tells one that is quite humorous but which he definitely would not tell in mixed company.

Since neither he nor his audience will be affected by his joke, there can hardly be a question of sin here for Mr. Baxter. However, if a youngster were present in this group or could overhear what was being said, it could easily turn into grave scandal which Mr. Baxter would be seriously obliged to avoid.

As far as the sinfulness of *listening* to such stories is concerned, it too is solved according to those same principles which govern all other indirectly venereal actions. Hence one would be guilty of serious sin if willful listening (with full realization and consent) would stir up the passions to such a degree that it would constitute a proximate danger of consenting to venereal pleasure or of committing other serious sins against chastity. Of course, if listening is done in order to arouse venereal pleasure in the first place, then it is done with an impure intention and is therefore matter for serious sin. Listening is considered *willful* (aside from full realization and consent) when one could either leave or change the trend of the conversation; sometimes people listen to such stories because there is nothing else they can do about it, as could easily happen in a factory or office, etc. If there is a *proximate danger* of consenting to sin, one must leave if possible. If we can reasonably do so, we are obliged to protect others out of charity. Thus, if the talk is really very dangerous, one should try to change the subject. Some people are naturally adept at steering the conversation away from such talk; others have developed this art and so can do it very gracefully; still others do more harm than good by trying to change the subject.

Also we may add that listening to impure talk out of mere curiosity, or smiling at an impure joke because one is afraid not to do so, is venially sinful. Occasional laughs at stories that sound funny are not sinful; however, there may be a danger of encouraging such stories in this way, so one should be cautious.

The reason why occasional laughs at stories that sound funny are not sinful is that these laughs are produced not by the off-color element but by the humorous element.

EXAMPLE:

Clement, who has a wonderful sense of humor, is not at all attracted either to the telling of "dirty stories" or to listening to them; but sometimes, when he does hear his fellow workers tell such stories, he can't help laughing at the really humorous ones.
He does not sin by this.

DETERMINING GUILT WHEN TEMPTED OR WHEN HALF-AWAKE

Whenever a person judges the sinfulness of his thoughts, words, or actions against chastity, he should always keep in mind that no one is gravely guilty unless he has *full consent* and *sufficient realization or reflection in conjunction with serious matter*. Many times one of these elements is missing; hence, no grievous sin has been committed.

A simple practical way of determining grave guilt is the one given by Father Bernard Haring: "A person who generally displays good will, and with earnest moral concern tried at least to avoid complete sexual gratification, has not committed a mortal sin. Nevertheless, penitents should be warned that those who decide, with full deliberation and freedom, directly to exploit their sexual urge in all degrees except orgasm cannot, psychologically, intend not to go further; in the end, they will succumb to this innermost and unruly tendency. A warning becomes even more imperative if arousal of another person's sexuality is involved, because of the sin against charity and the mutual implication in a waxing impulse" (*Shalom: Peace, The Sacrament of Reconciliation,* Farrar, Straus and Giroux, New York, 2nd edit., 1968, p. 191).

SECTION TWO

In the preceding section we have seen how God's plan includes the natural attraction of the sexes for each other and the sex urge. We have also seen why a person may yield to the promptings of that urge only in the married state — namely, because it is only in this state that the natural, threefold purpose of sex (biological, psychological and social) is fulfilled. The whole preceding section dealt chiefly with the morality of sex for the unmarried. Now we shall concern ourselves with the morality of sex for the married.

In acquiring a true knowledge of the use of sex in marriage and, hence, in forming a true Christian attitude toward it, both reverence and frankness are essential; this same is true of one who is imparting such knowledge. Our approach to marital sex life must be frank so as to impart real instruction and yet reverent so as not to profane the mystery of God's plan for human living. We must be frank in order not to leave confused and muddled impressions in regard to such tremendously important, sacred and intimate matters of married life — the life that the greatest majority of mankind is asked to live, since that is part of God's plan for them.

And such frankness is safe and sound if we really have a true and deep reverence for these matters, these plans of God, because in their deepest significance the fusion of body and spirit in man and woman united by God, and the birth of children with immortal souls, are very sacred and holy mysteries. If we have a true idea of these plans which God has made, we can hardly speak of them without experiencing awe and the inspiring hush — not a morbid Victorian hush but the hush of reverence — engendered by the presence of something that is very holy and near to God.

Truly, ignorance of these matters for the married is not a virtue; it is to be on the edge of a precipice. It is only by acquiring the knowledge and attitude that should be theirs by virtue of their call from God to the married state that they can best hope to fulfill His designs for them and thereby to gain eternal happiness.

MARRIAGE

First of all, every husband and wife should be thoroughly convinced of the high dignity of their calling. Somehow many have the impression that marriage is a second-rate vocation, one to be chosen only because a person believes that he or she is not good enough for the seminary or convent. True, some nuns, and priests, too, in their zeal to encourage vocations to the priesthood and the convent, sometimes do leave that impression but it is not right.

When theologians speak of virginity as being the highest vocation, they do not mean that virginity is the only call to perfection. To say this would be to debase the institution of marriage, which Christ raised to the dignity of a sacrament. There is no divinely established state of life that is not a call to perfection. God instituted marriage as one of the means of helping man realize a divine perfection in his life.

True, the Church, following the counsel of the Lord through St. Paul, teaches that consecrated virginity is, *objectively speaking,* the highest state of life. However, *subjectively* speaking, for the individual, the highest vocation is the one to which he is factually called. God gives a vocation to virginity to some; to others He gives a vocation to the married state. For these latter, marriage is the pathway to perfection.

Virginity takes its excellence from being something beautiful and holy in itself and not because there is something shameful and low about marital love. If the latter were the case, virginity would hardly merit the name of a gift offered to God; it would simply be a matter of giving up something defiled or evil, a thing which the Commandments already oblige us to do. The point is that a priest and nun by their vow of chastity or celibacy surrender to God something very good, something that will cost them much sacrifice, in order to show Him how much they love Him. Marriage is a very good and high vocation and it does not become less so simply because it can be given up for love of God. It is precisely because it is such a good thing that it makes such a great gift.

We should never forget that "he who condemns marriage, tarnishes also the glory of virginity. He who praises marriage, renders virginity more admirable and more sublime. . . . Marriage is good: hence virginity is to be admired in that it is better than good. . . . If you cast marriage from its pedestal, you betray the glory of virginity and reduce it to a low estate" (St. John Chrysostom, *On Virginity,* X, in Migne, PG, Vol. XLVIII, cols. 539-540).

Unfortunately, so many well-meaning husbands and wives forget about their third Partner in the marriage, God. Far from decreasing their love for each other, He will only increase and fulfill it. If they do not welcome God into their lives with their whole hearts, they are bound to miss the fullness of His grace and His love. And in proportion as they fail to do this, their love for one another must suffer. The need of love is always in us, the need to give and to receive it; that tremendous need of our whole being is satisfied only by God. And if, therefore, God is kept out of a marriage, even unconsciously, the married partners are left with a heart-hunger which cannot be satisfied by one another.

When this happens they know a hunger and an unconscious longing for that perfection of love which can be found only in God Himself; they turn desperately to one another for what only God can give. Their demands upon one another grow beyond any possibility of fulfillment, and in these desperate demands upon one another they put a strain on human relationships which such relationships were never meant to bear and which they cannot bear. So much, so very much of marital unhappiness is explained by this. So many marriages that were full of promise have really had no fair chance because of this separation — to a greater or lesser degree — from God, the third great Partner in every marriage; whereas, if the couple had willed to give God His rightful position in their lives, He would have become the very source of their great love-life. He would have satisfied them where they could not satisfy one another. He would also have shown them how to discern and fulfill those needs in one another which He had appointed in their human relationship. Without the inspiration of His presence in their hearts, they miss the full meaning, the richness, and the beauty of that human relationship; the pattern of their married life has then to depend entirely upon their own all-too-human minds and misruled emotions.

God, the Father of us all, is always a very willing partner. He thought so much of His married children that when He sent His own and only Son upon earth He wished to make of marriage a sacrament, one of the seven great channels through which grace is literally poured into their souls. He knew His earthly children, weakened and crippled by the fall of their first parents, need much grace or help to enable them to bear up under the difficulties that married life often brings. So, to make it easier for them, He made of the Christian marriage contract a sacrament, a bank, as it were, of graces or helps from which they can draw at will. Only to two special vocations, to the priesthood and to marriage, did He choose to give this storehouse of special aids.

This being so, the husband and wife, no less than the priest, can turn to their inexhaustible storehouse of grace for support in face of trial and trouble. God's married children, no less than Timothy, St. Paul's companion on his missions, are admonished to "stir up the grace of God which is in you." If husband and wife do this, they need not worry about fulfilling the tremendous promise they uttered when taking each other on their wedding day: "I (name) take you (name), for better, for worse, for richer, for poorer, in sickness and in health, until death do us part." When trial and temptation bombard their souls with a seemingly invincible blitz, they can ask their all-powerful third Partner to give them all the help they need not only to withstand the blitz but to carry on the battle into enemy territory to complete victory. God will come through always. That is precisely why God made marriage a sacrament: that the married might use it to make saints out of themselves as well as to bring new saints into the world.

THE MARRIAGE ACT

Marital intercourse, commonly called the marriage act or marital relations, is lawful and good when performed by the married couple in keeping with God's law. When properly performed, the marriage act, far from being something vile and vulgar, is an act of virtue, meriting divine approval in a special way, as an expression of divinely ordained sacramental union. Very truly a magnificent thing, this marriage act, and the attitude that would have an aura of shame and apology hovering over this act of procreating potential saints is next to blasphemous! The idea that there is something shameful in the intimate relations of husband and wife is definitely wrong and un-Christian. Such an attitude is due largely either to the lack of correct instruction or to a muddled miseducation in these matters.

Every married couple should realize once and for all that marital intercourse is very definitely an act of virtue, so long as it is *properly performed* and for any *one* of the following reasons: for the procreation of children, the fostering of mutual love and harmony, the restoration of peace, avoidance of incontinence in either one or the other partner, or for any other worthy motive. St. Paul would never have admonished anyone to do anything shameful or sinful and he says: "Let the husband render the debt to his wife: and the wife also in like manner to the husand" (1 Cor. 7:3).

Marital intercourse in its physical and psychological aspects is the most perfect form of tenderness and love, signifying mutual self-surrender. This self-surrender, in turn, signifies not merely the brief self-surrender of the physical union but even more the moral self-giving that continues through the days, the weeks and years of mutual love and understanding, consolation, sacrifice and support: in a word, they "become one flesh," the intertwining of two separate lives into one — truly, in both momentary physical union and in all things throughout life.

When two people love each other very much, they experience an ardent desire to be fused and lost, as it were, in each other; this tendency toward fusion is most perfect in conjugal love. The two become a part of each other, yet without losing their own personalities, without ceasing to be themselves.

God made everybody's heart that way. If it loves, it tends to union. A mother embraces her child and presses it to herself as if she would be one with this little being whom she loves so dearly; that is how God made a mother's heart. And that is how He made the hearts of husband and wife. Their attraction for each other, their overpowering happiness in possessing each other, finds expression in that intimate marital act by which they seek to make themselves one.

Love is an incomparable thing. By marital love and its consequent act of union, both of which were established by God Himself, two creatures are enabled to transmit life; an entirely new being arises from their union and is, as it were, the prolongation of the lives of the father and mother, their flesh, their blood and their bones.

When a cell from the father's body and a cell from the mother's body come together (in the mother's body), they form one cell, into which God, the third Partner of the marriage, infuses that life-giving element, the immortal soul. This cell will divide into two, into four, eight cells, and thus continues to develop into the full body of the infant which is born just nine months later. A new being, part of the flesh and blood of mother and father, comes into the world; this new life is destined to become part of the mystical body of Christ, a child of God, and will last forever! God has another creature to lavish His love upon and to be loved by in return. God and all heaven are waiting to be this child's inheritance! Therein lies the complete richness and beauty of the marriage act! There is the virtue of it, if all is done according to the plans of the Divine Architect. That is how God wants us to view marriage and its union of two as one; that is how we should see it.

In fact, St. Paul bids us to see in marriage a union comparable to that existing between Christ and His Church. Surely no one can blaspheme this union by saying that it is something improper, vile, ugly, or shameful. God forbid!

Only pagans would have us believe otherwise. Only a world that has forgotten its Maker has surrounded sex with the aura of nastiness which it has today even in the minds of many Christians.

There is another attitude, a spawn of Jansenism, which would tell the married that they should not enjoy, to a greater or lesser degree, the pleasure resulting from the marriage act. Far from it, the opposite is true. It is God who has attached keen physical pleasure to the exercise of the procreative faculties. He would not have put it there if He did not want it enjoyed within the bounds set by Him (properly performed intercourse in the married state).

He put this pleasure into the marriage act to make sure this faculty would be used to perpetuate the human race. Hence married people are justly entitled to all the delight they can reasonably procure from marital relations, for they pay fully for this joy and delight by assuming its consequences and the attendant responsibilities. So they need not scruple on that score. God wants it so.

EXAMPLE:

"This sort of thing is distasteful to me," is the attitude of Mrs. X when her husband requests the marriage act. "It's my duty to render it to my husband, but I know that God turns His face the other way at a time like this."

This is not only a positively un-Christian attitude toward the sacred power of sex, but it could be sinful. Such an attitude is almost enough to tempt a husband to unfaithfulness. The husband, unsatisfied, perhaps hurt, and certainly disappointed by his unresponsive yet "dutiful" wife, knows that outside his home other women have no distaste for "that sort of thing" and can be found on streets, in bars and in offices. A good man will resist such a temptation; a less good man may not — not that he would be justified; he would not. But our point is that the refusal, without sufficient reason to grant the marital rights, constitutes matter for grave sin.

MODERATION URGED

It may almost seem that since the marriage act, when properly performed, is an act of virtue, it should be performed very often. But this is not really so. It has to be moderated like everything else. To give a dollar to a beggar is an act of virtue, but to give him the whole pay check when wife and children are waiting at home to be fed and clothed properly, would not only *not* be an act of virtue but would be positively sinful. So also, moderation should be observed in exercising the rights of marriage. Common sense and prudence should always dictate the frequency of the act. Of course, the married couple is left with much freedom in this regard. Much will depend on their mutual will and need in this matter. Whatever is mutually agreeable and satisfactory to both partners can be assumed to be moderate *for them.*

At the other extreme is the very dangerous situation where there is an unreasonable refusal to render the marriage act when the other partner seriously asks for it. One of the purposes of marriage is the allaying of concupiscence, the desire of the body. This desire varies with each individual, and it is hardly likely that any particular man and wife will find themselves completely similar in this regard; it usually happens that one partner is disposed to a more frequent use of marriage rights than the other. This situation places the responsibility on the other to sacrifice personal inclination. Such a one should understand the other's needs with kindness and love. So long as the frequency of the request is not unreasonable, refusal would be matter for grave sin, not only because the marriage contract is broken but also because the partner refused is denied the legitimate satisfaction of his bodily urges and may be unable to use sufficient self-control to avoid committing either solitary sin or adultery.

However, if there is truly excessive demand, or rather if the frequency of the act is abused, then the frequency may be restricted without sin. There may be other circumstances entering into this problem of excessive demand; hence, consultation with one's confessor may be imperative in many cases. No problem of married life is a stranger to the confessor; so feel free to ask for advice and counsel there. Expert counsel is yours for the asking.

ACTIONS BOUND UP WITH THE MARITAL ACT

Because the marital act is good and sacred, it should be clear, then, that all actions, whether necessary or useful as a preparation to this act, are good and virtuous. The same is true of all actions accompanying it. This applies also to all actions which are conducive to rendering the act more pleasurable.

Moreover, whatever one is justified in doing, one is justified in thinking about or desiring and enjoying it. Of course, such action (both interior and exterior) cannot be intended to cause voluntary ejaculation (taking place outside the marital act), nor can one voluntarily expose oneself to the proximate danger of such pollution. The word *voluntary* in both cases must be emphasized, for if such pollution occurs involuntarily, that is, unexpectedly, unwished for, there is no sin.

ACTIONS NOT BOUND UP WITH THE MARRIAGE ACT

In addition to the marriage act, there are other sexual privileges granted to the married. Certain marks of endearment and expressions of love, such as kisses, embraces, caresses, touches, looks, and the like, are perfectly permissible even if done with no intention of performing the marriage act. They are almost an indispensable means of fostering and maintaining mutual love. The married can safely follow this principle: whatever they may do to foster or show mutual love, and however it is done, it is not sinful provided they do not intentionally or consciously cause pollution (in one or the other party) or voluntarily expose themselves to the proximate danger of it.

Also they may not only enjoy thoughts, desires, or imaginations of anything that they are allowed to do, but they may also take pleasure in the remembrance of past intimacies with their partner in marriage; here, again, there must be no intention or proximate danger of causing pollution.

Sometimes a married person may even be allowed to risk the danger of pollution by his or her acts of affection if there is proportionate reason to justify such an action; for example, to restrain one's partner from adultery, to avert suspicion, etc. Should pollution occur in such a case, the withholding of consent is a serious obligation.

Perhaps it may seem obvious but the married are seriously forbidden to enjoy thoughts or desires *not* about their wife or husband but about someone else. The guilt of such thoughts or imaginations and desires is judged according to the principles given for the unmarried, except that such desires also have the added malice of being adulterous.

IF PROCREATION IS IMPOSSIBLE . . .

It often happens that procreation of children is impossible either because the wife is beyond the child-bearing age, or because she is already pregnant, or because of some other reason. In such cases it is still lawful and good to perform the marriage act because the other purposes of marriage (the fostering of mutual love and the allaying of the sexual urge) can thus be fulfilled. The marriage act is likewise lawful even if it is certain that a stillbirth or a premature delivery will result (due to the poor health of the wife).

Marital relations are lawful at any time during the year. In seasons of penance, such as Lent and Advent, some pious couples, by mutual consent, either refrain entirely from the marriage act or perform it less frequently; but this is merely optional on their part; in no way is it prescribed.

Some may wonder whether such relations are lawful on Communion days (and the night before). Yes, because the act is good and virtuous, it forms no obstacle to the reception of Holy Communion.

RENDERING THE DEBT

Through the marriage contract the married partners give each other the use of their bodies and undertake to have marital relations whenever the other reasonably requests or wishes; that is the object of the contract. Therefore, to refuse marital relations without sufficient reason when the other reasonably requests it, is a gravely sinful matter, because a serious right of another is being denied. Besides, the partner wishing to have marital relations would usually have to make a sacrifice, great or small, to overcome temptation to incontinence when refused by the other. Frequently the refusing party is quite definitely placing the refused partner in real danger of incontinence.

If, however, only a mere suggestion or hint rather than a real request is made for the marriage act, and the partner requesting it is quite satisfied to take no for the answer, then there would be no question of sin (provided, always, no danger of incontinence exists on the part of the requesting partner). It would usually be venially sinful for one, when asked for the debt, only to postpone it briefly; likewise, when the use of the marriage right is frequent and its refusal rare (such a refusal is venially sinful).

Either partner may ask for marital relations at any time, even during pregnancy, menstruation, lactation or nursing, or during an ordinary sickness. The wiser course, however, during the months of pregnancy, especially the last months, is to restrict the frequency of relations; necessary precautions should also be taken to avoid injuring the coming child by adopting, whenever required, a less dangerous position; but the act still must be performed properly. If there is real danger of abortion, relations must not take place. During the menstrual period special consideration should always be had for the wife; though it is not immoral to perform the act at that time, it is not advisable. However, during the first two weeks following a birth, the marriage act is forbidden under pain of serious sin; and during the following four weeks, under pain of venial sin.

Husband and wife, if they truly love and cherish each other, will always be considerate of one another and no laws or rules regarding the rendering of marital relations are necessary for them. Mutual love and consideration will take care of that. On the one hand, each will be happy to be able through marital relations to give the other pleasure and joy; on the other hand, each will generously forgo their own pleasure if marital relations would be a burden for the other. True conjugal love is like that: unselfish. When it is that, marital intercourse will be the full and true expression of mutual love as it was meant to be.

True, sometimes rendering the debt may be a hardship for some women; St. Paul calls the marriage act a "debt" (and the name has stuck since), thereby implying that it would at times be a real and painful burden; for paying a debt is not infrequently painful, especially if it is a serious debt. Every wife must be very careful in this, lest by her refusal she expose her husband to the temptation of seeking sexual gratification elsewhere.

Still, there are some circumstances when either partner is completely justified in refusing to render the debt. Moral theologians tell us that the following circumstances excuse:

1. When the one requesting the debt has committed adultery. However, the adultery must be certain and it must have been committed voluntarily. Thus, this excuse does not hold if one has been raped. Also, there is no excuse after the adultery has been pardoned by the other — for example, by voluntarily rendering the debt, even once, in spite of knowledge of the adultery.

2. The marriage debt need not be rendered when the other is completely intoxicated or insane.

3. When there is great danger to health or life. Thus such a danger would be present if one has a very weak heart (a competent, honest physician should pass judgment), or if one partner is infected with venereal disease. But the ordinary hardships of pregnancy, nursing and care of children do not excuse (always remembering that the husband is bound by the law of charity); neither would intense but brief pains, nor prolonged but mild headaches, and the like. Neither does the fear (even if founded on experience) that the possible conception will result in a stillbirth or miscarriage excuse from rendering the debt; however, if by rendering the debt there is danger of causing the miscarriage of an already conceived fetus, the marriage act may not take place.

4. Moral theologians also affirm that the wife may refuse to render the debt during the six weeks following a birth.

5. When there is real abuse of frequency of relations; as we have said before, it may be restricted. Best to talk this matter over with one's confessor.

6. When there is danger of scandal, as can easily happen in certain circumstances, in crowded homes, etc., then the debt should be refused; in such cases the relations should be postponed until this danger is absent.

WHAT IS FORBIDDEN TO THE MARRIED

Because of the extremely serious consequences for the human race and because of the importance of procreation for time and eternity, God has placed very definite and rigorous limits around the sexual appetite. Those limits are precisely set within the bounds of lawful marriage. The "off-limits" signs are so definite that any deliberate (with full realization and consent) indulgence in sexual gratification is seriously sinful for those not united by the bonds of marriage. This is so, we repeat, not because the sexual appetite is something evil, but because something very sacred has been tampered with.

Even those united by marriage are not permitted the indiscriminate use of sex; although married, they still have to observe the limits which God has put around this sacred faculty. In addition to the above, the following actions are sinful to the married: *self-abuse* or masturbation, *sodomy, onanism,* and *artificial birth prevention* or the use of contraceptives, *adulterous incest* and *adultery.*

SELF-ABUSE

This act defeats even the biological purpose of sex. Some married people commit this solitary sin despite the fact that the use of marriage (by the marital act) should serve them as a virtuous outlet for concupiscence. It is precisely for this reason that self-abuse is, in a way, a more serious sin for the married. In confessing this sin, the married must mention the fact that they are married.

SODOMY

This very serious sin of impurity, when not committed by two persons of the same sex, is any sexual union between man and woman (or husband and wife) which imitates sexual intercourse in an unnatural manner. Because it would be imprudent to discuss this particular subject outside the confessional, we refer to the confessor anyone faced with giving unwilling cooperation in this sin and, again, do not be afraid — the confessor is there to help you.

ONANISM

This sin of onanism or withdrawal is committed, if in the process of intercourse the husband withdraws voluntarily and thus wastes the seed. It gets its name from Onan, who committed this sin (Genesis, 38:8). God struck Onan dead (just for what reason Scripture scholars disagree). Needless to say, onanism is a serious sin for both husband and wife if done deliberately with malice of forethought. Though withdrawal may render conception more unlikely, it definitely does not prevent it entirely.

ARTIFICIAL BIRTH PREVENTION

This is a sin of many names, but whether it is called artificial birth prevention, birth control, contraception, the art of "being careful," or any other such name, it is still regarded as onanism practiced artificially, if the couple act out of egoism in refusing the service of life. While it is carried out in various ways, by the use of pills, jellies, chemicals, or mechanical devices, the purpose is always the same — namely, to prevent conception from taking place from the marriage act. The Church has condemned all and every use of artificial contraception; according to the mind of the Church, every time an artificial means of contraception is used, it constitutes matter for serious sin.

According to the opinion of theologians, artificial birth prevention is evil, because it consists of performing a natural act (the marriage act) in a way that is contrary to the will of God and perverts His divine intention; it is an act of gross insubordination and rebellion against the natural law. Neither extreme poverty, nor delicacy of constitution on the part of the wife, nor the prediction of the doctor as to the danger of her death if she were to attempt to give birth to another child — in a word, no reason whatever can be a just cause for the use of artificial birth prevention.

If any types of sheaths are used in the marriage act, the act is unlawful from the beginning; hence, positive cooperation on the part of the wife is never permitted. She may not render the debt. However, if there is danger of serious harm to her if she refuses to perform the marriage act, her confessor, after judging the case, may permit the wife to act passively — only on the basis of averting a very grave evil. The wife in this case is gravely bound to try to withhold consent to the concomitant pleasure. If the woman is the one who uses means to prevent conception (jellies, chemicals, or even certain actions), the husband must use all his marital authority to prevent such practices on her part; if he cannot prevail, he must conduct himself in a manner similar to that of a woman in regard to a husband to the practice of onanism.

One of the purposes of marriage is mutual help in the sanctification of each other, and if one or the other or both have a mind to practice artificial birth control or any other sin against conjugal chastity, they drag down the person they hold most dear in life to the depths of degradation and sin. The husband or wife who endeavors to persuade the other to participate in gravely sinful actions may be persuading the other to eternal suicide. "Do you not know that you are the temple of God and that the Spirit of God dwells in you? If anyone destroys the temple of God, him will God destroy. For holy is the temple of God, and this temple you are" (1 Cor. 3:16, 17).

CONJUGAL ACTS AFTER VOLUNTARY STERILIZATION

Here we are speaking of voluntary sterilization undergone for the purpose of birth prevention or contraception. Subsequent to such an operation, all conjugal acts as attempts to enjoy the fruit of culpable sterilization without sacrifice are sinful. Their motivation and underlying disposition make them so.

Before marital relations may be resumed without sin, there must be a change of heart, true and sincere repentance for having undergone sinful sterilization. The marriage debt, however, may be requested and rendered for any morally good motive, e.g., fostering of mutual love, etc. True repentance requires the will to correct the sinfully caused condition so far as is reasonably possible. In this case, it would include the willingness to correct the condition resulting from the voluntary and culpable sterilization, i.e., the willingness to try reversing the biological act of sterilization, if this can be done with reasonable hope of success and the expense involved is not excessive to the person in question. Factually, present medical techniques in reversing vasectomy are still very imperfect and the success of the corrective operation, dubious: this, coupled with the serious expense involved would generally excuse a person from attempting to reverse the operation.

Also a person is not obliged to reverse the biological act of sterilization, if he (or she) judges, with an upright and enlightened conscience, that a new pregnancy now and at any time in the future would be against rightly understood responsibility (e.g., not being able to take proper care of the children they already have, because of ill health, etc.). In such a case, the act of restoring biological fertility for this person would be against enlightened reason.

'THE PILL' — SYNTHETIC PROGESTIN PRODUCTS

Medical science has introduced various synthetic progestin products (Enovid, Norlutin, Ortho-novum, etc.) whose chief effect is the suppression of ovulation and, therefore, renders the woman infertile. Many laymen refer to these products merely as "the pill," while others call them the "contraceptive pill," "steroid drugs," etc. Since these drugs make a woman infertile for as long a time as they are used, they are used chiefly for birth control or contraceptive purposes.

Even before Pope Paul's encyclical "On Human Life," there were certain clear-cut, moral principles taught by the Church regarding the use of progestational products or steroids:

1. The use of progestational steroids with the serious and direct purpose of birth control was condemned.

2. If such medication was used not with the purpose of preventing conception but on the advice of a physician as a necessary remedy for an illness of the womb or the organism (health of the whole body), it was allowed according to the principle governing actions with a twofold effect. (See Pope Pius XII's address at the seventh convention of the International Society of Hematology, Rome, September 12, 1958.)

These principles hold valid after the promulgation of Pope Paul's encyclical "On Human Life." Under principle number 2, we may include the medically indicated use of progesterone for normalizing a woman's periods; hence, its use is permissible even though ovulation is excluded during treatment and the couple may engage in marital relations without sin in the meantime. The same may be said when progestin products are used to normalize the woman's cycle in order that the couple may make use of the "safe" period. Formerly, menstrual irregularity prevented numerous couples from using rhythm in order to exercise responsible parenthood. This difficulty is now very considerably diminished. Also progestational steroids may be used without sin to cure the ills or difficulties of menopause or "change of life" if the physician so directs. In the meantime the couple may sinlessly engage in conjugal acts.

But what of the use of progestational steroids by married couples, free from selfishness, in order to avoid pregnancies precisely because they want to be responsible parents? In other words, how to solve the truly agonizing difficulty of reconciling the need to express conjugal love with the responsible transmission of human life? Discussions regarding this problem were many and varied in recent years. Many sincere Catholics, laymen and theologians, have entertained doubts about the validity of arguments proposed to forbid any positive intervention which would prevent the transmission of human life. "As a result there have arisen opinions and practices contrary to traditional moral theology. Because of this, many had been expecting official confirmation of their views. This helps to explain the negative reaction the encyclical ('On Human Life') received in many quarters." (From the "Statement of Canadian Bishops on the Encyclical Humanae Vitae," Plenary Assembly, St. Boniface-Winnipeg, September 27, 1968.)

In the encyclical "On Human Life," Pope Paul VI gave his decision, one of the most courageous given by any man in the modern world, regarding the morality of using steroid drugs for preventing conception. The encyclical forbade the use of such drugs for the purposes of contraception even though this would harmonize conjugal love and responsible parenthood and it reiterated the morally accepted means of harmonizing these two obligations by the use of rhythm.

Instead of diminishing, the controversy intensified. Thousands, perhaps millions of Catholics still faced grave problems of conscience. In fact, the problem was compounded, for the visible head of the Church had spoken. While he did not pronounce his decision *ex cathedra* and, therefore, his teaching was not *de fide,* he exercised his supreme, authentic teaching authority as head of the Church. The distress and confusion was genuine and intense. The Canadian bishops tried to put it into focus when they said: "We wish to reiterate our positive conviction that a Catholic Christian is not free to form his conscience without consideration of the teaching of the magisterium, in this particular instance exercised by the Holy Father in an encyclical. . . ."

Obviously, some kind of clarification regarding these difficult problems of morality was necessary from those who share the pastoral concern which led the Holy Father to offer counsel and direction in an area which, while controverted, could hardly be more important to human happiness. (See "Statement of Canadian Bishops," Number 2.) In fact, such clarification was obligatory. The encyclical "On Human Life" (Numbers 4 and 18) itself clearly indicated this. The bishops of the various countries of the Catholic world, in concert with theologians, endeavored to discharge their obligation to the best of their ability. They did this also out of concern and love for the Holy Father and in the spirit of service to all mankind. Though the statements of clarification and guidance given by the national conferences of bishops in the various countries of the world were not the same, that of the Canadian bishops was one of the most helpful. Certainly, it is a safe guide to follow for any loyal Catholic.

Pertinent to the problem at hand, the Canadian bishops offered some practical norms to help settle the consciences of distressed Catholics faced with difficulties arising from the encyclical.

A. *Each person must follow his honestly formed conscience:* "Christian theology regarding conscience has its roots in the teaching of St. Paul (Rom. 14:23, 1 Cor. 10). This has been echoed in our day by Vatican II: 'Conscience is the most secret core and sanctuary of a man. There he is alone with God, whose voice echoes in his depths' (The Church Today, Number 16). 'On his part, man perceives and acknowledges the imperatives of the divine law through the mediation of conscience. In all his activity a man is bound to follow his conscience faithfully, in order that he may come to God, for whom he was created' (On Religious Freedom, Number 3). The dignity of man consists precisely in his ability to achieve his fulfillment in God through the exercise of a knowing and free choice.

"However, this does not exempt a man from the responsibility of forming his conscience according to truly Christian values and principles. This implies a spirit of openness to the teaching of the Church which is an essential aspect of the Christian's baptismal vocation. It likewise implies sound personal motivation free from selfishness and undue external pressure which are incompatible with the spirit of Christ. Nor will he succeed in this difficult task without the help of God. Man is prone to sin and evil and unless he humbly asks and gratefully receives the grace of God this basic freedom will inevitably lead to abuse.

"True freedom of conscience does not consist, then, in the freedom to do as one likes, but rather to do as a responsible conscience directs. Vatican II applies this concept forcefully. Christians therefore 'must always be governed according to a conscience dutifully conformed to the divine law itself, and should be submissive towards the Church's teaching office, which authentically interprets that law in the light of the Gospel. That divine law reveals and protects the integral meaning of conjugal love, and impels it towards truly human fulfillment' (The Church Today, Number 50)." (See "Statement of Canadian Bishops," Numbers 9, 10, 12.)

B. *Those who honestly fail to agree with some points of the encyclical are not to consider themselves or are not to be considered out of the Church:* "It is a fact that a certain number of Catholics, although admittedly subject to the teaching of the encyclical, find it either extremely difficult or even impossible to make their own all elements of this doctrine. In particular, the argumentation and rational foundation of the encyclical, which are only briefly indicated, have failed in some cases to win the assent of men of science, or indeed of some men of culture and education who share in the contemporary empirical and scientific mode of thought. We must appreciate the difficulty experienced by contemporary man in understanding and appropriating some of the points of this encyclical, and we must make every effort to learn from the insights of Catholic scientists and intellectuals, who are of undoubted loyalty to Christian truth, to the Church and to the authority of the Holy See. Since they are not denying any point of divine and Catholic faith nor rejecting the teaching authority of the Church, these Catholics should not be considered, or consider themselves, shut off from the body of the faithful. But they should remember that their good faith will be dependent on a sincere self-examination to determine the true motives and grounds for such suspension of assent and on continued effort to understand and deepen their knowledge of the teaching of the Church." (See "Statement of Canadian Bishops," Number 17.)

C. *Those who, because of particular circumstances, find themselves in what seems to them a clear conflict of duties, e.g., reconciling of conjugal love and responsible parenthood, are given this practical norm by the Canadian bishops:* ". . . In accord with the accepted principles of moral theology, if these persons have tried sincerely but without success to pursue a line of conduct in keeping with the given directives, they may be safely assured that whoever honestly chooses that course which seems right to him does so in good conscience."

Among other counsels, the Canadian bishops also urged: "In the situation we described earlier in this statement (Number 17) the confessor or counsellor must show sympathetic understanding and reverence for the sincere good faith of those who fail in their effort to accept some point of the encyclical." (See "Statement of Canadian Bishops," Number 25).

In keeping with the directives of the Holy Father, obviously, the use of rhythm is of paramount importance for Catholic couples. Let us deal with it in detail.

RHYTHM

Rhythm is the restriction of the properly performed marital act to the non-fertile periods of the wife in order to avoid conception. In other words, the married couple are using their right to the marriage act, and the fact that generation does not follow is not due to their artificial obstruction of nature but only to the normal functioning of nature. This practice is based on the theory that the period of a woman's ovulation can be determined with reasonable accuracy. Without attempting to explain the physical aspects of ovulation (it is best to consult a reliable physician), we shall only mention that competent medical authority says that the periods of ovulation (fertility) recur at regular intervals. Determining the exact length of the interval between the end of one ovulation and the beginning of the next is essential to the successful practice of the rhythm theory; but this space of time between ovulations differs in different women. In some this interval may consist of twenty-four days; in another it may be twenty-eight days; and in others, thirty-two days. Since there is a biological connection between ovulation and the menstrual flow, knowing the time of the latter can aid in computing the occurrence of the former. In any case, the aid of a physician is nearly always necessary for any successful or very accurate computation. Even then, rhythm cannot be looked upon as a certain method of avoiding conception; but it does provide probability of securing the desired results.

As we have said before, those united to each other by valid marriage have the right of performing the marital act. Furthermore, if both the husband and wife freely agree to forgo the exercise of their right, there is no obligation on their part to perform the marital act at any particular time. They may, if they so sinlessly agree, lawfully abstain from exercising their marital rights for the whole of their married life or for a part of that time; hence, total abstinence, from the use of marital rights for either a period of time or the whole married life is sinless in itself. This, of course, has no reference to the use of the marital rights only during the sterile period: it is merely the lawful right of the married not to use their marital rights totally and exclusively in their married life if both so freely desire. For example, after Mr. and Mrs. J are told by a medical expert that a pregnancy would likely result in her death, they mutually agree to total abstinence from the use of their marital rights until Mrs. J is physically unable to have children because of age. Though this is an extreme case, it is an entirely sinless course of action which, though heroic, is possible with the grace of God.

If a married couple may, when they so agree, abstain from using their marital rights for the whole of their married life or for part of that time, may they also abstain from the use of their marital rights only during the *fertile period* of the wife? In other words, when is it lawful and when is it sinful for married couples to perform the marital act only at those times when conception is less likely? In itself the marital act, if placed in the normal way, during the so-called sterile periods of the wife is natural and sinless. Note we say *in itself* it is lawful, for it may become sinful because of certain circumstances.

1. First of all, married couples who choose to exercise the marital act at all have the obligation of contributing to the preservation of the human race. This obligation is not sufficiently fulfilled when the marriage act is restricted to the sterile periods merely by placing the act in a natural way with the willingness to accept children if they are conceived. In practice, we may say that married couples who exercise the marriage act have an obligation to have a family, if they can. This is a *serious* obligation, but there may be grave reasons which would excuse them from this obligation. Therefore, married couples who have not fulfilled this obligation and who do not have grave reasons excusing them from fulfilling it, may not use rhythm without sin.

What are some of the reasons that are considered sufficient for justifying the use of rhythm over a long period of time? The following: (1) if pregnancy would constitute either a serious harm to the health of the mother or danger of death; (2) if the coming child would very probably be stillborn or would inherit a serious defect; (3) if with the increase of the family there would be grave difficulty in supporting it responsibly. Some theologians also hold that couples may also use rhythm for long periods of time in countries with a serious problem of population explosion.

EXAMPLE:

Mr. Y is a factory worker who has four children. He thinks that it would be justifiable to use rhythm for the next few years to ease the burden. Mrs. Y agrees.

They may do so sinlessly.

Using rhythm without any justifying reason at all for a short period of time (e.g., two or three years) would ordinarily be venially sinful.

2. When practicing rhythm, the husband or wife still has the serious obligation of rendering marital relations if the other sincerely requests it outside the sterile period, or if one of them is in proximate danger of serious sin (self-abuse, adultery, etc.) because of the limited periods of time to which the use of rhythm restricts sexual relations.

EXAMPLE:

In the above case, after Mr. and Mrs. Y mutually agree to the use of rhythm for several years, four months later Mr. Y asks his wife for the marital act outside her sterile period.
Mrs. Y has the serious obligation to render relations then.

We judge the use of basal body temperature for the purpose of avoiding offspring in the very same way as the use of rhythm.

It is useful to know that rhythm can be used for a purpose other than that discussed above. If a married couple know the exact date of ovulation, they will be able to determine the time when the use of their marriage rights is most likely to bring about pregnancy; this may therefore help those married couples who are childless and want very much to have children.

TIPS TO HUSBANDS AND WIVES

Little things mean a lot. Most husbands and wives don't want diamonds and pearls, Cadillacs or yachts — they can't afford them anyway. And most who have them would rather have a spouse who is loyal, understanding and considerate, with a heart filled with love; one who will walk at their side, extending a helping hand when the going gets rough; a spouse who shares their hopes, their prayers, their joys and sorrows, their whole life in an intertwining union of love. These are the important things in any happy marriage but the trimmings, the little things, also mean a lot. The following tips, unashamedly lifted en masse from other works (Anselm Viano, *When You Are Married,* Staten Island, N.Y., Society of St. Paul, 1950) are good, so good in fact that we would like to share them with you.

FOR THE HUSBAND

A. Eat appreciatively of her cooking and express your appreciation often in words.

B. Give her a genuine, sweet kiss with natural frequency, and remind her that you remember her and the entire family daily in your personal prayers.

C. If possible, set aside at least one night each week for a "night out" with her.

D. Have only praise for her when talking with others.

E. Work together with your own children, or with adopted ones if you cannot have your own.

F. Develop spare-time hobbies that you can share with each other.

G. Plan many events together instead of going separate ways.

H. Have frequent words of praise for her.

I. Share with her all plans, problems, efforts and benefits for your home.

J. Remember all anniversaries and other special events.

FOR THE WIFE

A. Let him know continually that you are proud of and believe in him, and are saying a prayer for him each day.

B. While with others agree with him most of the time, if not always.

C. Dress attractively for him at all possible times.

D. Avoid any kind of deception or secrets kept from him.

E. Have an encouraging interest in his work.

F. Entertain married friends frequently in your home with him.

G. For each critical suggestion offer him at least two points of praise.

H. Have an encouraging smile and word for him, especially in "tough" times.

I. Even when there are children, save time and interest exclusively for him.

J. Accumulate with him many happy memories for the future.

'DON'TS' FOR THE WIFE

All your life you have been taught in song and story and drama that love is moonlight and roses and sharp ecstasy. It's not. It's understanding and loyalty and consideration of each other. It's drawing together in grief and success and failure. It's walking together in harmony.

It doesn't sound very romantic? Oh, but it is! It's all of the fine, good things that grow out of the wonder you're feeling now. Love doesn't remain the same. It grows in riches and poignancy, as you, too, will grow in wisdom and understanding.

And, as in everything else, there are a few "don'ts" to remember:

DON'T expect too much.

DON'T expect a movie version of marriage.

DON'T expect him to tell you every day how much he loves you. He expects you to take that for granted.

DON'T telephone him at his place of business unless it's extremely urgent.

DON'T pout because he forgets to kiss you.

DON'T nag him about his friends or the girls in the office.

DON'T bind him with possessive chains, no matter how fraught with love they may be. No one likes to feel that he is tied to a stake! Feed the brute, and love him, and pray for understanding and tolerance and patience!

'DON'TS' FOR THE HUSBAND

Husbands should observe a few DON'TS too, such as: DON'T leave clothes around on chairs or wet towels on the bathroom floor. DON'T be careless when dining. Here is a fine list from Father C. H. Doyle's *Cana Is Forever* (Tarrytown, N.Y., Nugent Press, 1949):

Never butt into the management of the kitchen.

Never say her hat is crazy. Praise her for her unusual headgear.

DON'T complain about the "junk" in her purse. Think about your own pockets.

DON'T keep telling your wife to "step on it" when she is trying to do her nails or pour herself into one of those new dresses. You'd be all thumbs then, too.

DON'T forget her birthday or the anniversaries. (The same goes for her parents'.)

DON'T pass remarks about her girl friends.

DON'T stay at a party when you can see that your wife is uncomfortable or bored. Take your cue from her when to leave.

DON'T neglect to compliment your wife often on her beauty and efficiency. It works wonders.

Remember that she loves attention. In public, really turn it on. Help her off with her coat, stand behind her chair until she is seated. Order for her. Light her cigarette. Look interested in what she is telling you. Just remember that women love attention. Pour it on!

Chapter XV

THE SEVENTH AND TENTH COMMANDMENTS

"You shall not steal" (Ex. 20:15).

"You shall not covet your neighbor's house" (Ex. 20:17).

God has given us a divine law forbidding us to steal or to desire unlawfully anything that belongs to another; from this we may deduce another great truth: *God has given men the right to own goods or property* (otherwise we could take anyone else's goods), a fact not a few men in our times refuse to recognize. This truth is also found in the natural law: each of us has a natural right to the goods necessary for preserving life (food, clothing and shelter), because each of us has the natural obligation and right to preserve our life. A man must not only provide for himself alone but for his family as well. He is therefore justified in striving to acquire and to keep as his own the things he and his family must have if they are to live a life worthy of human beings.

Without permanent property or capital a man cannot make adequate provision for his own support or that of his family, especially when old age, sickness or some other disability prevents him from working for a living day and night. Were the State to own everything, it would necessarily have to give man his livelihood. Then man would be compelled to depend completely on the State and this would contradict the right of every man to enjoy his personal independence. The State would then be his sole master, dictating what man's life should be, what he must do, what he must not do. Should he refuse to do the State's bidding in order to follow his conscience, then all the State would have to do would be to deny him his livelihood. As simple as that. Modern history has witnessed such cases many times.

Man, master of his own person, is also master of the fruits of his labor, his inheritance, his gifts or anything which he has acquired by lawful means. He has a right to hold and possess these things in order to reasonably assure himself and his dependents future livelihood. He has a right to claim these things as his own, and everyone must regard them as such; his right of claim implies an obligation for everyone else to act in accord with this claim.

The Seventh and Tenth Commandments protect this right by obliging everyone to respect a person's ownership of goods and by forbidding any violation of this ownership. The Seventh Commandment forbids theft, robbery, cheating, unjust damage, etc. The Tenth Commandment further safeguards this right of ownership by forbidding all *unjust desires* for another's goods, i.e., to *covet* our neighbor's goods (it does not forbid us *merely to desire* them). In other words, we are guilty of unjust desires when we want to acquire another's goods by *unlawful means,* not if we propose to acquire them by lawful means. Unjust desires for another's goods are sins of the same nature as the unjust deeds themselves would be, had they actually been carried out.

EXAMPLE:

Mrs. O'Shea, a wealthy widow, looks at a friend's stamp collection and ardently wishes she had a few of his "oldies" from British Guiana. She offers $10,000 for them.

She committed no sin whatever in desiring to have the stamps, for she did not want to acquire them by unlawful means but by lawful means: by buying them for a fair price.

THEFT

Theft is the secret taking of another's goods contrary to his reasonable wishes.

Usually we think of theft as secretly stealing something, shoplifting, or "swiping" something. But theft can take on more subtle forms; for instance, if I burden myself with debts (running up a charge account, etc.) to such an extent that I know I will not be able to pay, or if I live so lavishly now that I will not be able to pay my legitimately contracted debts of the past. Or, again, if I know the owner would refuse to lend me some particular thing but still I "borrow" it with the intention of giving it back, I am really stealing the temporary use of that article; hence, to judge the morality of this act, I would have to estimate the charge which would be billed me had I rented such an article for that amount of time from some rental agency. Thus, if I know an acquaintance of mine has made it a practice never to lend any of his books to anyone but still I "borrow" a bestseller which I want to read, I would have to assess my guilt by what a rental library would charge me for using the book. If I willfully kept the book for ten days and the rental library charged three cents a day, I would be guilty of a theft of thirty cents.

If I believe the owner would consent to lend me some article had I a chance to ask him, I may go ahead and borrow the article even though he would be quite displeased. In such a case, there is no question of theft for I would have what is known as the owner's *presumed consent.* If, however, the owner can conveniently be asked, one cannot use presumed consent. Whenever a person borrows with presumed consent, he must afterwards inform the owner about his action.

EXAMPLE:

Aunt Susie's neighbors are away for the weekend. Whenever asked, the

neighbors always lent Aunt Susie their garden equipment; so she borrows the articles for her own as well as her nephew's use. She is justified in presuming consent.

HOW TO DETERMINE THE GUILT OF THEFT

To judge correctly the gravity of any particular theft, we must keep in mind several circumstances that will affect it. In other words, we must judge the theft not only according to the *amount or value* of the goods stolen but also the *person* from whom it is stolen, as well as the *length of time* during which the stealing continues. Why do these circumstances affect the sinfulness of theft? Because the gravity of the theft has to be measured, logically enough, by the injustice, damage or inconvenience suffered by the victim. Obviously, a beggar will be much more affected by the loss of ten dollars than will a millionaire; public order will be violated more by the loss of a government car than by the loss of a hub cap of that car, etc. This tells us only what is obvious. Most cases will not be as clear-cut; hence, we must make a more detailed examination of the principles involved.

Principle I: *It would be grave matter (seriously sinful) to steal an amount of goods equivalent to the average day's pay of the person from whom the goods are stolen* (or the equivalent amount of what the man needs to support himself and his family with food, lodging and clothing for one day). Since this standard refers to a father of a family, the amount stolen from an unmarried person would be about twice as great before it becomes a serious matter. Naturally, this amount (which theologians call *relatively grave matter*) will vary from person to person, since one man may earn $30 a day while another may make only $15 a day. It depends on the job the man holds, the part of the country he is working in, and other similar circumstances. Because the injustice caused by stealing an equivalent of the victim's daily wage is grave, the sin is also grave if done deliberately.

When children steal from their parents (or *vice versa*) or steal from close relatives, the sum would usually have to be twice the daily wages of the victim in question before it would constitute grave matter. The reason for this is quite simple: theft, as we have already seen, is the unjust taking of another's *goods contrary to his reasonable wishes;* but parents naturally are less unwilling to lose their goods to their own children than to total strangers; hence the conclusion. This, however, does not mean that petty thefts of children from their parents are sinless. They definitely are sinful.

Principle II: *There is, however, an amount the stealing of which is always grave matter regardless of the wages or wealth of the one from whom it is stolen.* This is technically known as *absolutely grave matter* (or the *absolute sum*). The amount varies, of course, with circumstances of the times — the value of the dollar, for example — and with the place (the same amount has more or less purchasing power according to the place or the country). In general a sum is *absolutely grave* when it constitutes the equivalent of a week's wages received by a middle-class person.

In the matter of stealing from the wealthy, we do not so much regard the inconvenience sustained by the wealthy victim on account of his loss, but rather the serious violation of public order. If stealing unlimited amounts were only venially sinful, then private property and the welfare of human society would be seriously imperiled, with the result that stimulus for honest labor and industry would be seriously weakened. Also, confidence in the honesty of one's fellowmen, so necessary for normal functioning of business, would soon fade into complete distrust. Such a state of affairs would have dire, far-reaching effects for everyone.

Principle III: *Theft is venially sinful if the amount stolen is anything below the day's wages of the victim* (or below two days' wages if the victim is unmarried); or, *in the case of the very wealthy or companies* (corporations, governments, etc.), *if the amount stolen is below that known to constitute absolutely grave matter.*

We must emphasize, however, that sometimes repeated small thefts can add up to grave matter. This happens (1) when small amounts are stolen at intervals but add up to relatively grave matter (or, in the case of wealthy or collective ownership, absolutely grave matter) within the space of two or three months; (2) when the person committing the thefts has the intention of stealing a large sum from his victim by the repetition of small thefts. Let us examine this *time element* in greater detail.

THE TIME ELEMENT

A. When small amounts are stolen at intervals, the injustice ordinarily does not cause as much harm and inconvenience to the victim as would the same amount stolen from him in one lump sum. Therefore, *grave matter* is usually considered as being reached only when the sum stolen at intervals (but within less than two or three months) amounts to about twice the sum constituting grave matter when stolen in one lump sum. When stolen at intervals (but within less than two or three months) from an individual, then, the amount would have to be twice the relatively grave amount to constitute grave matter. When stolen from the very wealthy or from a corporation over a period of time, it would have to be twice the amount considered as absolutely grave.

EXAMPLE:

Betty, who is in charge of the petty cash for a large, prosperous firm, repeatedly takes small amounts ranging from 50¢ to $2, and then "pads" the account to cover the loss. She does not plan to steal a large sum in this way, only when she is short of snack money. There is matter for grave sin as soon as the amassed sums reach twice the absolute amount.

B. When the person committing the thefts has the intention of stealing a grave sum from his victim by the repetition of small thefts, then there is matter for grave sin *no matter how long* is the time over which the theft is spread. In other words, no matter how long the period of time over which the thief will stretch out his crime, if he has the intention of eventually, little by little, reaching a grave amount, the small thefts coalesce (add up) *through his intention.* What is the grave amount in this case? It is the *same* as that grave matter when stolen in one lump sum (principles I and II).

If a person steals small amounts *habitually* over a long time, however, he is regarded as having the intention of taking a large amount, though he may protest that he does not have such an intention. The very fact of habitually stealing from his victim indicates that he actually has the intention.

EXAMPLE:

Ralph habitually steals screws, nuts, bolts and small tools which are manufactured at the shop where he works. What is more, he intends to continue this practice indefinitely, for he finds it a profitable one — by selling these various items to the neighbors he makes enough to supply himself with money for his Saturday night poker games at Joe's place. These small thefts "coalesce" through his intention and hence there is matter for serious sin as soon as they eventually amount to grave matter.

There is matter for serious sin when a person steals what he believes is of great value, even though after the theft he finds out that the article stolen is only of small value; for example, if Mary, a maid working for the wealthy Smiths, steals what she thinks is an expensive diamond ring and later finds out it is merely of the "dime-store" variety (the obligation of restitution, however, obliges her to restore only what the ring is actually worth, that is, the "dime-store" price; hence, the obligation to make restitution would not be a grave one in this case, i.e., not binding under pain of serious sin).

Lest our explicit presentation of the principles regarding theft lead anyone to give in to the allurements of an "easy way" to acquire small luxuries, etc., we hasten to point out one thing: sooner or later a person must expiate his guilt of theft, even petty theft, by suffering for it in this life or in the next; then too, before God forgives him his sin of theft, he must promise to restore the ill-gotten goods anyway. Theft, even the smallest, is a sin; Christ suffered for it and it hurts Him now through His mystical body, the Church. It's not worth it, no matter how we consider it.

WHAT OF THE PERSON IN NEED?

Theft is the taking of another's goods *contrary to his reasonable wishes.* The last phrase is very important, for the mere act of taking another's goods is in itself not sinful (it is not an *intrinsically* evil act). Only when such an act is contrary to the reasonable wishes of the owner does it become sinful. Accordingly, it is not theft to take another's goods when we are in extreme need and must take them to get ourselves out of such need (presuming always the owner himself would not be placed in extreme need by our act).

Adjudged as extreme need are all circumstances in which a person would be in grave danger of losing his life, his health, his reputation or any other comparable situation. In such circumstances I may take as much of another's goods as will relieve my emergency, unless the other is in like necessity; I can do this even if the owner actually refuses to give up the goods needed by me. In extreme need the goods of earth become common property; the obligation to preserve life, health, or reputation takes precedence over the right of private ownership in these circumstances; or, rather, the rights of exclusive private ownership lapse until another's extreme need ceases to exist. The person in need, however, may take only what is absolutely necessary to relieve his present extreme need, and he must have no other way of acquiring the goods (for instance, asking for them).

If they are not used up, the goods taken must be restored when the need ceases. If the goods (money, food, drink, etc.) have been consumed, no restitution is necessary.

In all this a person may do for another what that other person could ethically do for himself.

EXAMPLE:

Old Hans has been bombed out of his home and is now starving. Because of his physical condition he cannot work. He sees a fairly fortunate family (at least they are well-fed) leave their house to take a stroll in the nearby park. They have previously refused him help. He slips into their house and takes some food from the kitchen. Old Hans was perfectly justified in his action.

Civil law does not recognize this right of taking another's goods by one in extreme need; however, this does not change the morality of such an action.

OCCULT COMPENSATION

Occult compensation is an act of secretly taking from another what is owed the taker in strict justice. Everyone has the right to possess what justly belongs to him. Attaining this possession generally should be accomplished through the ordinary channels. If, however, a situation arises in which a debtor refuses to pay and one cannot without grave inconvenience claim his right in a court of law, then one may pursue that right through occult compensation, provided the right is morally certain and in pursuing it one will come to no harm. This does not injure the proper order of society, for if a person cannot pursue his right in an ordinary way he may then pursue it in an extraordinary way.

In order to safeguard occult compensation against abuses, we must observe the following conditions:

A. The debt must be a *debt of justice* (otherwise the act would be unjust spoliation), and it must be *certain,* not doubtful (for everyone has a right to keep what he has until another's ownership is proved). Therefore, in cases where mere gratitude should persuade another to give me an article or sum of money, or when someone had promised to give me something but clearly had no intention of binding himself in justice, I cannot use occult compensation.

B. The creditor must be unable to recover his debt by any other means, either because such means would be useless or because they would seriously inconvenience him. Legal justice forbids a person to take the law into his own hands if there are other ways which can just as easily be used. Consequently, I cannot use occult compensation if I can conveniently achieve the same effect either by simply asking that the debt be repaid, or by threatening to file suit in the law courts, etc. But if such ordinary means would cause me great expense, create scandal, hatred, etc., I could justifiably use occult compensation as a last resort.

C. No unnecessary injury must be inflicted upon a third party (e.g., suspicion of theft); and the debtor must not be caused additional unnecessary loss or harm (e.g., deprivation of something he urgently needs for the day's work).

Since we are human and can easily deceive ourselves regarding the fulfillment of these conditions, we should as a general rule refrain from employing occult compensation until we have sought the advice of a prudent and impartial counselor. One's confessor would be the best adviser of all in such a matter.

EXAMPLES:

1. Mrs. Whosit lent $300 to Mr. Tenderhook, a business partner. After their quarrel and the breakup of the partnership, Mr. Tenderhook refuses to repay the loan. Though Mrs. Whosit could easily have her lawyer take care of Mr. Tenderhook in prompt order, she does not, but goes to his hunting lodge and takes $300 worth of camping equipment.

In this case it was unlawful for Mrs. Whosit to use occult compensation, because she could have easily recovered the debt by due legal process; thus the second condition necessary for occult compensation was not satisfied.

2. After Mr. Tenderhook finds that someone has broken into his lodge and made off with the camping equipment, he immediately suspects either the boys who have a cabin nearby (they are known to be light-fingered) or Mrs. Whosit. But he is quite convinced that Mrs. Whosit would not "stoop that low," for he has always known her to be scrupulously honorable. So it must have been those college hoodlums, he concludes.

The following weekend, when the boys are away at the university, he breaks into their cabin and takes an expensive camera which he thinks is worth about $300.

Again, in this case, it was not lawful to use occult compensation, for the first condition was not verified. Though this was not an act of vicious thievery on Mr. Tenderhook's part, it still was theft in the true sense of the word and hence not only a matter of grave sin but also a matter entailing full restitution. Whether or not Mr. Tenderhook was subjectively guilty of grave sin depends on his knowledge of the morality of his act.

3. Ronald worked three days for Mr. Tightfist. The wages agreed upon were $10 a day. After having asked Mr. Tightfist for his wages five times during the past two years, Ronald is still unpaid. So he asks his confessor whether he may use occult compensation; his confessor permits him to do so, but with the stipulation that he not exceed the thirty-dollar limit.

This was a just case of occult compensation, for all the conditions permitting it were verified.

4. Arthur, a carpenter, buys lumber from a company he has dealt with for years but which has just changed hands, and in his haste neglects to get a receipt for payment. The new owner sends him a bill, and when Arthur refuses to pay, sues him. Arthur is forced to pay a second time for the lumber. He is entitled to use occult compensation to recover what is owed him.

OCCULT COMPENSATION AS REGARDS AN UNJUST WAGE

Occult compensation is the secret taking from another of something (money or goods) which that other owes the taker. Clearly, such an action is fraught with possible danger of abuse, both moral and practical. It is therefore justly permitted *only* under very limited and special circumstances. Before we consider these regarding a just wage, let us remind ourselves of this: *Anyone who wishes to seek occult compensation is prudent and well-advised to consult with a competent and unbiased adviser.*

Workmen, servants and other employees have a right to a just wage, and when they do their work the payment of their wages is a debt of justice. What is a just wage in any particular case? That is not always easy to determine, even when we know all the circumstances surrounding a particular case. We must remember that, if a worker has freely contracted to work for a certain salary, even though later he may decide he is being underpaid, he must honor that contract. In order to use occult compensation an employee must not only make sure that the above conditions are fulfilled but he must also be sure of the following: (1) that the employer did not pay the original salary contract; (2) that the employer, without any need of help, has not hired him out of mere pity; (3) that the employer could pay more and still not suffer hardship; and (4) that the low wage was not already compensated for by tips, better food, etc. Obviously, employees are not always the best judges as to what is a fair and just wage.

The first means of obtaining a just wage which we must use is to take up the matter directly with our employer. Whether it is effective or not remains to be seen but it certainly has the advantage of not causing us useless worry and anxiety in settling our conscience in this complicated matter. We are, in fact, obliged to use this method unless we know that our efforts would be useless.

Another point to remember: if employees do additional work freely, they must not insist on being paid for it, since they have no claim in justice to such pay; if the employer asks, even implicitly, to have some extra work done, the employee then has a just claim.

EXAMPLE:

During the depression, Farmer Jones hired Mr. Green, the father of a large family, to work for him one summer, since the latter badly needed a job. The fact is Farmer Jones himself was trying desperately to make ends meet and could easily have taken care of the work himself but, pitying the large family of Mr. Green, he offered him the job with the best pay he could afford; though that, true, was far below the wages paid elsewhere for the same type of work. Farmer Jones even told Mr. Green not to quit looking for a better job.

That winter Mr. Green thinks he is justified in using occult compensation to make up for what he estimates his wages should have been: an extra $50 for the summer.

In this case Mr. Green is definitely not entitled to occult compensation; if he does, he is gravely obliged to make the required restitution.

OBLIGATION TO MAKE RESTITUTION

By *restitution* we mean an obligation arising in strict justice to repair the injury caused, or to restore the property taken in violation of justice. Actually, it is nothing more than putting the harmed person back into the same condition which was his before the injury. Restitution is obligatory (a) when a person is in unjust possession of something belonging to another, or (b) when he has inflicted unjust damage or loss on another.

Now to examine each in detail.

A. NECESSITY OF RESTITUTION
BECAUSE OF UNJUST POSSESSION

Because a person may be in possession of another's goods either (1) *in good faith,* (2) *in bad faith,* or (3) *in doubtful faith,* the corresponding obligations of restitution will be different in each of these three cases.

1. Possessor in Good Faith

A possessor in good faith is a person who, through no fault of his own, is not aware that he has (or has had) goods not really belonging to him. The goods may have been acquired by him in a perfectly legitimate way; for example, by purchase, gift or inheritance, and at the time he acquired them he had no idea that they were actually not becoming his property. Now he finds that the person from whom he received the goods was not their real owner and so was incapable of handing over a just title of ownership. What must be done about restoring such property?

First of all, we must ask ourselves these three questions about the goods:

(a) Are they or any part of them still in our possession?

(b) If the goods have been sold, were they sold during the time when we did not know they belonged to another?

(c) If the goods have been consumed, were they consumed while we still had the conviction that they were really ours?

We must ask these questions, because our obligation will differ with each of the above-mentioned instances.

a. If the goods (or any part of them) are still in our possession, we must return them (or whatever remains of them) to their true owner, if such goods have been given to us as a gift. For example, Mr. Fingers, a friend of mine, gave me a lawn mower. Now I find that the lawn mower had been stolen from Mrs. Grass. I must give it back to Mrs. Grass, even though it has deteriorated considerably through my use of it during three years. However, I need not pay for its use nor am I obliged to make good its deterioration. This is true even if it has deteriorated through my carelessness.

If the goods are still in my possession and I did not get them as a gift but *bought them from a thief (not knowing they were stolen),* then I am permitted to return them to the thief and recover my money (we do not in this section advert to the complicated matter of legal prescription — a way of acquiring title to ownership of goods by reason of having in good faith used and possessed them during the time and in the manner fixed by law; a person may take the benefit of such a law when it applies to his case), for I am not placing the property in any worse situation than it was before I bought it and I am not bound to retain property for the sake of the real owner at my own probable loss. If, however, the true owner should happen to claim the goods (by prosecution) before I get a chance to return them to the thief and recover my money, I must give them up to the true owner, even if this means a complete loss to myself.

b. What happens if the goods *have been sold* while we were still in good faith? If I, in good faith, sold or gave away goods which really did not belong to me and *the goods no longer exist* (they have either been consumed or destroyed), then I am held to no restitution. However, if I have made any profit from such property (through natural increment; e.g., a valuable animal produces offspring), I must restore *to the real owner* the profit or its equivalent, less maintenance expense. In case of doubt as to whether I made any profit from the property, I am *not obliged* to restitution. Nor need I make restitution of profits accruing through my own industry (e.g., sale of cheese made from cow's milk).

EXAMPLE:

Not knowing that a valuable watch was really not my property, I sold it to Mrs. Goodkind at the same price I paid for it (that is, at no profit). While Mrs. Goodkind is on vacation in Michigan, her summer cottage burns down and the watch is lost forever. Now we learn that the watch really belonged to Mrs. Gem. Am I, or is Mrs. Goodkind, obliged to restore the equivalent of the watch to Mrs. Gem? No, neither of us is so obliged, for the goods have perished.

If I sold such objects in good faith and they are still *in existence* and now the real owner discovers and claims them from the person who bought them from me, what are my respective obligations? First of all, the goods such as they are must be given back to the real owner (the real owner, however, must get them at his own expense; that is, he must pay for the hauling, etc.). The person who bought the goods from me may demand his money back from me (the price at which I sold him the goods). If he does, I must give the money back to him; if he does not ask, then I have no further obligation.

EXAMPLE:

My Aunt Penelope willed me a summer cottage which she thought was hers. I sell the cottage to Jack for $8,000, and now we find that the cottage *really belonged to a Mrs. Scott. There is no doubt about the matter, for she has documentary proof to substantiate her claims. Jack must restore the cottage to Mrs. Scott (he is entitled to make a deduction for all the improvements which he has made on the property). If he demands that I restore the $8,000 which he paid me for it, I must give him that amount; if he does not make any demands, then I am not obliged to restore anything.*

c. If the goods *have been consumed* while being used in good faith, then there is no obligation of restitution to the real owner.

EXAMPLE:

I and my family have consumed the five cases of beer which we had received from a friend a year ago; the friend claimed that he obtained the beer from his boss at the brewery. Now we find that the beer had been stolen. In this case there is no obligation of restitution. In consuming the beer we thought that we were consuming something which was ours and so we committed no sin of injustice; now we cannot restore the beer itself to the real owner because it no longer exists. Hence we have no obligation to make restitution. The real owner is the loser this time.

2. Possessor in Bad Faith

A person who *knowingly* and *unjustly* retains another's property is called a *possessor in bad faith.* His are the following obligations of restitution:

(a) If he *still has the goods,* he must give them back immediately to the rightful owner. If the goods have deteriorated while in his unjust possession, he must also make good that loss. We must emphasize that money in our present economic system is productive and, hence, a long delay in paying legally claimed debts (or retention of stolen property) would at least mean the loss of the interest which that amount could earn; consequently, there is an obligation to restore to the owner, at least at bank rate, the interest lost. If the possessor in bad faith, through natural increment or his own industry, makes any profit from the property while it is in his hands, this profit, less the expenses of maintenance, must also be restored.

EXAMPLES:

1. Joseph steals a car from a parking lot. Finally, he decides to go to confession. He must now restore the car to the parking lot or put it in such an obvious place near the lot that the owners can easily recognize and promptly claim it.

2. Mr. Delay borrows $1,000 from Mr. Smith and signs a notarized statement that he will repay in full at the end of six months. A year and a half elapses before Mr. Delay repays the debt. He must also now restore that amount of interest on the $1,000 that Mr. Smith could have easily earned from the local bank during the overdue time (one year).

(b) If the possessor in bad faith has either *destroyed, given away,* or *lost* the goods (i.e., rightful owner cannot recover them), he must make good the loss to the owner. The amount to be restored may be estimated according to the value of the property at the time it was stolen.

EXAMPLE:

Dorothy stole a diamond ring valued at $1,000. Later, she lost it in a lake where she went boat-riding. She must restore to the rightful owner the full value of the ring at the time she stole it.

3. Possessor in Doubtful Faith

Whenever a person is *really doubtful* as to whether he has in his possession property which belongs to another, he is said to be a *possessor in doubtful faith.* Such a person must make a reasonable investigation of the matter. His investigations, naturally, must be proportionately greater in regard to objects of greater value. If his efforts fail to clear up his doubt, he may, with a clear conscience, keep the property in question. If he neglects to make a reasonable investigation, he becomes a possessor in bad faith.

EXAMPLE:

Mr. Goodhart buys a fur coat for his wife on their wedding anniversary. A week later he hears that the fur shop where he bought the coat had been involved on more than a few occasions in selling stolen furs. Mr. Goodhart begins to doubt whether the coat he bought was a stolen one. His investigations reveal nothing to show that this was the case. He may now keep the coat, for he has made a reasonable investigation.

A person who has been in possession of stolen property in good faith and then begins to have doubts, remains in good faith until the doubts are resolved by the investigation; in the meantime such a person may use the goods according to his good pleasure. When the real owner is discovered, the possessor need restore only such portions of the goods as still remain. Of course, he must restore any profits coming his way in consequence of his temporary possession of the goods, except those due to his ingenuity or industry.

We have by no means treated the problem of restitution exhaustively. The problem is necessarily a complicated one. We have given the general principles, it is true, but any number of circumstances may arise which can change the solution; hence we strongly advise anyone involved in such matters to seek guidance from a priest, either in or out of the confessional.

B. UNJUST DAMAGE

Moral theologians usually define *unjust damage* as an injury or harm done to another with or without material benefit to oneself. If John purposely wrecks Jane's car (e.g., he secretly despises Jane), he is said to have inflicted un-just damage on Jane.

Restitution must be made by the person who has inflicted the injury only if the following three conditions are all verified:

Condition I: *The damage must actually have been accomplished.* Thus, there is no restitution to be made — though the intention is, of course, sinful — if the intended damage is not carried out. If the intention has been carried out only partially, restitution must be made only for the damage actually caused. For example, Pat sets fire to John's barn with the intention of completely burning it down; but the fire is discovered in time and only slight damage is actually done. Pat does not have to make restitution for the whole barn but only for the small damage actually inflicted.

Condition II: *The act that is placed must have really caused the unjust damage.* We cannot say that the agent is the true author of the damage caused if he performs an act which is *merely incidental* to the damage; in such a case no obligation of restitution exists. The following case illustrates such an act (merely incidental to the damage done).

EXAMPLE:

Mr. Jones offers his services to his neighbor, Mr. Farmer, for burning down a barn to make space for a new structure. Farmer, very busy with other work, cannot be present for the burning but knows Jones is experienced and always careful. Despite his care, however, an unexpected wind carries the flames to Farmer's house, and considerable uninsured damage to the homestead results. Jones's act is merely incidental to the resulting loss. He is not obliged to make restitution.

Condition III: *The act causing the damage must be deliberately and consciously unjust.* As we have seen, any act done without advertence and consent is not a sinful act. Hence, no one is bound in conscience to repair any damage which he did not intend to do, barring sinful negligence, of course.

EXAMPLE:

Bill, driving past a dry wheat field, is momentarily but completely distracted by his wife just as he lights his cigarette; he automatically throws the match out the window. When they reach the other end of the field, they see the blaze. In this case Bill is not bound in conscience to restitution because his act causing the damage was not deliberately unjust.

In becoming aware of the blaze, however, Bill must do his best to prevent the fire from spreading (further damage) and so he must help to put out the fire.

But when the damage caused is deliberately and consciously unjust, the amount of reparation is the full damage or as much of it as was foreseen at least indistinctly by the one inflicting the damage. If a person did not foresee even indistinctly the full damaging effect of his action, he need only repair whatever he foresaw; thus, if in anger I shoot a neighbor's prize bull, thinking it is an animal of ordinary value, I would be bound to restore only the equivalent of the animal I thought I was destroying. Other factors, however, could easily change the amount of restitution in such a case; hence, it is imperative that the directions given by one's confessor be followed.

C. CIRCUMSTANCES WHICH EXCUSE FROM RESTITUTION

Once we have certainly and completely fulfilled an obligation of restitution, that obligation ceases absolutely and forever. If we are doubtful whether or not we have made restitution, we may presume that we have, provided we had always been in the habit of meeting our obligations promptly and have at least probable reasons for believing that we have also made the required restitution this time.

Important as the obligation of restitution is, still some reasons can excuse from compensating for the harm done through unjust damage and theft. These reasons are: (1) *remission or condonation* by the rightful owner; (2) *physical or moral inability to pay* on the part of him who has to make the restitution; and (3) *honest bankruptcy.*

1. *Remission or condonation by the rightful owner* simply means that the real owner is truly willing to give up his claim of restitution.

EXAMPLE:

Before she starts for New York, young Bernice steals a watch valued at $150, and then "hocks" it when she runs out of money. On her way home she thinks the matter over and is thoroughly repentant. She tells her employer, from whom she stole the watch, the whole truth. The kind-hearted employer tells her to forget about restoring anything to him because, he says, it took a lot of good will to come back and confess to him. Bernice is thus released from the obligation of making restitution.

2. *Physical or moral inability to pay* on the part of him who has to make the restitution also constitutes a valid excuse as long as the *inability lasts.* The reason for this is simple; no one is obliged to do what is beyond his power. One is morally unable to pay when he cannot make restitution either without serious loss to his goods of a higher order — such as life, honor or good name — or without serious loss to his honestly acquired goods or without exposing himself and his dependents to grave want. It is presumed, of course, that in such cases the rightful owner will not be exposed to the same fate if the restitution is not made.

EXAMPLES:

1. Mr. Face cannot make restitution now because his theft would be exposed; or, at any rate, he would be strongly suspected of thievery and would thus lose his good name. He is justified in waiting for an opportune time, even though this will mean considerable delay.

2. Mr. Finevoice maliciously wrecks my car: the repairs cost $500. He has some fine paintings which he could sell to pay me, but he could do this only at a great loss to himself — for they are worth much more than the present buyer offers. Mr. Finevoice is justified in refusing to sell now in order to get the money for me.

3. *Bankruptcy.* Any person declared insolvent by judicial decree or pronouncement (officially declared unable to meet the just claims of all his creditors) is called a bankrupt. All men are liable to misfortune. After something has gone wrong in a man's business, it would be unfair (economic conditions being what they are in the United States) if he had to spend the rest of his life striving to reduce overwhelming financial debts which, in all probability, he could never discharge anyway without a fresh start in business. Such a man would not and could not live a life worthy of a human being with such a superhuman burden. The United States civil law recognizes this fact and hence not only forbids all legal action against an honest bankrupt for the recovery of debts but also (after the bankrupt has been legally discharged from bankruptcy) cancels the debts themselves. Court procedure in most cases includes, among other things, appointing an administrator who pays such debts as can be taken care of from whatever assets exist or from the sale of things still owned by the person or enterprise filing for bankruptcy.

This law of bankruptcy also extinguishes such debts in conscience for the following reasons: All businessmen in the United States realize what this law means and still willingly assume the risk of bearing the loss of certain amounts of money through the bankruptcy of others with whom they deal; they too want to protect themselves in the same manner if some similar misfortune befalls them; finally, this law itself was enacted for the common good. That a bankrupt thus released by the pronouncement of the courts, is again received into business circles is proof enough that these risks incidental to business are freely undertaken.

This moral release, of course, holds true only for honest bankruptcy. A dishonest bankrupt (one who wishes to avoid paying his debts by deceiving the civil courts into pronouncing him legally bankrupt) still has the moral obligation of making good all his debts; he has the same obligation in conscience concerning his debts as he had before the court pronouncement.

EXAMPLES:

1. Mr. Ingbing, who owns a department store, has debts amounting to $100,000. He conceives of a scheme whereby he can have the civil court declare him bankrupt, though he has secret assets and is still far from being reduced to the state of being unable to pay his debts.

After he is legally declared a bankrupt, he is told by his wife that he still has the obligation in conscience to pay all those debts. He consults his pastor and finds she is right.

2. *The J.J. Twinkles Co., in 1972, was forced into bankruptcy. The owner had debts amounting to $75,000, when he filed for bankruptcy. The sale of his assets netted $35,000, which the administrator used to pay off the creditors having first claim; other creditors were paid in proportion to the amounts owed them. The owner considered himself legally and morally free of all financial obligation as soon as he received a court discharge from bankruptcy. He was correct; honest bankruptcy released him from his remaining debts.*

PROPERTY RIGHTS OF MINORS

By a *minor* is meant any boy or girl under twenty-one years of age. Here we are not concerned with those persons under twenty-one who have been "emancipated" by marriage, entrance into religious life or the armed forces, or simply by parental consent. But even a minor not emancipated thus still has certain property rights which the parents must respect.

First of all, whatever comes to a minor by *inheritance* or by *gift* truly becomes his property. Parents have no right to such goods simply because of their being the parents. Yet, the father should ordinarily administer such property for minors. Any interest or profits accruing from these possessions belong to the minors and not to the parents.

EXAMPLE:

Anna Busch, a six-year-old, inherits $5,000 from her grandmother. Her parents put the money into a bank, but they consider all the accrued interest on the invested money as their own. "Anna will still have what was willed to her," says her father, "and she has no right to more than that."

Anna's father is incorrect; Anna is entitled not only to the principal but also to all the interest. Her father, therefore, when she comes of age, must in conscience restore all the interest as well as the principal due to her.

Now as regards earnings, if a minor lives away from home and his father in no way supports him, then he owns all that he earns. If the minor lives away from home but the father still supports him (pays for the minor's room and board, buys his clothes or pays his tuition), the minor must reimburse his parent insofar as he can from his own occasional earnings, if his father insists on being reimbursed.

What if the minor lives at home but is a wage earner? Certainly he is bound in justice to compensate his parents (if they demand it) for his maintenance (food and shelter, etc.) and for all those expenses that his parents must incur *because of him.* Whether a minor is unjust in retaining a portion of his earnings for his own use against the parents' will, will depend on the circumstances. Generally speaking, parents act unwisely if they do not allow such a minor any pocket money. But if they happen to be clearly unwilling to let him keep any part of his earnings, *the minor is not bound in justice to hand over more than is reasonably sufficient to cover his maintenance.* If such be the case, the minor should not rely wholly on his own judgment but should seek counsel from a reliable adviser on the matter. Moreover, charity may require him to help support the family, if there is need.

EXAMPLES:

1. *Roger, seventeen, not living at home and making his own way in the world, refuses to give his parents any part of his pay checks.*

He is not obliged to, but if his parents are in grave need at times, charity would oblige him to help them out.

2. *Eugene, a minor living with his parents, pays his father the same amount for room and board as is required at boarding houses in that city. His father demands more, in order to compensate at least in part for his upkeep when he was a child.*

Eugene can in conscience decline to pay more than what he has been paying.

LOST AND FOUND ARTICLES

I do not become the owner of money, jewelry and other articles simply because I happen to have found them; they still have a rightful owner somewhere. Certainly I may keep such things until the true owner is found, and I may do this against the claim of anyone except the rightful owner. In the meantime, too, I am bound only to take ordinary care of the lost article — such care as I would take if it were my own property. Since we usually have proportionately more solicitude for our own articles of greater value, we must have this same proportionate care for found articles of greater value.

Also, I am bound to make reasonable efforts to find the owner; the efforts made must be proportionate to the value of the found article — the more valuable the article, the more effort must be made. Of course, we would always fulfill our obligation of finding the rightful owner by simply turning the lost article over to the police; this requires little effort on our part and also has the advantage of not incurring any expenses involved in advertising, etc., expenses we may not be able to collect when the owner is located. If, however, we prefer to rely on our own efforts in finding the rightful owner and should the article happen to be of great value (e.g., expensive jewelry, costly gems, etc.), one should see what the civil law of his State requires by way of trying to find the owner. If sufficient time has elapsed and due effort has been made and the owner has not been found, then the finder may regard the article as his own.

What is to be done if the real owner appears later, say, a year or two later? If I still have the goods, I must hand them over to him, for he has not lost his claim to them. I may, of course, deduct justly or ask recompense for all expenses incurred in my search for the owner (the advertising in the lost-and-found column, etc.).

EXAMPLE:

Ouch O'Day found an envelope containing $100. There were no names or

*other identification on it. He puts an ad in the local newspaper for three days
and keeps a sharp lookout in the lost-and-found column of the same paper.
After waiting two months for the rightful owner to show up, Ouch treats his
wife and children to a day at the seashore with two meals at good restaurants.
Several weeks later, the rightful owner shows up. What is Ouch's obligation?*
   He is not obliged to restore the $100.

BUYING AND SELLING OBLIGATIONS OF BUSINESSMEN

In the matter of buying and selling, the first question most businessmen
ask is: What is a just price to demand for goods? In general, the price is just
when it is reasonable, that is, equivalent to the value of the thing sold. But this
is too general a principle to be of much practical use and, besides, it does not
even apply in certain cases. Obviously, the answer must be more detailed and
certainly more practical.

Without delving into the various theories and laws of economics to see
what determines the price of a thing, we can say price usually depends on the
product's utility and upon the supply of and demand for that product; usually
it is the public itself that ultimately determines the price (except in unjust
monopolies). This yardstick usually influences those dealing with the commod-
ity, including producers, distributors, dealers, sellers, etc., in arriving at their
judgment of the price that ought to be placed on a product. In our present economic system businessmen are highly sensitive to public reaction and opinion.

But public valuation differs within certain limits, according to the circumstances of time, place and other varied factors. Accordingly, it is usual to find
three different prices in the open parket: the *lowest,* the *medium* and the *topmost* price. Any of these is, morally speaking, a *just* price to ask and to pay. To
sell above the highest, or to force prices below the lowest, would usually be unjust and hence sinful. Special circumstances, such as the risk of not getting paid
by an individual customer, may justify charging above the highest price prevailing in the open market. Modern trade and commerce is extremely complex,
as well as intensely competitive; hence it may be morally impossible to fix
beforehand the topmost price which may be charged and received and still be
just. *In practice, therefore, one may ordinarily (excluding unjust monopoly) consider that price as just and fair which the purchaser is willing to pay, and the seller
to accept, always provided that no deception is practiced by either the seller or the
buyer.*

The buyer is presumed to know his own business, his own interests; also
he is free to decline buying and to go to another merchant for a better "buy."
This is the only workable solution of a fair and just price and it can be reconciled with the theory of three prices as stated above; if Joe is willing to give
$1.50 for a particular article, that of itself shows that $1.50 does not really
exceed the highest price in public estimation. Joe could easily refuse and go to
another store. So, given an open market (thus, excluding monopoly, which is
unjust in many, many cases) and the absence of fraud or pressure, the best bargain a man can make is the only practical definition of a fair and just bargain.
When a shopper or buyer happens to have paid much more than the article is

worth, without fraud or deceit, he has had a common experience — an experience he should not forget when going out shopping the next time. However, to raise the price simply because of the buyer's special need is profiteering and is unjust.

Above, we mentioned the exclusion of fraud or deliberate misrepresentation of the quality of goods; misrepresentation must be scrupulously guarded against, for it is perhaps one of the commonest offenses against justice in the matter of buying and selling, i.e., through false advertising. What then, are a person's obligations in this regard?

First of all, a buyer has *a right not to be deceived* into paying more because the goods are falsely represented as being of better quality than they really are. Naturally, those very *general and conventional praises* which all advertisers employ to extol the goods of their clients should not be regarded as fraudulent. This is a custom of the trade which deceives no one and should be regarded as such.

If the article offered for sale is not what the seller claims or what it appears to be (through advertising, or has substantial defects, etc.) or is useless for the known purpose of the buyer, the sale ordinarily would not be a just one in conscience. The word *ordinarily* here needs a little explanation. If the buyer had opportunities of examining whatever he is going to buy and is not deliberately deceived by the seller, but deceives himself, then, *Caveat emptor* ("Let the buyer beware"); he is the one taking the risks. Merely accidental defects, obvious defects of minor importance need not be pointed out at all, provided that the charge is never more than the topmost just price. However, if the seller is explicitly asked about such a defect, he is bound in conscience either to disclose the defect or he must decline to guarantee the article.

EXAMPLE:

Mr. Y who owns a photography shop, sells a light meter to an uninitiated amateur for the regular price, though the photo-electric cell in it is very weak and needs to be replaced. In order to make a sale, Mr. Y does not point out the defect.

He commits a sin of injustice; he is also bound to restore the money of which he defrauded the customer.

To sell an article at the current price is permissible, even though the seller knows for certain that the price will soon fall.

The extremely high prices paid for rare objects, works of art, antiques, curiosities and such may be foolish but they are not unjust. Neither is it unjust to demand an increased price for an article which is very dear to one personally.

EXAMPLE:

I treasure the stamp collection my father gave me before he died. A stamp collector wants to buy it now. I am justified in compensating myself according-

ly; the collection is really worth only $5,000 but I ask $6,000 for it; I tell the prospective buyer why.

We can ask much, much more than the prevailing market price for articles dear to us for only sentimental reasons, but we must inform the buyer how much such articles are actually worth. If we do so and the buyer is still willing to pay the price we ask, we commit no injustice.

BETTING OR WAGERING

Betting or wagering is a contract by which the persons involved agree on a reward to be given to the one correctly guessing an unascertained event, past or future. Thus I bet my brother $10 that Notre Dame will be undefeated during this coming football season. Notre Dame loses a game and so my brother wins the bet. I give him the agreed sum, $10.

Is it sinful to bet? No if (1) both the bettors are uncertain as to the disputed point; if (2) each intends or agrees to pay if he loses; if (3) the object of the bet is understood by both in the same way; and if (4) the matter of the bet is not sinful or not an incentive to sin (e.g., to bet that one person can consume more beer than another at a beach party would not fulfill this condition).

If one of the bettors is certain about the disputed matter, and does not inform the other of his certainty, the contract is not valid or just, and the winner is bound in conscience to make restitution of the sum won. But if he informed the other bettor that he is betting on a certainty, and the other still insists on making the bet, the winner may keep the sum won, for in such case the person informed by the other bettor is considered making a free gift.

EXAMPLE:

Gertrude wants to bet me a dollar that the city of Danzig is spelled Dansig in English. I am certain of the spelling and tell her so, but she insists on making the bet. I may lawfully keep the dollar thus won.

Though betting is a luxury but not sinful if all the above conditions have been fulfilled, yet it can easily become a habit if carried to excess. It can, therefore, become sinful if it leads a person to risk money needed to satisfy his just obligations, paying debts, supporting dependents, etc. Like many other things, then, in itself betting is not ethically wrong; it is the abuse of it that leads to evils.

LOTTERIES

A *lottery* is a scheme in which people pay for tickets qualifying them to become possible winners of prizes; the winners will be determined by lot or chance, usually by the drawing of written names from some receptacle, such as a barrel or a hat. The sweepstakes are an example of a lottery. It is a valid contract by which a price is paid for the chance of drawing a prize. A lottery is not sinful if there is no fraud in the drawing of the names, if the chances of winning are equally shared by all ticket holders, and if there is some reasonable proportion between the price of a ticket and the chance of winning a prize. Again, this practice may be abused — for example, by inducing people to buy beyond their means.

EXAMPLE:

The president of the Farmers' Union local suggests raffling off an electric range in order to pay for the trip of a delegate to Washington. Therefore all the union members sell tickets for the range and thus make more than $600. At the next meeting all the ticket stubs are put into a box and a girl draws one. The one she pulls is, of course, the winner.
There is nothing morally objectionable in this affair.

GAMBLING

Gambling is a contract in which the participants agree to give to the winner in a game of chance a certain prize or sum of money as a stake. Thus, playing bingo, dice, poker, euchre, etc., for money (or anything of value) is gambling. Strictly speaking, if the outcome of the game does not depend wholly on chance but at least partially on skill, such a game is not gambling, even if stakes are offered for the winner — for example, playing billiards, checkers, baseball, etc., etc., for stakes. Either type of game, whether that of skill or pure chance, is in itself licit even though money or some other valuable is staked on the result of the game.

What is a practical rule of morality for gambling? We shall put it thus: gambling is sinful only if one of the following four conditions is *not* fulfilled:

1. Whatever is put up as stakes (money, etc.) must justly belong to the person who gambles; and it must not be necessary for the support of his family or for paying his debts. Quite obviously, I can't take my brother's car and stake it in a game of cards. Neither can I use half of my pay check as stakes when the money is badly needed for the support of my family.

2. All cheating and fraud, such as using loaded dice, marked cards, card stacking, etc., must be excluded. Any type of "poker face," grimace, looking sad, happy, etc., in order to deceive the opponent is permissible; such actions are part of the game and if any player is so naïve as to be taken in by these, that is his own fault.

3. The participants should all have a reasonably equal chance of winning. If one of the participants is less skilled than the others (and so has little chance of winning) and yet knowingly enters the game, he is freely exposing his goods to loss in an honest contract. His losing therefore constitutes no injustice. If one in a group of inexpert players is a "card shark," he should make his advantage known.

EXAMPLE:

A stranger drops into the back room of Elmira's general store. It is Saturday night and "the boys" are having a game of poker. The stranger is invited to join in the game by the men, who are merely run-of-the-mill players; they have no idea that the stranger is a professional gambler. He must inform them of his expert skill or he would be acting unjustly toward these unsuspecting players.

It would not be sufficient for him simply to say half-jokingly: "Aw, you fellows have no chance with me," and let it go at that. But if he sincerely states his position and they still insist that he join, he may do so and with justice keep his winnings (presupposing that the other conditions are not violated).

4. The players must freely consent to play; that is, they must play without force or real threats.

A WARNING TO THE UNWARY

Anyone going to professional gambling houses or casinos should be on his guard against risking his chances. The devices which can be used to enable such establishments to win regularly are legion.

Wherever State law prohibits gambling and makes such contracts invalid, the loser is not bound in conscience to pay his stakes to the winner. Similarly, the winner in such States is not obliged to restore to the loser the winnings once he has received them, unless a court of law compels him to do so. Everyone is free to avail himself of a law enacted for the welfare of the public in this regard.

The basic reason why gambling, *in itself,* is not sinful is that every man, having a just right to possess property and being its master, can give it away absolutely and so may also give it away under various conditions whether depending on chance or on more conventional reasons.

Even so, many are the social evils of gambling. Though modest gambling may not, in itself, be illicit, it serves to whet the appetite and feed the passion for immoderate forms of gambling. The habit, like any vicious addiction, is difficult to control. Immense stakes and losses lead to desperation, marital troubles, nonsupport of families, as well as the more obvious evils of lying and cheating. The brood of social evils resulting from immoderate gambling is the reason why many States have enacted and enforced anti-gambling legislation.

Chapter XVI

THE EIGHTH COMMANDMENT

"You shall not bear false witness against your neighbor" (Ex. 20:16).

We read in the Book of Proverbs (22:1): "A good name is more desirable than great wealth; the respect of others is better than silver or gold." A man's good name or reputation is indeed one of his most valued possessions. Just as the Seventh and Tenth Commandments protect man's material possessions by forbidding all injustice, so the Eighth Commandment protects his good name and reputation from injury by explicitly forbidding lying in giving testimony about another in or out of court and by implicitly prohibiting anything which leads to such false testimony, that is, all lies, detraction, contumely, rash judgments and suspicions and the violation of secrets.

How all such actions and speech injure another's good name and reputation is self-evident. The faculty of speech has been given to us for expressing faithfully whatever is in our mind whenever we have reason to convey our thoughts to others; we abuse that faculty if we do the opposite. If man's words did not mean anything, if lying were not forbidden, society would suffer greatly; man's life would be a nightmare of uncertainty. Unbridled lying would sow mistrust, suspicion and complete lack of confidence in all human endeavor, as well as great positive harm to individual persons and their good name.

Those tempted to take this matter of truth lightly should think over the following words of Scripture: "Lying is an ugly blot on a man and ever on the lips of the ignorant. A thief is preferable to an inveterate liar, but both are heading for ruin. Lying is an abominable habit, so that disgrace is the liar's forever" (Sir. 20:24-28).

THE SIN OF LYING

Lying is the expression by which we convey to another something contrary to what we think in order to deliberately deceive him. To put it another way: lying is the contradiction between our outward expression and our interior conviction.

From the definition of lying we see that three elements constitute a lie and if any of these elements is missing there is no lie. Thus:

1. It must be an expression either by word or deed which communicates my ideas to another person. If nobody is around and I talk aloud to myself, expressing something which I know is false, there is no lie; the same is true if I talk thus to animals — to my dog or cat, for instance — for here there is no second *person* present to whom I am communicating my ideas. We have used the word *expression* instead of *speech* because ideas can be communicated to another not only by speech but also by writing, gestures and nodding of the head. All are included under the term *expressions,* and hence all are under discussion when we treat of lying.

2. Furthermore, lying is an expression by which we convey to another *something contrary to what we think;* that is, we want another to believe what we ourselves do not. In other words, there is a real opposition between what we say and what we think. Hence, if I speak what is really false, believing that my statement is true, I do not lie: I am merely mistaken in my judgment. But, on the other hand, if I say what is actually true, believing I am saying something false, I am telling a lie.

3. Finally, lying is done *in order to deliberately deceive another;* there must be the intention of knowingly deceiving another. If I am greatly distracted, and therefore without realizing it, say something which I habitually know is false, this is no lie but merely a misstatement. The same is true of statements regarding anything clearly impossible or manifestly false, certain exaggerated expressions of politeness, all fiction, such as novels, dramas, narrative poems and the like; figures of speech, such as metaphors, irony and hyperbole are obviously not intended to be taken literally and thus are not lies. Some of these need a little more explanation but first we want to point out that there are many circumstances, such as time, place and manner of speaking which modify the meaning of what we say, and so they are rightly considered a part of the *total expression* conveying our ideas to another. Everyone recognizes that such circumstances help determine the meaning of what is said — no need to worry and fret, then, about the possibility that the truth was not expressed literally.

The following examples will illustrate:

EXAMPLES:

1. It is five o'clock and Lois, who is downtown, wants a ride home with her father, who usually goes to the Nibble-Inn Diner for a cup of coffee immediately after work. Lois rushes into the diner and asks the waitress: "Has father been here?" The waitress answers: "No, he hasn't." Now, of course, he has been there nearly every day for the last five years, but the circumstances modify the meaning of the literal words spoken. Thus Lois' question is modified to mean, "Has father been here yet today?" which the waitress correctly understood and which she herself answered by a statement modified to mean, "No, he hasn't been here today."

2. Mr. X, witness to a strange murder on Row Street, had finally been located by the police. He was the only man known who could give the police important information. When the D.A. finished his interview with Mr. X, the newspapermen rushed in to get the story. The D.A. simply dismissed them with, "There's nothing new about the case," for he would jeopardize the case if he revealed anything Mr. X had told him. In these circumstances the D.A.'s answer simply meant: "There's nothing new about the case for you." So, even though there were many things new about the case, the D.A. did not tell a lie.

HYPERBOLE

Hyperbole is the use of extravagantly exaggerated statements, easily understood as such, and hence are not lies. Thus, when Lois is asked, "What sort of man is this Ted living at Cortland?" she replies, "Oh, Ted is the best man who was ever born in Michigan!" What she really means is that Ted is a very fine man. We Americans are especially prone to use hyperbole. Our everyday life abounds in these exaggerations. Ask a European what he thinks of some good man he knows and generally he will be more exact in expressing his opinion: "Oh, he is a very kind chap, considerate and good-hearted." The American will answer something like this: "Ah, he's a prince of a fellow, has a heart of gold, the best man you can ever meet!" Both are correctly understood as meaning the same thing.

IRONY

Irony is a mode of speech used to express a sort of humor or ridicule, with the intended implication of a meaning exactly the opposite of the literal sense of the words used. As such, it is not a lie. For example, at the dress rehearsal for the senior class play, John, Jr., nearly outdid himself in a horrid performance. His chum, Jimmy, nudged him as he brushed past, remarking, "You certainly were the most tonight, Junior! Tony Curtis hasn't got a chance!"

JOKES

When the nature of our jokes *as* jokes is obvious, so that a reasonable person would readily discover the jest, they are not lies and so are not sinful in the least. Some style such jokes as "jocose lies," but this is not correct terminology for, as we have said above, the circumstances (the jovial manner in which the story is told, or its preposterous nature, or a sly smile, twinkling eyes, etc.) modify our words to mean that this is just fiction. But there is a *jocose lie that is a lie,* told merely to amuse, true, but whose jocose nature is not evident. That is the real difference between a joke and a jocose lie. In other words, if the joking is known as a joke, it is not sinful in the least; but if our joking is not known as such, it is a jocose lie and so is venially sinful.

EXAMPLE:

Theobald is noted as a teller of tall tales. One night at a poker game he fabricated a "tall one" about his hunting in Mexico. He told it in such a way that his audience was held spellbound, but from certain details about impossible feats, knew that Theobald did not intend them to believe.

He commits no sin in telling this story.

FICTION

To present fiction as fiction is not lying; this includes any type of literature whether it is in form of the drama, poetry, the novel, a riddle, or a fable.

MORALITY OF LYING

All lies are intrinsically evil; that is, their very nature is evil and cannot ever be otherwise, for it involves the use of a faculty directly contrary to its natural purpose or end. We were given the faculty of speech mainly for communicating to others the thoughts in our mind. When we tell a lie, when we are communicating to another, in order to deceive, something opposite of what we are thinking we are misusing that faculty. In itself, a lie is a *venial sin.*

A lie will become a serious sin only because of some added circumstance, as, for instance, when grave harm is done by a particular lie or some great dishonor is thus shown to God. So we may say that a lie is a venial sin unless: (1) we do some grievous harm by it (then the gravity depends on the extrinsic circumstance of injustice); or (2) we commit perjury because of it (lying under oath); or (3) we lie to deny our faith.

MENTAL RESERVATION

At times we are questioned by some Susie Pry about something we cannot reveal or about some secret we must guard, and so we must evade giving the correct answer; in fact, sometimes our very silence might betray the secret. What should we do in such cases? We cannot under any circumstances lie, for that is always sinful; the only thing we can do and the thing we must do is to veil the truth legitimately. This is done by what moralists call *broad mental reservation.*

Broad mental reservation means limiting our answer to a particular sense, but one actually connected with the question asked. In other words, we use expressions which can be known to correspond to our interior thought by a sensible, prudent and reasonable hearer familiar with the circumstances.

We tell no lie by doing this, for the words we use can be understood in two senses: one, which we mean; the other, which the hearer takes. We express what is actually in our mind, and the hearer can possibly understand the intended meaning of the words used both from the words themselves and from the circumstances, if he had sense enough to do so. But just because the hearer will probably take the other (the wrong meaning of the words), we are not the ones to deceive him; he deceives himself by his own interpretation of the words used. For a sufficient reason we may let others deceive themselves thus, even if the hearer in his ignorance is entirely unaware of another meaning to the words we use.

We do not, therefore, lie when we use this kind of reasonable mental reservation; we may perhaps be the occasion of deceit, but this is because our hearer deceives himself. Still, we must always have sufficient reason for thus concealing some fact and the hearer must have no right to the truth; otherwise, we cannot licitly employ this kind of mental reservation. If we could use broad mental reservation without any reason whatever, widespread mistrust, suspicion and loss of confidence in all our social intercourse would result. We would have to figure out, then, the hidden meaning of everything we are told — an enervating procedure, not to mention the irksome annoyance involved.

A genuine utility for ourselves or others, and this proportionate to the importance of concealing the truth, is considered a sufficient reason for using broad mental reservation.

There are numerous examples of broad mental reservation licitly used in everyday life.

EXAMPLES:

1. Mrs. Moose sees an importunate visitor coming up the walk. Quickly she instructs her husband to answer the doorbell and to inform the visitor that she, Mrs. Moose, "is not at home." The husband does so. Both husband and wife are justified, for the phrase "not at home" has indeed two meanings: one, that the particular person is actually not at home; the other, that the person is not at home to the caller. Everyone knows that this is a conventional way of expressing a truth. And even if the caller were ignorant of the convention, the form of words would still not be a lie, for the words express the truth; but the truth is hidden from the caller, not by the form of the words used but through the caller's own ignorance.

When visiting we may employ all kinds of conventional courtesies: expressing our delight with our visit, certain dishes at table, the drapes, etc., though these may actually be disagreeable to us. We may always praise someone's beauty, poise and charm, or say how smart we think someone's new hat is; similarly, in answering invitations we may say, "I am happy to be invited," or "We accept with pleasure," etc. These are not lies, even though our feelings about these matters may be just the opposite. These are accepted forms of courtesy which convention recognizes as polite, urbane and not intended to indicate our genuine sentiments. And they are to be considered as such.

2. Everyone entrusted with secrets which may not be revealed — confessors, statesmen, secretaries, lawyers, physicians, nurses, notaries, magistrates, etc. — may always answer: "I am ignorant of the matter," or "I know nothing about it," meaning ". . . as far as you are concerned"; or they may use other similar phrases, even though they have exact knowledge of the matter. Here again the circumstance (of being a priest, a lawyer, etc.) colors the answers so that it means: "I have no communicable knowledge on this particular subject." The same holds true if a person, guilty of certain offenses, is asked by another who has no right to the information, whether he had committed such a sin or crime. The person questioned may legitimately avoid answering yes if the other has no right to this secret knowledge. This is legitimate self-defense against the unjust wordy aggression of another, and the action is, under such circumstances, permissible. But if the inquirer has a right in justice to the information, as for instance, a parent or teacher questioning a child, this type of mental reservation is then unlawful.

3. A defendant in court may plead "not guilty" even though he is guilty; for the phrase "not guilty" is always understood as meaning "not juridically guilty until you have proved otherwise."

For instance, John Doe is accused of embezzling funds and is brought to trial. He pleads "Not guilty," though he actually committed the crime. This plea is not to be considered a lie, because the words can be understood in two ways: in one sense, they signify not actually guilty, and in another (in court), "Not guilty before the law until proved to be so." All reasonably well-informed people understand this as one possible meaning of the phrase.

If we have sufficient reason (to avoid incriminating ourselves) we may use broad mental reservation even under oath in court, for we need not give any proof of our own guilt. We do not violate the oath because there is a tacit limitation understood, "as far as the law requires me to reveal this matter." In the United States, it is best to plead the Fifth Amendment in such a case.

STRICT MENTAL RESERVATION

Another kind of mental reservation, called *strict mental reservation,* is never permitted, for it is a lie simply and purely. This consists in limiting the meaning of words and giving no clue whatever (by circumstances, etc.) to the true meaning of the words, so that no one, however wise, could understand. For example, if Daphne asks Dorothy whether she is staying home during the Christmas holidays, Dorothy replies, "Yes," meaning that she will stay there in imagination. This is a downright lie.

Another example: Sailor Jones is asked by a friend whether he has enough money for the train fare home. Though Jones has more than enough for the trip, he wants additional funds for a "good time" on the way home; he therefore answers, "No, I haven't," meaning in his own mind, "I haven't enough *in my wallet* — the money's in my locker." He avoids answering the next question as to how much he needs to get home by saying, "Give me thirty bucks." There is no doubt as to why this type, the strict mental reservation, is sinful: it is merely another name for a lie.

Some may contend that since both strict mental reservation (or lying) and broad mental reservation produce the same results, that is, the hearer does not obtain the answer he wants — it does not matter very much how the results are achieved. But it matters very much how the results are achieved, for we may never produce a good result by immoral means. *The end never justifies the means.*

SECRETS

A secret is hidden knowledge or information which we are bound not to reveal to others. There are various kinds of secrets. Moral theologians usually divide them into three classes: the *natural,* the *promised* and the *entrusted* secret. There is another kind, the *sacramental* secret, which is in a class apart and is protected by the seal of confession; this is without doubt the greatest of all secrets. The obligation not to reveal knowledge gained in confession is derived from divine precept, also from natural and ecclesiastical law. The sacramental secret can never under any circumstances be revealed, for it binds absolutely and at all times.

But here we are concerned with the three other kinds of secrets. Since each kind entails different obligations, we shall examine each separately.

I. A *natural secret* is one in which hidden knowledge is acquired either accidentally or purposely through effort, but which cannot be revealed without causing harm or reasonable displeasure to another. Natural law makes such a secret binding, not convention or agreement. For example, Susie Pry happens to know that Mr. Car committed adultery several times. Susie is in possession of a natural secret.

The possessor of a natural secret is bound under pain of serious sin not to reveal it if the matter is of grave importance. This is so if the revelation of the secret causes grave harm to the person about whom we know the secret. If, without just reason, a natural secret is revealed, charity is always violated and it may be that justice is too. Thus, in the above example, if Susie without a just reason reveals Mr. Car's misbehavior and he thereby loses his job or his good name, Susie gravely violates both charity and justice.

Just reasons for revealing natural secrets are: Whenever the keeping of such a secret would involve harm or grave inconvenience, either to the one holding or sharing the secret, or to an innocent third party, or to the common good. There is no obligation to keep such a secret once the general public becomes aware of it.

EXAMPLE:

Joan, a good Catholic young lady, is keeping company with Mr. Young, and they plan to get married soon. I happen to learn that Mr. Young has been twice married and divorced under different names in California. To protect Joan I tell her of this secret knowledge. In this case Joan is the innocent third party who would suffer greatly if that knowledge were not made known to her.

II. A *promised secret* is one which we have promised not to reveal after we have received knowledge of it. Since the obligation connected with this kind of secret arises primarily from the promise, it obliges either under mortal or venial sin depending on whatever obligation the one making the promise wished to impose upon himself.

If the secret has been discovered and then a promise of secrecy given, the obligation of secrecy binds not only in virtue of the promise but also in virtue of the natural law; hence such a secret would be called a *promised natural secret,* binding in fidelity and in justice. This type of secret would bind under serious sin if its revelation would cause either reasonable and great offense or grave harm to the person with whom the secret is concerned.

As in the case of the natural secret, we may reveal a promised secret for a just reason, that is, when the keeping of the secret knowledge would involve grave harm or serious inconvenience to the holder or sharer of the secret, to an innocent third party, or to the common good. There is this exception: if we have expressly promised to keep the secret even at the cost of grave inconvenience to ourselves, we are obliged to do so unless this would result in grave harm to an innocent third party.

EXAMPLE:

Luella discovers that Mary is planning to enter the convent this summer; then Mary asks Luella to promise not to divulge this secret. Luella makes the promise and thus takes upon herself the obligation of a promised secret. If Luella promised to keep this secret even at great inconvenience to herself, she is bound to keep the secret despite serious inconvenience to herself.

III. An *entrusted secret* is one which is confided to another with the understanding that the latter will not disclose it. The agreement to keep the secret is had before (not *after,* as in a promised secret) we entrust that secret to the other. Such an agreement may be explicit or merely tacit, the latter in cases of advice sought from professional men, such as physicians, lawyers, nurses, social workers, student counselors, etc. A tacit agreement is always had whenever we consult such professional people in virtue of their office, and whatever is revealed to them is then termed a *professional secret* (which is merely a specific type of entrusted secret). Excluding the seal of the confessional, a professional secret is the most binding of all the secrets.

The obligation to keep entrusted secrets is derived from the contract which preceded the giving of the information, hence it binds in justice. It matters little whether the agreement was explicit or implicit (the professional secret). In matters of serious consequence, the violation would be in the category of a grave sin.

EXAMPLE:

Fourteen-year-old Ned has been having problems concerning purity. His father is dead and there is only one person with whom he feels he can speak about this problem without extreme embarrassment, his Dad's old friend, the elderly Mr. Walsh. Mr. Walsh is understanding and kind, and Ned knows that he will certainly keep everything under his silvery hair. So Ned, first asking Mr. Walsh to keep the information secret, makes a clean breast of his troubles and gets valuable advice from the older man.

Mr. Walsh is gravely bound not to disclose any of this matter.

The obligation of keeping such secrets ceases, however, whenever their revelation is necessary to:

A. *Avert serious harm or danger to the public good or to the good of the community.* The good of the individual in such a case must be sacrificed for the greater good.

EXAMPLE:

Mr. Hopeless is selling narcotics to many high-school students in a small midwestern city. Lawyer Sawyer suspects this because of certain things Mr. Hopeless let slip when he came to seek legal advice regarding narcotics sales, supposedly for "a friend." Lawyer Sawyer informs the police about it and eventually Mr. Hopeless is arrested. Lawyer Sawyer's action was justified.

B. *Avert serious harm to an innocent third party.*

EXAMPLE:

Mr. Dudd, who has a hidden infectious disease, is about to marry the unwary Miss Truly. Though warned by Doctor T that he will bring untold misery to the healthy young woman and her future children, Mr. Dudd refuses to tell his prospective bride. Doctor T informs Miss Truly of the disease. He acted rightly.

C. The obligation to keep a secret also ceases when continued secrecy would work *serious harm either to the one who had entrusted the secret or to the one to whom the secret had been entrusted.*

EXAMPLE:

Jimmy made his chum Jack promise not to tell anyone before telling Jack about some pot parties he had been attending . . . and that he has been smoking pot now for three months. Jack informs Jimmy's parents about the matter in order that they may do something before it's too late. Jimmy in this case is the one who had entrusted the secret and to whom serious harm might come. Jack's action was justified.

If professional men were not able to divulge secrets under such circumstances, they could reasonably refuse to accept such secrets, an attitude which would be injurious to the common welfare.

We may reveal an entrusted secret, even a secret of grave importance, to *one discreet* person who will keep the secret, if we have a good reason for doing it (e.g., we feel that we need advice on what to do, etc.). If we do not have a justifying reason, then it would be venially sinful for us to tell such a secret even to one person, no matter how discreet that person may be.

EXAMPLE:

Miss Slagel, a social worker, is confidentially entrusted with a problem involving the morality of a whole rooming house. She does not know what is to be done and so she consults her old professor at college, Doctor Perkins.
She is justified.

AS REGARDS ALL SECRETS

Generally all secrets (except the secrets told in confession) cease to bind when they have become public property or if permission to reveal them may be reasonably presumed from the person about whom the secret knowledge is had.

PRYING INTO THE SECRETS OF OTHERS

Just as we have the duty not to reveal the secrets of others without just reasons so we have the duty not to pry into their secrets. To pry into someone else's secret without reason or from sheer curiosity is venially sinful; however, to extort a secret of grave importance by fraudulent or violent means is matter for serious sin; moreover, the obligation to keep such a secret is assumed as soon as the person obtains the hidden knowledge.

OPENING AND READING THE LETTERS OF OTHERS

The letters (or private notes) of another may be opened and read with the reasonably presumed consent of the writer or the recipient. Otherwise, it is sinful, because there is always the risk of finding out secrets or of causing reasonable offense; however, if we sincerely think that it is necessary to open and read some particular letters in order to avert serious harm to ourselves, to the State, or to an innocent third party, or if we think that it is necessary for the common welfare, we may do so. Hence parents may open and read the mail of their children who are still under their parental authority, if they think it is necessary for their children's protection. A married person may read the letters of his or her spouse only when it is necessary to avert some grave evil — unless reading each other's mail is a family custom. In such cases, one is free to follow what is customary. During wartime governments may censor all mail.

To read without permission another's letter which, it is presumed, contains nothing important is venially sinful. But a reader is gravely bound to desist reading another's letter if he foresees he will unjustly acquire important secret information through the letter. Needless to add, such a reader is bound to maintain secrecy just as if the matter had been confided to him.

EXAMPLES:

1. Jane knows that one of her co-workers is involved in a serious personal lawsuit. When he is absent she finds in his desk — and reads — personal mail from his lawyer; she knows she may thereby learn grave secrets. There is matter here for serious sin.

2. Geraldine wonders what a girl could write to a boy friend; so she opens and reads her brother's letter from his girl friend. Geraldine's action was venially sinful.

DETRACTION AND CALUMNY

Detraction is the unjust injuring of another's good name by revealing his true faults to others. If what is said of another (or is imputed to him) is false and is known to be false, then we have the sin of *calumny* or *slander*. Calumny has the additional malice of lying.

Every man has a right to his good reputation, to his good name; even deceased persons and moral persons (i.e., communities, religious orders, organizations, and every organized body of men) have this right. This good reputation may be genuine or it may be merely apparent. If the good reputation is genuine, then the right of the individual or corporate body to it is *absolute;* but if only apparent, then the right of the individual or corporate body is *relative,* and therefore whenever the revelation of secret faults or sins is necessary or very useful either for the common good or for protecting the rights of an innocent person, the secret sins or faults may be revealed.

The latter would hold true, for example, when the faults of others are revealed to their parents, superiors, or to someone else for the purpose of seeking needed advice and help. Revelation of faults is also allowed to prevent harm to others, harm which is at least proportionate to the detraction, as could well happen in cases of choosing another for office, marriage, a teaching position, medical adviser, etc.

EXAMPLE:

In building her new house Miss Good has hired as contractor Mr. B, who recently caused homeowner Mill a great loss by using defective materials in the latter's new home and refusing to replace them when their inadequacy was proved. In confidence Mill tells Miss Good about this, so that she may guard against being victimized. This is permissible.

May a person who is accused and actually guilty but not yet convicted reveal the true, secret faults of the witnesses for the prosecution, in order to weaken their deposition? Yes, provided this is necessary for self-defense and provided the harm thus done to them will not be out of proportion to the benefit which the accused person will derive from such a revelation.

Neither is there detraction when the faults mentioned are already publicly known. A fault is said to be *publicly known* when (1) it is commonly known; or (2) will soon be generally known; or (3) after a legitimate court sentence has been passed for some crime. However, if some fault is *publicly known only in a private community* such as a college, a seminary, or some other institution, it may not be revealed to outsiders. A fault publicly known in one place and not in another may be made known in the latter provided it is foreseen that the news will soon reach that place.

EXAMPLES:

1. Detective Smith had known, in his official capacity, of Gilroy's guilt in a certain robbery. Now Gilroy makes a complete confession to the police and the news is going to press. Detective Smith is no longer bound to keep secret that matter which will be in the evening papers.

2. Yesterday XX was sentenced to two years in prison for sex offenses. Mr. Murry, who had previously known about XX's immoral conduct, now tells his neighbor about those offenses.

It was not sinful to disclose that matter, since it became public by virtue of the sentence imposed on XX.

SINFULNESS OF DETRACTION

Since detraction is the injuring of another's good name or reputation, its sinfulness is to be gauged in any particular case according to the gravity of the harm done to the good name. If the harm is serious and great, the deliberate detraction is grievously sinful; the revelation of a single grievous fault committed by our neighbor may sometimes have this result; some will say that this is usually the case. If the fault revealed is slight, then the detraction is venially sinful.

In order to make a fair estimate of the harm done, we must take into consideration not only the nature of the defect revealed but also the circumstances surrounding the case: (1) whether the detracting person is a reliable source (is he a known liar, an untrustworthy newsmonger, or a conscientious man?); (2) whether the person detracted is generally highly respected, a man of honor and dignity or of shady repute; (3) whether the listeners are persons who would readily believe the detractor or simply let the remarks pass without much thought. The number of persons hearing the detraction also makes a difference; to tell several persons even one serious, hidden sin of another may easily be gravely sinful: but to tell only a person who will certainly not carry the matter further is usually venially sinful, unless, of course, there is some *special reason* why the person detracted does not want that particular person to know of his fault.

If some grave fault of a particular person is already known, to tell of another fault generally going hand in hand with the fault already known would be venially sinful, e.g., to say of a notorious drunkard that he curses or instigates fights.

EXAMPLES:

1. At a bridge game Mrs. Cowslip reveals what she thinks is a choice bit of gossip: that Mr. Cook, who is a respected family man, has been caught by his wife in the act of committing adultery.
There is grave matter here.

2. Mrs. Serious tells her neighbor Mrs. Green that Mr. Tilt, known to be a "heavy gambler" and negligent of his family's welfare, came home in a drunken stupor last night. This detraction is matter for venial sin.

3. Mrs. Bad, without a justifying reason, reveals that Jones, a respected retired worker living nearby, once served a prison term for misappropriation of

public funds. There is matter for grave sin here in depriving Jones of his good name.

REPARATION TO BE MADE FOR DETRACTION

Like any other sin violating justice, detraction involves the obligation of making restitution for the harm done, as far as possible. This includes both the restoration of the injured person's reputation and the reparation of any *foreseen material harm* which has resulted from the injured reputation. Thus if the detracted person suffered some loss of customers, or failed to close a particular business deal because of the detraction, the detractor is bound in conscience to make good that material loss if he foresaw it.

This obligation of restitution binds venially if the harm done by the detraction was only slight. If, on the other hand, the detractor deliberately caused grave damage (and foresaw it at least indistinctly) he is seriously obliged to restitution, even if this would involve great personal inconvenience.

The manner in which we are to make restitution for *calumny* is different from the way we are to repair for mere *detraction*. The calumniator, we must remember, has lied, and so must admit that he had spoken falsely about his neighbor (e.g., by saying, "I was mistaken in what I said about so and so," etc.; or, "I find that the statement I made about so and so is not true"; or some other such statement). The detractor who did not also calumniate, could not say this or he would lie; for he has revealed a true fault or crime. He must therefore try to restore the other's reputation in some other way; for instance, by either excusing the faults committed by the detracted person or by discreetly praising him for his good qualities, especially those tending to make up for the qualities which have been the subject of detraction. This can be done with great tact and without any embarrassment. If one person has defamed another in a newspaper or magazine, he can usually make the proper restitution only by use of the same medium.

EXAMPLES:

1. When Mrs. Twostep goes to confession, she finds that she must make reparation for her sin of detracting Mr. Clover. So, at the next meeting of the bridge club (whose members heard the detraction), she tactfully praises Mr. Clover and especially his loving consideration for his wife. In this way she repairs, partially at least, the harm previously done by her uncontrolled tongue.

2. News-commentator Jones had accused Mr. Leader of being a liar. In order to repair for this now, he brings out some of the really fine things that Mr. Leader did for his community during his term of office. Thus he repairs for the sin of detraction insofar as he is able.

REASONS WHICH EXCUSE FROM MAKING RESTITUTION

When no one believed the detraction, with the result that no actual harm was done, there is no obligation to make restitution. If actual harm has been inflicted on another's reputation, restitution is necessary unless one of the following reasons holds true in one's case (any one of these reasons releases either a *detractor* or a *calumniator* from the obligation of restitution): (1) if some kind of reparation has previously been made; (2) if the matter has been completely forgotten; (3) if it can reasonably be presumed that the defamed person excuses the detractor from the obligation of making restitution (e.g., the defamed person either says in so many words that he wishes no more to be said about the matter, or the detractor can reasonably gather as much from the defamed person's conduct toward himself); (4) if the crime which the detractor revealed to a few has now become public through other sources entirely independent of the detractor's sinful action: for example, if a newspaper or magazine has exposed it, etc.; (5) if restitution is morally or physically impossible. This is the case if the listeners to the detraction are either unknown, or cannot be reached, or if it is known that they will not change their opinion about the defamed no matter what is said or done. Moral impossibility is also said to hold if the detractor would suffer much more actual harm in making the restitution than the defamed person suffered as a result of the detraction.

EXAMPLES:

1. Mr. Snow had revealed to a few of his friends a secret crime of his colleague. Before he had a chance to repair his detraction, the police (acting on evidence entirely independent of Mr. Snow's revelation) arrested his colleague and the newspapers printed the whole story.

Mr. Snow is now excused from the obligation of reparation.

2. Mrs. Mouthful defamed Mrs. Black, the lady next door, by telling a few of the neighbors about some of Mrs. Black's secret sins. Now Mrs. Mouthful and Mrs. Black are again on speaking terms; in fact, they have resumed their former friendship despite Mrs. Black's knowledge of the detraction.

Here Mrs. Mouthful can reasonably presume that she is excused from repairing the detraction.

CRITICIZING PUBLIC OFFICEHOLDERS

Not a few people will ask: "Is it sinful to expose the faults of those holding *public* office, Father? A distinction must be made between their reputation as public officials (that is, as regards their conduct in the performance of public duties) and their good name in private life as members of families, as fathers, husbands, businessmen, etc. We are allowed to openly criticize the public defects or mismanagement of public officials; many times this acts as a restraining influence on such officials. But there is no justification whatever for exposing the *private misconduct* of such men, unless, of course, in some particular instance the good of the State and the prevention of serious injury to public interest (an injury to be feared as a result of the official's private delinquencies) should render an exposure for that purpose not only necessary but effectual. The exposure of private misconduct, however, would be unlawful if it would be useless and ineffectual. Journalists and other public sources of information are bound by these same principles, and must be careful to practice discretion in such delicate matters.

EXAMPLE:

At a press conference Mr. Jones, who is a city councilman, truthfully accuses the mayor of deliberate misappropriation of public funds.

There was nothing morally wrong in thus exposing a serious defect of a public official. However, if Mr. Jones revealed a moral defect of the mayor's private life, say, marital infidelity, there would have been very serious detraction (if true) or grave calumny (if false and known as such) on the part of Mr. Jones; also Mr. Jones would then be obliged in conscience to restore to the best of his ability the harm done by his detraction (or calumny).

LISTENING TO DETRACTION AND CALUMNY

There is a difference between *hearing* detraction or calumny, a thing hardly possible to avoid in this world of chatter, and *listening* to it. By *listening* here is meant taking an active interest in what is being said and enjoying it. Listening to grave detraction and calumny can become a matter of grave sin, if done out of *positive hatred* toward the defamed person and *with internal approval of and rejoicing over the grave detraction or calumny* (and, of course, with full realization and consent). In such cases, since the sin is merely internal, there is no obligation of reparation on part of the listener.

Inordinate *curiosity,* and the morbid satisfaction which some take in hearing secret things or secret sins, will be venially sinful, malice being absent. The same holds true if one merely refrains from trying to put a stop to detraction or calumny (by not trying to change the subject, etc.); it is venially sinful, because such a person acts thus through human respect or through carelessness. A scrupulous person would usually not even sin venially in not trying to put a stop to detraction or calumny. Neither would a person be guilty of any sin if he would suffer inconvenience by trying to stop such talk or if his attempts would be useless.

Deliberately leading others on to detraction or calumny, provoking and encouraging them, may be a matter of either grave or venial sin depending on whether the detraction or calumny spoken by the other person is seriously or slightly injurious. If, however, one leads another into detraction simply because he desires to obtain this knowledge for himself and is firmly determined that the information will go no further, such a person generally would not sin seriously.

CONTUMELY

Contumely is the act of unjustly dishonoring another person in his presence, thus showing one's contempt for that person; contumely is what most people mean by "insulting him to his face." It is done by insulting words or deeds, such as a slap on the face, spitting on a person or performing any other act which insults and expresses contempt. Contumely is a sin against justice and charity, for it is positively injurious to the honor due to another.

Contumely may be either venially or seriously sinful. If only a slight injury to another's honor is done, it is venially sinful; but if the contumely is calculated to cause serious harm, it is a gravely sinful matter. The opprobrious or insulting language common among people of lower social conditions or among persons in violent anger is not usually taken seriously and is not thought to do any dishonor.

Since contumely is a sin against justice, it entails the obligation of repairing the insult offered. The reparation is to be made publicly or privately, depending on whether the person was insulted in public or in private. Reparation can simply be made either by asking pardon of the injured person, or by showing him special signs of esteem and good will, or by any other similar signs of honor.

If the insulting was mutual and equally grave on both sides, there is no obligation of reparation.

RASH JUDGMENT

Rash judgment is a person's firm mental assent (undoubting assent), without sufficient reasons, concerning a supposed sin of another. Such judgment is formed with the knowledge that the grounds for it are not valid. Every man has the right to the good opinion of others unless he has proved himself unworthy of it. Rash judgment can be gravely sinful if all the following conditions are verified in one's case: (1) if the matter or sin of another about which the rash judgment was formed is serious; (2) if there is firm conviction, not merely doubting; (3) if the judgment is fully deliberate; and (4) if there are insufficient reasons for forming the conclusion. If any of these is absent, the sin is not grave.

We may exercise caution (e.g., not "trusting people too far," etc.) in practical life without any sin at all. When we do this, we are not thinking any evil of our neighbor; we are merely reckoning with the factual possibility of our being deceived.

EXAMPLE OF RASH JUDGMENT:

Mr. O'Neil's secretary is in trouble. She asks him for advice and he invites her to have dinner with him so that they can have a good long talk. While they are at dinner, Mrs. Blacktongue comes in and immediately sums up the situation thus: "Hmm, O'Neil is snugly settled in a booth with his pretty secretary where they can't be seen easily. How intimate the tête-à-tête. She even has tears in her eyes! Obviously both are in love! My, but I should have known that old man O'Neil was like that." She goes away firmly convinced that Mr. O'Neil is madly in love with his secretary.

Chapter XVII

ANNUAL CONFESSION AND COMMUNION

Every Catholic who has reached the use of reason must confess at least once a year (Canon 906); this is a serious obligation. Strictly speaking, however, this precept binds only those who think that they have sinned gravely (committed mortal sin); so those guilty of venial sins only are not obliged by this law.

A sacrilegious confession does not fulfill the obligation. If a person fails in his obligation one year he must confess as soon as possible during the following year. By so doing he fulfills the precept for both years. Children who have the use of reason before seven years of age are also bound by this precept; on the other hand, children who do not possess the use of reason, no matter how old, are not obliged.

No special time is set during the year in which this annual confession is to be made. A person may begin the year on the first day of January, or at Easter, or within a year from his last confession. Whichever way one counts, the law is fulfilled, provided that not more than a year has elapsed between one confession and another. If, however, a person is accustomed to going to confession at Easter time (in preparation for fulfilling the precept regarding reception of Holy Communion during Easter time), he fulfills the law, even though more than a year has intervened between the two confessions (e.g., Joe goes to confession on the first Sunday of Lent one year, and the next time he confesses on Holy Saturday of the following year); though more than a year has intervened, he always goes to confession and Holy Communion during the Easter time (which extends from the First Sunday of Lent through Trinity Sunday).

Annual confession may be made to any priest who has the faculties and jurisdiction; the Church thus gives penitents complete freedom in the choice of a confessor.

EXAMPLE:

Mrs. Hood is not conscious of having sinned gravely during the past ten years. Although she communicates every Sunday, she had not been to confession for three years because, she says, she would be terribly worried about not having sufficient sorrow for her peccadilloes.

Though she has not sinned in not going to confession every year, she should remember all she needs in any confession is to have sorrow for any grave sins of her past and to include one of them in her confession. In that way she can confess frequently and thus get the full benefit of the graces which the Sacrament gives.

PRECEPT OF EASTER COMMUNION

The Church commands every Catholic who has reached the use of reason to receive Holy Communion at least once a year, during the Easter time (Canon 859). This is also a serious obligation. If a person does not receive during the Easter time (whether deliberately neglecting or perhaps forgetting) he is still bound gravely (under pain of serious sin) to communicate during the year.

A sacrilegious Communion does not fulfill this obligation. If one communicates worthily but without advertence to the fulfillment of the precept, he still satisfied the obligation and is not obliged to receive again.

Our Easter Communion does not have to be made in our own parish church, but we are urged to make it there. Those receiving their Easter Communion in a strange parish should notify their own pastor of the fact, but this duty of notification does not bind under any sin.

A person who foresees he will not be able to receive during the Easter time is not bound to receive before that time but this does not excuse him from the obligation of receiving at least once during the year.

Easter time in the U.S.A. extends from the First Sunday of Lent to Trinity Sunday inclusive.

RECEIVING COMMUNION WHEN IN DANGER OF DEATH

The faithful in danger of death from any cause whatsoever are seriously obliged to receive Holy Communion. The phrase *in danger of death* means a sufficiently serious reason for fearing death on account of ill health or on account of any circumstances which would result in probable death.

EXAMPLE:

Private Holt, a Catholic, volunteers to go with five others behind enemy lines to get some vital information. An extremely dangerous mission, it is likely to result in the death of one or several of the participants.

In this case Private Holt is gravely obliged to receive Holy Communion before he goes, if at all possible.

Chapter XVIII

THE EUCHARISTIC FAST
— FASTING — ABSTINENCE

The modern, simplified form of Eucharistic fast aims to enable Catholics to receive Holy Communion more frequently. The many factors of modern life, the considerable changes in working conditions, in public offices and generally in all social life had made the reception of Holy Communion very difficult or even impossible for many Catholics, if the previous forms of Eucharistic fast had to be observed. This, coupled with the insistent requests of the bishops, prompted the Holy Father to issue modified legislation regarding the pre-Communion fast. The Church does not and cannot change anything in which doctrinal principles are involved, yet it tries to harmonize Church discipline with the circumstances of changing times.

Here we shall deal with all the fasting requirements as they now apply to the Catholic laity.

The drinking of natural water does not break the Eucharistic fast. Hence, before going to Holy Communion, anyone may drink as much water as he wishes. Because natural water does not break the fast, no permission of a priest is needed for this, nor need any interval of time intervene between the drinking of water and the reception of Holy Communion. One may take a drink of water immediately before Holy Communion as far as the legislation is concerned, and he need not be suffering from weakness or thirst.

We must not add any other element to the water, however; we cannot put sugar, for instance, into the water. If natural water contains certain substances, such as iron or calcium, we need have no scruple in drinking it just before Holy Communion. The same holds true of fluoridated or chlorinated water.

To receive Holy Communion, we must abstain from food and liquids (other than water) for one hour. Thus, Catholics must fast for one hour from food and drink (other than water) before receiving Holy Communion. Any time up to an hour before receiving Holy Communion, everyone may eat and drink, including alcoholic beverages such as beer, wine, whiskey, etc. (in moderation, of course). No permission from a priest is needed for this, nor need a person be suffering from weakness or hunger. The only thing which we must observe is to finish eating or drinking, one hour before actually receiving Holy Communion (not before the beginning of the Mass at which we receive).

When a person is *in doubt* whether or not he has broken the fast, he may receive Communion with a clear conscience. This doubt may either be concerning the exact *time* (doubt whether it was before or after the beginning of the hour period prescribed), or it may be concerning the fact (doubt whether one had actually drunk or eaten something within the respective hour period). This, of course, does not mean that, when actually eating or drinking, one is permitted to neglect making sure of the time, and later trying to justify oneself by saying that he then doubts the exact time, etc.

Smoking does not break the Eucharistic fast; nor does the swallowing of particles of food that remained between the teeth. We may even take food into the mouth and spit it out again, as, for instance, in tasting pie-filling, soup, etc., to see whether it is seasoned enough, etc. We may also brush our teeth. Nervous people need not worry either: fingernails do not break the Eucharistic fast! The chewing of gum (its juices), however, does break the fast; hence, the hour limit must be observed.

THE SICK

The sick or infirm have further concessions of which they may take advantage: they may take nonalcoholic beverages, such as coffee, milk, fruit juices, etc., before Holy Communion without any time limit at all. Also, no time limit before Holy Communion is imposed on the sick or infirm in taking what is really and properly medicine, either in liquid or solid form (pills, etc.). Again, no permission from a priest is necessary.

A person need not be bedridden or even confined to the home to avail himself of these concessions. Thus, anyone suffering from ulcers may take milk, medicine, etc., within the hour limit, if he wishes. It is not necessary to consider what the medicine taken is made of; it may even contain alcoholic elements.

TRADITIONAL FASTING URGED

Priests and laymen who are able to continue observing the old and venerable form of Eucharistic fast before Holy Communion are urged to do so. By the old and venerable form of Eucharistic fast is meant the traditional fasting from midnight. While not to be taken lightly, this is an exhortation and not a law. All who make use of the modern concessions "should compensate for the good received by becoming shining examples of a Christian life and principally with works of penance and charity." These words mean exactly what they say. They are to be taken as a sincere *exhortation,* but in no way do they entail obligation.

FASTING AND ABSTINENCE AS PENANCE

Although Christ told us that we must fast and do penance, He did not tell us when, how, or how often. Before Vatican II, the Church decided for us exactly when and how we were to fast, to abstain from meat, or to do both. Many decried this as excessive legalism; perhaps it was, for not rarely curious quirks developed. How many "good" Catholics, for example, would not have tasted an ounce of meat on Friday, yet would presume to cut their neighbor's heart to shreds with vicious tongues?! And the legalists with their lobsters on Friday may now just have to think of other ways of doing penance!

Now the Church has left the choice of penance and fasting to each individual conscience. The emphasis too has changed — to the important ways of doing penance and mortification, hopefully for the better. The Church still very definitely insists on fasting and penance, as Christ did, but left their kind, form and time up to us. In addition, the Church has suggested many positive forms of penance such as performing acts of kindness toward the sick, the aged and the poor; to give generously to charitable and religious works; to practice voluntary self-denial, especially in regard to alcoholic drink and worldly amusements; to pray more frequently and more fervently; to receive the sacraments more often and to attend daily Mass (especially during periods of penance).

The choice of penance and mortification is left up to us to tailor according to our own particular needs and weaknesses. If, for example, I tend to overeat, fasting and abstinence in the traditional sense would be very profitable to my soul. But, if I find that I am selfish and greedy, perhaps helping the poor and the aged by performing acts of kindness and charity will be much more appropriate. If I am very opinionated and hypercritical of liturgical changes, perhaps the best form of penance for me would be not only total silence but unstinting cooperation with the parish liturgical committee and wholehearted participation in liturgical celebrations, however distasteful to me personally.

Sometimes merely remaining in a neighborhood where families of different color from us have moved in will do more for our soul than any amount of fasting and penance of abstinence. Our soul's needs are best known to ourselves alone and therefore we should be the best judges of the form which our penance and mortification should assume. Of one thing we can be sure, some kind of devils, some kind of weaknesses, can be cast out "only by prayer and fasting" (Mk. 9:28). For the most part, now, the Church has left up to us the when, how and what of penance and mortification.

Keeping all this in mind, what is the absolute minimum which still binds Catholics under the traditional form of fasting and abstinence? In the United States the traditional form of fasting (one full meal a day) and abstinence from meat and meat products must be observed on Ash Wednesday and Good Friday. In Canada there are no obligatory days of fasting and abstinence. (These are Church laws pertaining to Catholics of the Latin Rite only and not those binding Eastern-Rite Catholics. The latter have special legislation and so they must follow the regulations of their respective Eastern-Rite bishops.) The rest is up to the faithful to choose their own ways of truly doing penance and mortification, tailored to their own particular needs.

Chapter XIX

AFRAID OF
CONFESSION?

When the Master instituted the Sacrament of Reconciliation or Penance, He said emphatically, "Peace be to you!" He said it not once but twice. This was to show the one aim of confession: that of imparting peace, not worry, trouble and uneasiness. He intended that penitents should never be harassed by fear any more, that forgiven sins should never bother them again.

To most Catholics confession is just that, the best way of attaining peace of soul, a sacrament from which they derive a special solace, comfort and joy. They love it and would be miserable without it. Now, mind you, they do not find it easy, especially if they have a load to get off their chest, but once they are through with it they can dance and sing like children again because of the peace it brings them. For them it is still the same gentle Master who whispers, "Courage, my child, your sins are forgiven" (Mt. 9:2); and they take Him at His word.

There are some, however, to whom confession is almost everything else but a sacrament of mercy and peace. To these, confession is a worrying, nerve-racking effort — even after their ordeal, they find a short-lived peace if they find it at all — all because they misunderstand the whole idea of confession and the requirements for its valid and fruitful reception. There are many who go infrequently to confession precisely because they have a false notion of its requirements.

In the first place, we must never forget that confession is preeminently a sacrament of mercy. If it is not that to us, we are definitely misunderstanding the main purpose of confession; we are not using it according to the mind of Christ. The truly sincere and contrite are always pardoned as quickly as the Good Thief. Many do not seem to realize that if they make an act of perfect love (or perfect contrition) they have already received God's forgiveness before confession — though in case of grave sin the obligation of confession remains. In requiring confession, God intended that, through His priest-representative, He should hear from the sinner's own lips what wrong he has done and his sorrow for having done it; also that He might tell the penitent, through the same priest-representative, that He forgives him, that he has been reunited with his God and the Church which has been harmed by his sin. (This last is the main reason for the obligation of confession, even though the sin has been forgiven outside the confessional. The confession is a public act of reunification with the Church which has been harmed by the penitent's sin. The sinner is reconciled to the Church through his "public apology" in the confessional.) Anyone who loves us very much will not want to pounce on us when we make any slip-ups; neither does God, who loves us without limit.

"But we want to be 'on the safe side'!" We are not "on the safe side" if we work ourselves into a frenzy, making an extraordinary effort when we go to confession or worry about our confession afterwards. Christ does not want us to do that. What would you think of a friend whom you have forgiven from the bottom of your heart but who still insists constantly that you haven't forgiven him? You would rightly feel insulted.

All Christ asks of us is that we try to make our confession sincere. When we have confessed sincerely, we absolutely need not worry because we did not confess with the greatest possible earnestness and intensity. A simple straight-forward effort with moderate diligence is all that Christ demands.

Many people are afraid of confession not for what it is but for what they think it is; most of their difficulties arise *from their own grossly exaggerated ideas of the requirements of confession.*

Let us examine what is actually required for the valid reception of the Sacrament of Reconciliation (Penance).

THE REQUIREMENTS

I. We are obliged to confess all mortal sins according to their kind and number, which we have committed since our last good confession. There is no obligation to confess our venial sins, unless we have no other matter; then we must confess *at least one venial sin or some sin of our past for which we are truly sorry.*

Nothing could be clearer. The ordinary Catholic instead of having difficulty remembering a grave sin committed since his last confession will have trouble trying to forget it. The thought of his grave guilt will have been nagging at him ever since he committed the sin. So, as soon as he begins preparing for confession, it will stick out like a gigantic oil derrick in his backyard. Thus a sincere person can find necessary matter for confession in a very short space of time.

Provided we are sorry for our venial sins, they are forgiven by the absolution without being specifically mentioned in confession. However, if after examining our conscience, we can find nothing but venial sins, we must confess at least one of these or some sin of our past for which we are sorry. To reiterate: it is not necessary to make a complete accusation of our venial sins, one or two will do, or some sin of our past. Better to mention only a few and do something about them, rather than ransack every nook and cranny of our soul in an attempt to search out all our venial sins.

II. Now for contrition. This, too, is not so difficult as some think; many people torture themselves because they hold exaggerated or even false notions of what is the sorrow required for a valid confession.

Contrition for sin is of two kinds: *perfect* and *imperfect* (or attrition). This distinction is important because the latter is required for confession but the former, though more desirable, is not. Perfect contrition is sorrow for sin because we have offended God, whom we love above all things for His own sake. Imperfect contrition (attrition) is sorrow for sin because sin is hateful in itself or because we fear God's punishment (loss of heaven, punishment in hell, or in purgatory, etc.).

Now, all that is absolutely required for the worthy reception of the Sacrament of Reconciliation (Penance) is *imperfect contrition* (attrition) *for all our mortal sins.* Even if we are not sorry for any venial sins at all, the Sacrament is not invalidated, provided we have at least imperfect contrition for all our mortal sins, including *those past and previously confessed.* Naturally, such imperfect dispositions lessen the grace received from the Sacrament, but in no way do they nullify it.

Whenever you are tempted to worry about contrition, remember that if you are not *deliberately insincere,* the very fact of going to confession proves contrition, for otherwise, why would one go? If you wish to have contrition, says St. Francis of Sales, "then you have contrition by the simple fact that you wish to have it."

Imperfect contrition plus the Sacrament of Reconciliation (Penance) is always sufficient to restore to grace the person guilty of grave sin; but imperfect contrition *without the Sacrament of Reconciliation (Penance)* does not. For example, after having sinned gravely, Andrew cannot get to confession; if he has only imperfect contrition, he is not restored to grace. But if he gets to a priest and confesses, still with imperfect contrition, then this is sufficient. On the other hand, perfect contrition alone always restores the mortal sinner to grace; so does an act of love for God, for it actually includes perfect contrition. Many people erroneously think they cannot be restored to the grace and friendship of God until they go to confession! True, we must submit every mortal sin to the power of the keys, and we must do this before we approach Holy Communion. But we can, indeed, be restored to God's grace any time by making an act of love for God or by having perfect contrition — and this we should try to do as soon as possible after any fall.

Some people also worry about their *purpose of amendment.* Yet it, too, is not a difficult requirement when properly understood. In fact, if genuine contrition is had, this implies a hatred of sin which, in turn, implies a determination to avoid mortal sin in the future. So, in case a person goes to confession in a hurry and sincerely tells God he is sorry (contrition) but forgets to make any explicit purpose of amendment, he need not worry about the worthiness of his confession.

Naturally, the better our dispositions for confession, the more grace we will receive and the more fruitful will our confession be. But this is no cause for anxiety or worry.

As the old catechism book put it, the purpose of amendment must be firm, but this does not exclude one's fears or "feelings" that he may commit this sin again; it must be efficacious — he must *want* to take the necessary means to avoid grave sin; and it must be universal, that is, it must include all mortal sins.

Many habitual sinners do not approach confession because they think they would not be honest and sincere regarding the purpose of amendment. They say: "But I honestly am convinced that I will fall into that sin again tomorrow; if not tomorrow, soon." They know that they have an inveterate habit and despair of breaking it. Looking back into their spiritual past, they see many falls and much weakness of the will; looking into the future, they see that the same old difficulty will be encountered — the same weakness of will. Naturally, considering all this, their mind judges that there will again be falls. But again, what a misconception of the purpose of amendment!

To *know* something is not the same as to *will* it; the purpose of amendment, although dependent on the intellect, is elicited by the will. If, here and now, the penitent sincerely *wants* to avoid sin in the future and is determined to take the proper means of avoiding it, his purpose of amendment is sufficient. This is so despite the nagging fear that, because of past conduct, the habits acquired, and one's naturally weak tendencies, the penitent may very well fall into the same sins in the future. But *knowing* this and *wanting* it are two very different things. Sincerely *wanting* to avoid grave sin in the future is sufficient for a worthy confession.

The third requirement for the worthy reception of this sacrament is probably the easiest — *satisfaction*. We must accept and be willing to perform the penance which the priest gives us. This willingness must be had at the time the penance is given. If afterwards a penitent omits the penance, he may commit a sin; but the sacrament would still be valid. So if one forgets the penance or a part of it, no need to fret, the confession was indeed valid and good.

Distractions, even voluntary ones, while saying a penance do not hinder its fulfillment as an obligation; such distractions, if voluntary, constitute a venial sin of irreverence. The penitent can still perform a penance even after he has fallen into grave sin.

If a person forgets what penance was given him in confession, he is not, strictly speaking, obliged to perform any penance. He may, of course, return to the confessional and ask the priest what the penance was, or get a new penance (in case the priest does not remember either). Or he may ask for a new penance in his next confession after giving a general idea of his last confession. A third alternative is for him to say the penance he is usually given for such sins. However, none of these things is obligatory.

Some people also spend a considerable amount of nervous energy trying to fix the exact time since their last confession. Telling Father how long it is since your last confession is a useful but actually a *nonessential* constituent of confession; even if you omitted it altogether, your confession would be valid. So, no need to worry or be anxious about it. An approximate estimate is sufficient; if you say, "about a month," it would cover three to five weeks. If you discover after confession that your estimate was far off, don't worry. All's well.

How about the act of contrition after the telling of sins? A set, memorized act of contrition is not necessary though it is useful. All that is strictly necessary is that the penitent be sincerely sorry in his will and express his sorrow in some audible way. God reads the heart and knows when the heart is sincere. Provided you were truly sorry before entering the confessional and have not retracted that sorrow, all is well. Why worry, then, if you should become completely distracted, with the result that you do not think of what you are saying or get tongue-tied and mixed up? It may happen that you are so distracted that you start saying the Grace before Meals (if you are sorry, Christ can only smile at your very human conduct)! Remember that confession is neither a test of human composure nor of memory.

HOW ABOUT DOUBTS?

People often worry about doubtful sins. Some are tormented by every uncertainty: they are uncertain whether they consented to a temptation, uncertain whether they have confessed some particular sin, whether they have made it black enough, whether they confessed it exactly, uncertain whether they were truly sorry. The litany of uncertainties can be endless.

First of all, as regards doubtful sin: if you are doubtful whether or not you committed a grave sin (doubt whether you had sufficient advertence, full consent, etc.), you have no obligation to confess the sin. In a catechism (approved by St. Pius X for the Diocese of Rome) is this very question. The answer given is: "If a person is not sure of having committed a sin, he is not obliged to confess it; but if he wishes to, he must add that he is not sure of having committed it." That is and has always been the teaching of the Church.

Plain common sense tells us that uncertainty can never, of itself, produce a certainty; neither can a doubt ever produce a sure obligation. Confession of doubtful sin, "doubtful mortal sins," therefore, can never be an obligation. In fact, it is advisable for those prone to scrupulosity not to confess such doubtful sins. Period. No ifs or buts!

How about those who are doubtful whether or not they had confessed a certain past sin (a grave sin, that is)? First of all, those obsessed with doubts about past sins will not rid themselves of that obsession by repeating confession. Anyone plagued by such doubts would do better by trying to resolve them in another way, by following the suggestions and remedies for scruples for they are definitely in the scrupulous class. Secondly, everyone should be consoled with this fact: even though a person may perhaps have omitted a serious sin in confession, provided the omission was not deliberate nor due to gross negligence (and who could accuse the usually careful, much less the scrupulous, of that?), the sin was covered by the absolution. The sin was forgiven and one cannot make things "safer" by worrying that he *may* have left one out; he must let bygones be bygones. Let's quote about this very matter from an excellent book:

". . . No further obligation can arise unless a *certain unconfessed mortal sin comes spontaneously to mind.*

"The next move is with the Lord. If there is still a serious outstanding sin which He wishes you to confess, it is up to Him to bring it to your mind; and if He does not trouble to do so, it is safe to conclude that He wishes bygones to be bygones. If He does not recall the sin to your mind, He has no one to blame but Himself. Of one thing we can be certain and it is this: He will not half-do anything; whatever He does, He will do thoroughly and well. If He chooses to recall a sin to your mind, He will recall it with clarity and certainty, and not in a vague, foggy, disturbing way. His inspiration *never* destroys our peace of mind" (Alfred Wilson, C.P., *Pardon and Peace,* B. Herder Book Co., St. Louis, Mo., pp. 130-131).

One simple thing to remember about your past sins: you must be *certain* that you have not already confessed them, before you ever have an obligation to go back on your past. If you were sincere at each confession, you need never go back over the matter of past confessions; for it is morally impossible that you could have left out any really serious sin.

ANOTHER WORRY

Another worry, and not a few are affected by it, is the question of accuracy. Many torture themselves needlessly because they think that what they say in confession must correspond *exactly* and *to the letter* with what they did. The plain fact is that if this were the case confession would be of very little use to us; for we seldom, if ever, tell our sins exactly as they are before God. God does not demand it; so neither should we demand it of ourselves. All that is necessary is that we try to express ourselves correctly; and if we have done this we should not worry, for that is all that the Master demands of us. Remember the simple rule that all we are obliged to do is to confess mortal sins according to their *kind* and *number* and any circumstances *changing the nature of the sin.* By "kind" here is meant the particular class to which a sin belongs; for example, whether it is a sin of blasphemy, Mass-missing, impurity, disobedience, etc. By *number* we mean how many times (approximately, if we do not remember exactly) we have committed that sin since our last good confession. The circumstances *changing the nature of the sin* are those circumstances connected with the sin which change the species of the sin: for example, committing the sin of impurity *with another who is married,* or stealing money *which belongs to the church.*

And here is some good, solid advice: "When confessing sins of impurity, it is neither necessary nor wise to go into details, unless the circumstances change the nature of the sin. All that is required is to tell the kind of sin and the number of times it was committed. 'Immodest touches once' would include any number of such touches at the one session. In this matter quite a lot is taken for granted; if, for example, intercourse is confessed, it is taken for granted that there were accompaniments; and so it is unnecessary to mention the fact. The time element need not, as a rule, be mentioned; because it makes no essential difference whether the sinful acts endured for five minutes or five hours" (*Pardon and Peace,* p. 135).

If you do not know how to confess some sin, do not be afraid to be blunt; there is nothing against true modesty in calling a spade a spade. Father will understand. Try your best; that is all our Lord asks.

In regard to this matter of expressing yourself accurately, a lot is taken for granted: ". . . *It is not necessary to express yourself very accurately.* When you go to the doctor with measles, you may and probably do explain your symptoms badly, but unless the doctor is very fifth-rate, he soon realizes what you mean, because he has heard all that so often before. Therefore, it is not unfair to say that if you imagine you are so difficult to understand, you either make too much of yourself or too little of your confessor.

"If the priest does not understand it, it is up to him to ask more questions, and if he neglects to do that when he should, it is his responsibility, his funeral, not yours; though, of that you are most certainly not the judge. It is presumption and uncharity for you to decide that the priest is failing in his duty. Even if he is, provided you have done your duty, his omissions need not trouble you" (*Pardon and Peace,* pp. 204-205).

'BUT WHAT WILL FATHER THINK OF ME?'

When you are ashamed and wonder, as a penitent of St. Francis of Sales did — "What must you think of me now that you know my ignominies?" — remember that every priest would want to answer you as did that great saint and confessor: "Why do you place me in the number of the Pharisees who regarded Magdalene, after she was forgiven, as a sinner? I regard you as a vessel of election."

'FEAR NOT, MY LITTLE FLOCK'

If you have a shameful tale to tell and are afraid, ask the confessor to help you; tell him that you are afraid. The priestly heart melts within him every time a sincere, aching soul is struggling to rid itself of some particularly heavy shackles. Try that and see!

With Christ, the priest offers you the warmth of his heart, the peace of your conscience. The flame of his love is yours; the joy of your return will also be his. He spends his life, as fathers toil, for your daily spiritual bread; he wants to care, with a mother's care, for your happiness. He longs to give you that atmosphere of love in which you can take your ease; he wants you there in the other Jerusalem, at the family table with all of us sitting around it. For the love in his heart is looking for the joy in your eyes when you get up from your knees. He knows that your life is hard but that your burdens are not so heavy when your conscience is clear, when Christ is with you. Come to him with your burden, so that when the angel of death at last appears you will have no more of it to carry with you. If you have lost the way through the darkness, turn your steps to the Master, and His servant who is waiting for you; he will guide you home again.

With Christ, his consecration as priest is to bend over you, fallen, bleeding, to hold you in his arms, to form you in soul and heart. With Christ, his consecration as shepherd is to have a heart full of love, to be watchful for everyone's needs; to give without reckoning; to do the most beautiful thing in the world . . . TO SETTLE YOUR CONSCIENCE!

INDEX

Communion — *continued*

parents' obligation to provide for their child — 125

Commutation of vows — 109

Compensation, occult — 204f:
concerning unjust wage — 206

Concupiscence, *see* Passion

Condemned person, killing of — 147

Conditions affecting guilt in regard to an act — 37ff, 50

Condonation of debts by rightful owner — 212

Conduct incompatible with prayer — 76f

Confession — 33, 65, 242ff:
accuracy in — 245, 247
annual, obligation of — 237
before receiving Holy Communion, obligation of — 244
doubts and doubtful sin in — 37, 65, 246f
during Mass — 114
examination of conscience for — 243
fear of — 242ff
imperfect contrition (attrition) necessary for — 244
lies in — 100
penance received in — 78, 245
purpose of amendment in — 244f
requirements for — 243ff
satisfaction (penance) in — 78, 245

Confessor, power of, to commute vows — 108

Confirmation, parents' obligation to provide for their child — 125

Conjugal relations, *see* Marital act

Conscience — 16ff, 49:
antecedent — 18
certain — 21
consequent — 18
correct — 12, 18
definition of — 12, 17
delicate — 24
doubtful — In *Preface*, 21f
effect of, on guilt — 19f
examination of, for confession — 243
false — 12, 17, 19f
formation of a certain — 22ff
lax — 24f, 37
remedy for scrupulous — 26ff
scrupulous — 25f

Conscientious objectors — 151

Conscription, military — 134, 151

Consent:
and passion — 41ff
full, in mortal sin — 35f, 164
"half" — 36f, 180f
presumed, in taking another's goods — 200

Consequent passion — 41

Continence, periodic, *see* Rhythm

Contempt of God — 104

Contraceptives:
sale or distribution of — 61, 62

Contraceptives — *continued*
use of — 190
use of "the pill" as — 191ff

Contract:
in betting or wagering — 218
in marriage — 183, 187
regarding wages — 206

Contrition:
imperfect, in confession — 244
perfect — 33, 244

Contumely — 235f

Convalescents, *see* Sick persons

Conversation, impure or obscene — 178ff

Cooperation, in sin:
definition of — 55
formal — 56
material — 57
special examples of — 59ff

Corporations:
guilt of, in corporate acts — 55f
thefts from — 202

Correct conscience — 12, 18

Country, love of one's — 133f

Courts:
and pleading "not guilty" — 226
and Sunday observance — 119
and use of broad mental reservation in — 226

Craniotomy — 145

Creditors:
and bankruptcy — 213
and use of occult compensation, *see* Occult compensation

Criminal, killing and wounding of — 147

Criticizing public men — 234

Crystal gazing, *see* Fortunetelling

Cursing — 103f

— D —

Damage:
unjust — 210ff

"Damn," use of — 103f

Dances:
cooperation in immoral — 62
strip-tease and fan — 174

Danger of sin, *see* Occasions of sin

Dangerous work, engaging in — 140f

Deaf-mutes, gaining of indulgences by — 78

Death:
as capital punishment — 147f
cooperation of soldiers in, of the innocent — 62, 151
directly intending another's, *see* Murder
directly intending one's own — 140; *see also* Suicide
desire for — 138
"easy" death, mercy killing (euthanasia) — 144f

Death — *continued*

Holy Communion, obligation of in danger of — 238

indirectly intending another's, *see* Principle of double effect

indirectly intending one's own — 137f, 141; *see also* Principle of double effect

in feticide, *see* Abortion

in lynching — 147

in manslaughter — 143f

in unjust aggression — 148f

sentence of, guilt resulting from giving false testimony — 143

Debts:

condonation of by creditor — 212

in bankruptcy — 213

interest accruing to debts legally claimed — 209

marriage debt, *see* Marital act

payment of — 200

Decalogue, *see* Commandments

Decapitation — 145

Deception:

in buying and selling — 217

in confession — 100

See also Lying

Defamation, *see* Detraction and calumny

Defects:

in articles sold — 217

revelation of another's, *see* Detraction and calumny

Defendant pleading "not guilty" in court — 226

Defense against unjust aggressor — 148f

Defensive war — 150f

Deliberate act — 49

Delivery, premature — 146

Desecration, *see* Sacrilege

Desire to die — 138

Desires:

impure — 168ff

unjust — 200

Determining guilt when tempted — 36ff, 180f

Detraction and calumny:

definition of — 231

in oaths — 106

listening to — 235

of public men — 234

reasons excusing from reparation for detraction — 233f

reparation for — 233

sinfulness of — 232

Devil:

existence of — 85

invoking of — 84ff

Devotion:

articles of — 87f

at Mass, *see* Mass

at prayer — 76ff

Direct intention — 51f; *see also* Motive

Direct scandal — 156

Directly venereal actions — 163f

Disease, venereal, and rendering the marital act — 188

Disobedience, *see* Obedience

Dispensation:

for performing servile work on Sunday — 119

from hearing Mass on Sunday — 116

from vows — 108f

Disposition of penitent for confession, *see* Confession

Distraction:

during Mass — 114

in prayer — 77, 79

in unjust damage — 211

Divination — 88ff

Divine positive law — 13, 30, 34

Divining rod, use of — 87

Divorce, cooperation in — 63

Doctors:

cooperation of, in abortions and sinful operations — 56f

keeping of secrets by — 228f

obligation of, in inconveniencing themselves seriously by reason of their office — 68

use of mental reservation by — 225

Double effect, principle of — 51ff, 137f, 146

Doubtful conscience — In *Preface,* 21f

Doubtful faith, possessor in — 210

Doubtful sins, confessing of — 37, 65, 246f

Doubts:

about goodness and badness of an act — 21ff

about grave guilt — 36f, 41ff

about just war — 151

about lawful ownership — 210

and doubtful sins in confession — 37, 65, 246f

settling of, before acting — 22

Dreams, belief in — 97f

Drinking:

cooperation in, of others — 59f

driving under influence of alcoholic drink — 142

immoderation in — 141ff

licitness of — 141

sinfulness of — 43, 141ff

treating others to alcoholic drink — 60

Druggists and clerks, selling of contraceptives by — 61

Drugs (and narcotics), guilt in using of — 43, 143

Drugs, steroid, for birth control — 191ff

Drunkenness, sinfulness of — 43, 141ff; *see also* Drinking

Dueling — 150

— E —

Earnings of minors — 214

Full consent — 35f, 164